AF522343

THE PHILOSOPHY OF EDUCATION

THE PHILOSOPHY OF EDUCATION

J.K.F. Rosenkranz

Translated from the German by

Anna C. Brackett

First LG Edition 2018

ISBN 978–93–83723–31–7 (Hb)

Published by
LG PUBLISHERS DISTRIBUTORS
49, Street No. 14, Pratap Nagar,
Mayur Vihar Phase I, Delhi 110091
Email: lgpdist@gmail.com

Printed at
Sapra Brothers, Delhi 110 092

EDITOR'S PREFACE.

This work was translated originally for *The Journal of Speculative Philosophy*, appearing in volumes vi, vii, and viii of that periodical (1872–'73–'74). It was intended for the use of philosophical students—who, in general, admire precise technical terms—and the terse German of the original was rendered by equally terse English. An edition of two thousand copies was reprinted in a separate volume. Demands for the work continuing after the first edition was exhausted, it was determined to publish a new one. For this purpose a revision has been made of the translation with a view to better adapt it to the needs of readers not skilled in philosophy. Where it has been thought necessary, phrases, or even entire sentences, have been used to convey the sense of a single word of the original. Typographical errors that had crept into the first edition, through careless proof-reading, have been carefully corrected. It may be safely claimed that no obscurity remains except such as is due to the philosophic depth and generality of the treatment. In this respect the translation is now more intelligible than the original. In addition to these helps, a somewhat elaborate commentary on the whole work has been undertaken by the editor, who has also prefixed to it a full analysis of the text and commentary.

It is believed that the book as it now appears will meet a want that is widely felt for a thorough-going Philosophy of Education. There are many useful and valuable works on "The Theory and Practice of Teaching," but no work that entirely satisfies the description of a genuine Philosophy of Education. To earn this title, such a work must not only be systematic, but it must bring all its details to the test of the highest principle of philosophy. This principle is the acknowledged principle of Christian civilization, and, as such, Rosenkranz makes it the foundation of his theory of education, and demonstrates its validity by an appeal to psychology on the one hand and to the history of civilization on the other.

This work, on its appearance, made an epoch in the treatment of educational theory in Germany. It brought to bear on this subject the broadest philosophy of modern times, and furnished a standard by which the value of the ideas severally discussed by radicals and conservatives could be ascertained. It found the truth lying partly on the territory of the established order and partly on the territory of the reformers—Ratich, Comenius, Rousseau, Pestalozzi, and their followers. It showed what was valid in the idea that had come to be established in the current system of education, and also exposed the weakness that had drawn the attack of the reformers.

Its Author.—Johann Karl Friedrich Rosenkranz was born at Magdeburg, April 23, 1805. He took up his residence in Berlin in 1824, distinguishing himself as a disciple, first of Schleiermacher, and afterward of Hegel. In 1833 he became Professor of Philosophy at Königsberg, and occupied for forty-six years, until his death in 1879, the chair held for twenty-four years by the celebrated Herbart, and for thirty-four years by the still more celebrated Kant. He wrote extensive works on philosophy and literature, and published the present work in 1848 under the title of *Paedagogik als System*.

Points of Great Value.—Special attention is called to the deep significance of the principle of self-estrangement (*Selbst-Entfremdung*) as lying at the foundation of the Philosophy of Education (p. 27). It furnishes a key to many problems discussed by the educational reformers from Comenius to Herbert Spencer. Since man's true nature is not found in him already realized at birth, but has to be developed by his activity, his true nature is his ideal, which he may actualize by education. Hence the deep significance of this process. Man must estrange himself from his first or animal nature, and assimilate himself to his second or ideal nature, by habit. At first all things that belong to culture are strange and foreign to his ways of living and thinking. Education begins when he puts aside what is familiar and customary with him, and puts on the new and strange—that is to say, begins his "self-estrangement." The nature of such important matters as work and play (p. 28) and habit (§§ 29–34) becomes evident from this insight.

The distinction of corrective and retributive punishment (§§ 38–45) is of great value practically in deciding upon the kind of punishment to use in an American school where pupils have a precocious sense of honor.

The part of this work devoted to educational psychology (§§ 82–102) is believed to possess great interest for the thoughtful teacher, as tracing the outlines of the only true science of the mind. The phases most worthy of the educator's attention are certainly those that relate to the development of the intellectual and moral powers; it is their *development* rather than their mere *existence* that the practical teacher wishes to know about. This treatise is commended to the notice of those who have hitherto been unable to find a satisfactory psychological basis for their educational theories. They are invited to ponder what is said about attention (p. 73); how the lower faculties grow into higher faculties, and how the higher faculties re-enforce the lower (pp. 75, 76); the function of the imagination in forming general types and in leading to abstract ideas (pp. 84–87).

The methods of treating the three grades of capacity—the blockhead, the mediocre talent, and the genius—are especially suggestive to the teacher (p. 109).

The subject of morality is treated with great care, and all will admire what is said on the inadmissibility of vacations in moral obedience (p. 153), as well as what is said (p. 147) on the subject of urbanity (politeness with a dash of irony), as the flower of social culture.

Rosenkranz very properly makes religious education the last and highest form of the particular elements of education. In no place may one find deeper insights in regard to the proper culture in religion in an age abounding in unbelief and skeptical influences. His distinction of three stages of theoretical culture in religion

—(*a*) pious feeling, (*b*) enjoyment of religious symbols, (*c*) interest in the dogmas as such—to which he adds the three practical stages of (*a*) self-consecration, (*b*) performance of church ceremonies, (*c*) the attainment of a pious trust in the divine government of the world —these distinctions are thorough-going. What he says (p. 167) on the dangers of unduly hastening the child from the stages of religious feeling to religious thought and reflection, or, on the other hand, of unduly repressing religious reflection in those who have begun to ask questions and suggest doubts, is very instructive to religious teachers, whether in the Sabbath-school or in the family. So, too, is the distinction (p. 170) drawn between the provinces of morality and religion.

The entire third part of the work is taken up with a history of education, based on the philosophy of history. It is rather an outline of the history of human culture than a special history of schools or of pedagogics. As such, it is highly valuable, not only for the teacher or parent, but also for all who desire to see in a condensed form the essential outcome of human history.

In this brief survey of the philosophy of history the reader will take note, first of all, of the deepest contrast —that found between the Oriental and Occidental world-principles. The former is that of obedience to external authority, the latter that of independence in all its forms. The educator will here find practical hints on all points of school management. In China, for instance, he may see exactly what kind of education will make conservative citizens—mere mechanical memorizing will do this (p. 197). He may see how too much stress on education for one's vocation may lead to castes like those of India (p. 200), while abstract asceticism in education may produce something akin to Lamaism. The enlightened reader will find it of great interest, in these days of the study of Buddhism ("The Light of Asia"—as well as the so-called "Esoteric Buddhism"), to read the distinction between Buddhism and Christianity (pp. 205 and 256), i. e., the distinction between the renunciation of selfishness and the annihilation of selfhood itself.

The "active" or restless peoples of Western Asia are of very great importance in the history of culture—mediating as they do between the extremes of the East and the West (p. 212). But, above all, we of modern times are most eager to study the three kinds of individuality which Europe has furnished us (p. 218) in the Greek, the Roman, and the Teutonic peoples. For these three elements of individuality, dominated by the spiritual idea which we received from Judea—the idea of God as a Divine Person—are the elements that enter our civilization and compose it. We have to study these four strands of our civilization in order to know ourselves. What is said about the religious significance of the games to the Greeks (p. 220) and the interpretation of Nature by the unconscious poetic power of the Greek mind (p. 223), as well as the characterization of the Roman principle (p. 230), will be recognized as a new elaboration of Hegel's insight given in his "Philosophy of History"—a work which alone would give its author a rank among the foremost of the great thinkers of the world. The Roman idea of *genus humanum* and its relation to the ideal of the Hebrew prophets—the *Messiah*, Prince of Peace, to be worshiped of all nations—is the key to the explanation of the adoption of Christianity as a world-religion (p. 249). The spirit of modern history is characterized as that which seeks to realize the good of all men in each man (p. 251).

The reader will find a mine of important ideas by following out the lead of any one of these thoughts. Especial mention, however, should be given to the application of the principle of self-estrangement in explaining the study of the classics (pp. 277, 278), and to the remarks on Rousseau (p. 283).

Omissions.—Occasional references to contemporary educational literature, to German customs, and to local or temporary interests have been omitted, and the fact of omission has been indicated by . . . . . . , or, if it is of the slightest importance, by express notice inserted in the text. Nearly all that is omitted may be read in the first edition of the work.

W. T. Harris.

Concord, Mass., *August* 18, 1886.

SCHEME OF CLASSIFICATION

OF THE

PHILOSOPHY OF EDUCATION.

PART I.—Education in its General Idea:

- A. Its Nature. §§ 13–32.
  - Possible only to self-active beings ... 19
  - Education by Divine Providence, by experience, or by teachers ... 21
  - Relates to body, intellect, and will; must be systematic; conducted in schools ... 23
- B. Its Form. §§ 23–45.
  - Self-estrangement, work and play ... 27
  - Habit ... 30
  - Authority, obedience, punishment ... 38
- C. Its Limits. §§ 46–50.
  - Subjective limit in the pupil's capacity ... 47
  - Objective limit in the pupil's wealth and leisure ... 48
  - Absolute limit in the pupil's completion of school-work ... 49

PART II.—Education in its Special Elements:

- A. Physical. §§ 53–79.
  - Dietetics ... 61
  - Gymnastics ... 63
  - Sexual [omitted].
- B. Intellectual. §§ 80–136.
  - Psychological epochs.
    - Intuitive—sense-perception ... 77
    - Imaginative—fancy and memory ... 82
    - Logical ... 94
  - Logical order.
    - Of development of the pupil ... 96
    - Of development of the subject ... 97
    - Of demonstration..
      - Analytic ... 101
      - Synthetic ... 101
      - Dialectical ... 102
  - Instruction.
    - Pupil's capacity ... 106
    - Pupil's act of learning—mechanical ... 115
      - dynamical ... 115
      - assimilative ... 116
      - living example .. 120
    - Method of instruction—text-book ... 121
      - oral ... 126
- C. Will-Training. §§ 137–174.
  - Social usages ... 143
  - Moral Training.
    - The Virtues ... 151
    - Discipline ... 154
    - Character ... 155
  - Religious education.
    - a. Feelings; b. Symbols; c. Dogmas ... 160
    - a. Self-consecration; b. ceremonies; c. reconciliation with one's lot ... 165
    - a. Family worship; b. union with church; c. religious insight ... 175

PART III.—Education in its Particular Systems:

- A. National. §§ 178–226.
  - Passive.
    - Family—China ... 196
    - Caste—India ... 200
    - Monkish—Thibet ... 206
  - Active.
    - Military—Persia ... 207
    - Priestly—Egypt ... 211
    - Industrial—Phœnicia ... 214
  - Individual.
    - Æsthetic—Greece ... 218
    - Practical—Rome ... 229
    - Abstract individual—German tribes ... 240
- B. Theocratic. §§ 227–233.
  - Jews ... 249
- C. Humanitarian or Christian. §§ 234–260.
  - Monkish ... 253
  - Chivalric ... 258
  - Citizen.
    - For special callings.
      - Secular life ... 263
      - Jesuitic ... 270
      - Pietistic ... 272
    - To achieve an ideal of culture.
      - Humanist ... 276
      - Philanthropist ... 279
    - For free citizenship ... 284

ANALYSIS OF CONTENTS.

INTRODUCTION.—§ 1. The Science of Education, a mixed science—presupposing and using others—resembling medicine. What other sciences it presupposes—its place in a complete arrangement of all the sciences (p. 1). § 2. The shallow character of educational treatises due to the vagueness of the definition of the province of education (p. 9). § 3. Business competition in education increases charlatanism (p. 10). § 4. The science of education belongs in the same department as the ethical sciences. It begins in the family (p. 10). § 5. The science of education contains the principles—the art of education relates to the devices of applying them, taking into consideration the local circumstances (p. 12). § 6. The local circumstances must not be elevated into general principles (p. 13). § 7. The science of education unfolds the general idea of education, and shows the divisions and the historical systems that have prevailed (p. 13). § 8. The general idea different from the system (p. 13). § 9. The divisions into physical, intellectual, and moral education (p. 14). § 10. The history of civilization shows the various ideas of education that have prevailed (p. 14). § 11. How the present one has arisen (p. 16).

The FIRST PART considers the general idea of education. § 12. (1) The nature of education in general, (2) its form, (3) its limits (p. 19).

CHAPTER I.—The Nature of Education. Education is possible because (§ 13) the mind is self-active (p. 19). Hence the human being is (§ 14) the only fit subject of education (p. 20). The guidance of the race by Divine Providence (§ 15) may be called education (p. 21), or (§ 16) the molding of the individual by the influences of life (p. 21), or, in the narrowest sense (§ 17), the influence of the teacher on a pupil (p. 22). The general problem of education (§ 18) includes development of intellect and moral nature (p. 23). It must be systematic (§ 19), or it will effect but little (p. 24). Necessity of dividing the work of education (§ 20) into special departments (p. 24), and (§ 21) hence special schools (p. 25). Possibilities and limits of education (§ 22), the capacities of the individual (p. 25).

CHAPTER II.—The Form of Education. § 23. The mind at first undeveloped; second, occupies itself on strange and foreign subjects; third, gets familiar with them, so that it is at home in a world of objects (p. 26). 24. Self-estrangement and its removal belong to all culture (p. 27). § 25. Definition of work and play (p. 28); necessity of insisting (§ 26) on respect for work (p. 29); equal necessity of play in order to develop the pupil's individuality. § 27. Recreation found for the educated man in change of work (p. 30). § 28. Education seeks to transform into habit whatever ought to belong to one's nature (p. 30). § 29. Indifference of habit—anything good or bad may become a habit (p. 31). Hence education should cultivate a sensitiveness for what is ethical. § 30. Utility a relative standard of judging what habits are to be cultivated (p. 32). § 31. The absolute standard is the moral one (p. 33). § 32. Active habit and passive habit defined (p. 33). § 33. Habit the end of education, but the power of breaking habits to be acquired (p. 34). § 34. Too much supervision of the pupil *versus* too much exposure to temptation (p. 35). § 35. Importance of studying the historic growth of defects of character (p. 36). § 36. When mere authority is sufficient (p. 37), and when explanations and arguments should be addressed to the pupil's reason. § 37. Scolding (p. 38). § 38. Punishment defined (p. 38); it should be given for particular and specified acts, and not for general disposition to evil action. § 39. Corrective *versus* retributive punishment (p. 39); school punishment the former. § 40. Punishment for correction should be regulated by the needs of the offender (p. 40), and not by the magnitude of the offense, as in the case of retributive punishment. § 41. Corporal punishment, isolation, punishment based on a sense of honor (p. 40). § 42. Corporal punishment defined (p. 41); the rod the best means. § 43. Isolation, its effect explained (p. 42). § 44. Punishment through the sense of honor—the danger in its use (p. 43). § 45. Necessity of careful discrimination in selecting the kind of punishment to use and in deciding its amount (p. 44).

CHAPTER III.—The Limits of Education. § 46. When work has become a habit, and the pupil has learned to practice the right methods from his own impulse rather than on account of external authority, his education in school has ended (p. 45). § 47. The subjective limit of education (p. 47) is the limit found in the pupil's capacity. § 48. The objective limit depends on the leisure and means of the pupil (p. 48). § 49. The absolute limit of education is found in the mastery of the means and methods, and the formation of correct habits on the part of the pupil (p. 49). § 50. Self-culture succeeds school education (p. 50.)

SECOND PART.—The Special Elements of Education (p. 55). INTRODUCTION. § 51. Education defined as the development of the inborn theoretical and practical reason of man (p. 55). Its three stages described. § 52. The special elements: 1. Education of the body; 2. Of the intellect; 3. Of the will (p. 56). The fivefold system of education—family, school, vocation, citizenship, and the Church—defined in the commentary (p. 57).

CHAPTER I.—Physical Education. § 53. The essential point in hygiene is an insight into the relation of assimilation to elimination in the bodily processes (p. 59). § 54. Perpetual process in the organism; balance between activity and rest (p. 59). § 55. Fatigue explained (p. 60); true strength arises only from activity. § 56. Physical education divided into dietetics, gymnastics, and sexual education (p. 61).

CHAPTER II.—Dietetics. § 57. What is the method of sustaining the repair of the organism (p. 61)? § 58–§ 63. Summary of contents. § 64. Cleanliness explained (p. 62).

CHAPTER III.—Gymnastics, § 65, is the art of normal training of the muscular system (p. 63), and depends on the relation of the voluntary to the involuntary muscles. § 66. Gymnastics corresponding to the national military drill (p. 63); Turner-halls; effect of invention of fire-arms on gymnastics (p. 64); why the Greeks paid so much attention to gymnastics (p. 65). § 67. Gymnastics should aim to make the body an energetic and docile servant of the will (p. 65); it should not aim at making acrobats. § 68. Classification of gymnastic exercises (p. 66). § 69. The foot-movements (p. 66). § 70. The arm-movements (p. 66). § 71. The whole-body movements (p. 67).

CHAPTER IV.—Intellectual Education. § 80. Didactics, or the science of the art of teaching presupposes physical education, but chiefly deals with psychology and logic (p. 69). § 81. The psychological presupposition. There must be a brief discussion of the outlines of psychology in didactics (p. 69). § 82. Attention the most important subject in educational psychology. Mind is essential self-activity (p. 70). Deduction of the powers or faculties of the mind from self-activity (p. 71); sense-perception, analysis, abstraction, perception of necessary relation, reflection, reason, etc. (p. 72). § 83. Education of attention (p. 72). Attention is the combination of intellect and will. Aristotle's distinction between first and second substances (p. 73). Avicenna's first and second intentions of the mind. Fichte's psychology. § 84. The mind does not consist of different faculties, but of different activities of the same power (p. 73); sense-perception, representation, thinking; intuitive, imaginative, and logical epochs of mind; fairy tales (p. 74); dialectical development of one stage of mind into another (p. 75), and the reaction of higher activities on lower ones so as to strengthen the power of the lower, illustrated by examples—Agassiz and Asa Gray—how science re-enforces the power of sense-reception (p. 76).

Chapter V.—§ 85. The intuitive epoch. Sense-perception, how educated by isolation of the object, by discovery of relations between objects, by connecting objects in one system (p. 77). § 86. Pictorial representation, its function (p. 78)—type or general form of an object *versus* individual specimen. § 87. Picture-books, their history—Comenius's picture-book (p. 78). § 88. Collections and cabinets; drawings; children should not attempt works of art (p. 79); the outlines which serve to characterize an object (p. 80). § 89. Explanations essential to instruction by means of pictures (p. 80). § 90. Educate the ear as well as the eye—music—careful articulation and quality of voice in reading—Plato and Aristotle on the importance of music; piano-playing; German musical dramas—symphonies and sonatas (p. 81).

Chapter VI.—The Imaginative Epoch. § 91. The formation of mental images and their verification; creative imagination; memory (p. 82). § 92. Comparison of mental image with the sense-perception of the object in order to verify and correct it (p. 82.) § 93. Emancipation from particular objects through generalization—ability to see the type of all objects of a given species—also the ability to recognize a particular object as belonging to a given species (p. 83). § 94. Art and literature as cultivation of imagination—furnishing the images which every educated person is obliged to know, because the mind of the race does most of its thinking by means of the images derived from literature and art, and communicates its thoughts likewise by their aid (p. 84). Homer and the Old Testament as furnishing the typical specimens of human nature which all must know (p. 85). § 95. Fairy stories of a nation furnishing the images with which children first learn to think (p. 85); list of the books which all youth should read at some time—what the nursery-tale gives the child (p. 86). § 96. Genuine fairy-tales immeasurably superior to those made to order, because they contain an unconscious reproduction of universal types, purified and made universal by passing through the minds of innumerable individuals in the course of oral transmission from one century to the next (p. 86). § 97. In later youth the pupil should approach more closely the study of noteworthy historic characters, and be moved by the stories of famous men (p. 87); he should attempt to understand the world, and grapple with its problems rather than remain content with passively viewing its pictures (p. 88); in what sense tragedy purifies the mind from passions (p. 89); necessity of gallant attacks upon works of great difficulty. § 98. How general conceptions are derived from works of the imagination (p. 90); memory and its relation to imagination—mnemonic helps (p. 91); distinction between recollection of particular objects and memory by means of general types, such memory as the scientific mind possesses; symbolic stage of culture *versus* conventional stage (p. 92); how recollection may be strengthened (p. 93). § 99. Repetition and writing down as a means of memorizing (p. 93).

CHAPTER VII.—The Logical Epoch. § 100. General concepts or schemata (p. 94); logical distinctions of particular, individual, and universal (p. 95). § 101. The cultivation of the sense of truthfulness; illusion and deception (p. 95). § 102. Logical forms, their use in education (p. 96).

CHAPTER VIII.—Method. § 103. Method the order in which a study or topic develops in the mind; the three elements of instruction (p. 96). § 104. The order of arrangement that belongs to the nature of the subject (p. 97). § 105. The order in which the pupil can best learn a subject, depending upon his stage of intellect, whether in the stage of sense-perception or imagination or abstract thought (p. 98); progress from the known to the unknown; function of illustration; symbolizing (p. 99); discovery of relations—finding the definition or complete description of a subject; necessary conditions of being (p. 100); the dialectic method which investigates the necessary presuppositions (p. 101). § 106. Method of demonstration—analytic, synthetic, and dialectic proofs—invention and construction, or heuristic and architectonic methods (p. 101); the genetic or dialectic method (p. 102); ascent from particular fact or event to the Cause of All by the dialectic method (p. 103); the notion or idea—the judgment as distinction of universal and particular—the syllogism as distinguishing and uniting the universal, particular, and individual (p. 104). § 107. The adaptation of the subject taught to the actual capacity and need of the pupil by the teacher (p. 104); the teacher must know the individual case, and use the necessary means to make the subject understood (p. 105).

Chapter IX.—Instruction. § 108. The pupil lacks what the teacher possesses and can give him by instruction (p. 106). § 109. Apprentice and master; true basis of authority found only in superior knowledge and ability (p. 106). § 110. Apprenticeship, journeymanship, mastership (p. 107). § 111. Three degrees of capacity in the pupil—dullness, mediocrity, talent and genius (p. 107); mediocrity the general rule among pupils—dunces and geniuses the exceptions (p. 108); genius has unbounded inclination and capacity, and is clear as to the methods which it should use—talent lacks insight into the best methods (p. 109). § 112. Difficulty of educating talent and genius wisely on account of precocity, which must be repressed (p. 109); vanity, affectation, and self-consciousness to be repressed (p. 110). § 113. The traditional learning which controls a sphere of knowledge (p. 110); the dilettant or amateur neglects the necessary preparation, but hastens to produce without it (p. 111); self-taught men and their obstacles; genius can teach itself (p. 112); the professionally educated; the *rôle* of reformer. § 114. Correspondence between apprenticeship and professional education, etc. (p. 113).

Chapter X.—The Act of Learning. § 115. The first object of the teacher to arouse the pupil to self-activity (p. 113); difference between didactic and artistic expositions (p. 114). § 116. Three elements in learning (p. 114). § 117. The mechanical element defined—punctuality, regularity, and system (p. 115). § 118. Dynamical element or self-activity of the pupil (p. 115). § 119. How to develop the power of the pupil to assimilate or digest knowledge by his own activity through attention and repetition (p. 116). § 120. Industry defined; laziness, over-haste, and over-exertion (p. 117). § 121. Seeming laziness and seeming industry (p. 118).

Chapter XI.—The Modality of the Process of Teaching. § 122. Three methods of instruction (p. 120). § 123. The lessons of experience; what is learned in the period of infancy (p. 120); in learning one's trade or vocation; in partaking of citizenship; in the church

(p. 121). § 124. What is learned through books; convenience of such learning—necessity of translating into elements of one's own experience (p. 121). § 125. Text-books should give us the principal results in any department, omitting no essential elements (122); good and bad text-books described (p. 123). § 126. If intended for private study the book should go more into details (p. 124). § 127. Oral instruction the most powerful agent of education (p. 124); the latest discoveries, the pronunciation of foreign languages, and similar matters, require oral instruction (p. 125). § 128. Oral and text-book instruction contrasted (p. 125). § 129. Acroamatic or lecture system and erotematic or catechetical method described and criticised (p. 126); system of Bell and Lancaster; Diesterweg's opinion of the lecture system in German universities (p. 127). § 130. Technical and popular lectures contrasted (p. 128); Kant's opinion of popular lectures. § 131. The order of educational institutions (p. 129); general education to be given to all citizens in the elementary schools; *Realschule, Gymnasium,* and university (p. 130); self-educated men compared with university educated men (p. 131); academies of art; natural science and modern languages *versus* Latin and Greek (p. 132). § 132. Rules and regulations of the school; programme of work (p. 133); struggle between the *Gymnasia* and the industrial interests of the community (p. 134). § 133. The teachers should manage the programme, course of study, methods of instruction (p. 135); in other matters it is governed by the civil power (p. 135); historical origin of the school through the Church (p. 136). § 134. State and church contrasted; their relation to the school (p. 137); disposition contrasted with overt act; freedom from authority in matters of science (p. 138). § 135. Limitations of church and state in their control over the school (139). § 136. School inspection ought to extend over the entire system so as to properly co-ordinate the several departments and give unity to the work (p. 140).

Chapter XII.—Education of the Will. § 137. The third special element of education is will-training (p. 141). § 138. The will-training consists in discipline, or the voluntary putting on of the forms of action prescribed by civilization, in preference to following one's natural impulses; morality and religion furnish the highest forms to which the natural will must be subjected (p. 142); politeness or conformity to the social code the least essential form (p. 143).

Chapter XIII.—Social Culture. § 139. The beginning of education of the will is the training in obedience to social manners and customs—i. e., training in behavior toward others (p. 143). § 140. The family training for the will begins with requiring obedience to elders (p. 144). The accident of birth determines this relation of superiority and inferiority. § 141. After the family comes the education of civil society, which insists on obedience to a social code of etiquette; politeness celebrates the form of devotion to the welfare of others (p. 146). § 142. Dangers of the mania for attracting attention of others, or of too much restraint and slavish dependence on the social code (p. 147). § 143. Urbanity is the mastery of the social code rather than slavish subordination to it. It obeys forms, but with a sort of irony (p. 147). § 144. The necessity of training one to prudent wariness against the dangers that arise from human selfishness in the world (p. 149).

CHAPTER XIV.—Moral Culture. § 145. Morality is the true essence of social culture. Its categories are duty, virtue, and conscience (p. 150). § 146. Unconditional obedience to duty is the first demand of moral education; not happiness, but duty, must be the guide of the will (p. 151). § 147. The training of the will to obey duty results in virtue; three things to be noticed—dialectic of virtues, moral discipline, character (p. 151). § 148. Dialectic interdependence of virtues (p. 151); the doctrine of the mean (p. 152); no unessential virtues; no vacations to be permitted in moral obedience (p. 153); missteps undo the whole work (p. 154). § 149. Self-government to be attained by disciplining the will to renounce some things that are permitted it (p. 154). § 150. The development of character is the final result of discipline of the will in self-control (p. 155); the factors that form it are temperament, external events, the energy of the will. § 151. Conscience is the consciousness of one's ideal self (p. 156) in contrast to the real self.

CHAPTER XV.—Religious Culture. § 152. Conscience is the bridge that leads over from morality to religion; the difference between the atheistic moralist and the religious moralist (p. 157); the unconscious irony of atheism (p. 158). § 153. The change of heart (p. 159). § 154. Three things in religious education—the theory or view of the world taught in religion, the discipline in the practice of religious observances, the union with a particular church (p. 160).

CHAPTER XVI.—The Theoretical Process of Religious Culture. § 155. Three stages of religion—feeling, religious images and symbols, religious insight into dogmas (p. 160). § 156. Feeling or emotion the basis of religion; but, if only a feeling, then only fetichism is possible; Schleiermacher's opinion (p. 161). § 157. Above mere emotion is the religious act which forms mental images of the Divine Being and his relation to man (p. 162). § 158. Mysticism an arrested development of the mind on this stage of religious feeling (p. 162). § 159. Religious imagination not an idle exercise of the fancy, but the fancy under the control of unconscious reason (p. 163). § 160. By reflection on the meaning and significance of the religious images, there arises a clear insight into the essential nature of the divine (p. 163). § 161. If the mind is arrested in its development at this stage of religious imagination, polytheism and idolatry arise; education must not for this reason reject the religious imagination altogether (p. 164). § 162. Religious thought, as a higher stage than religious imagination, has three stages—abstract, reflective, speculative (p. 165). § 163. The abstract stage, which sets up dogmas without any attempt to show their connection or their necessity in reason, is forced to give way before reflection, which, unless guided properly, will discover difficulties and become skeptical (p. 167); education must take care not to attempt to develop the reflective stage prematurely; it should, however, be careful to direct the inquiries of those already advanced to the stage of reflection, so that they may attain the speculative insight into the necessity of religious truth. § 164. The final stage of religious instruction in doctrinal matters therefore endeavors to give philosophical insight (p. 168).

CHAPTER XVII.—The Practical Process of Religious Culture. § 165. The three phases of religious discipline—consecration of self, performance of religious ceremonies, religious reconciliation with one's lot (p. 169). § 166. Distinction between the moral and the religious standpoints—the latter looks upon duty as the action of the Divine Will, and thus comes into personal relation to God (p. 169); distinction of sin, crime, and evil as the categories of religion, civil authority, and morality (p. 170). § 167. Consecration of self, the renunciation of selfish egotism; observance of religious ceremonies is intended to make consecration easy, because it gives the support of the whole church to each member of it (p. 170); but there is danger sometimes of confounding ceremonies with religion itself (p. 171). § 168. Religious peace and reconciliation may come through consecration of self, or through that and the practice of religious ceremonial (p. 171); but often it is only the rough discipline of life which brings home to the mind the truth of religion (p. 172); reconciliation must not be mere stoicism or fanatical asceticism, but cheerful activity in one's vocation (p. 173); discontent with one's lot; the *blasé* mood (p. 174).

CHAPTER XVIII.—The Absolute Process of Religious Culture. § 169. Three stages—feeling and consecration, symbolism and ceremonial, religious insight and reconciliation (p. 175). § 170. The first stage of religion a mysterious impulse toward the infinite (p. 176). § 171. The family instructs the child in its own chosen form of worship (p. 176). § 172. Reflection on the dogmas of revealed religion leads to insight into their rational basis (p. 177). § 173. The three stages are all essential to complete religious experience (p. 178). § 174. Religious education is the last and highest form of the particular elements of education (p. 179).

THIRD PART.—Particular Systems of Education. INTRODUCTION.—Historical systems of education. § 175. The number of pedagogical principles is limited to a few ideas, and hence there are only a limited number of historic systems (p. 183); the deduction of the fundamental ideas and the three general forms of civilization and their corresponding systems of education (p. 185). § 176. Civilization conditions all education and furnishes its object and aim; an outline of the three great phases of civilization (p. 185)—the Oriental civilizations, together with the Greek and Roman, form the first; the Jewish, the second; Christian civilization, the third (p. 187). § 177. The national, the theocratic, the humanitarian systems of education based on the three types of civilization (p. 188).

CHAPTER I.—The System of National Education. § 178. The family is the natural germ out of which grow the other institutions, and it furnishes the basis of national education (p. 190); the meaning of *pietas;* Des Coulanges and ancestor-worship; Hegel's definition of *Geist* (p. 191). §179. National education includes three systems—passive, active, individual (p. 191). § 180. The passive a subjection, first, to the family authority (China); second, to the caste (India); third, to the cloister (Thibet) (p. 192). § 181. The active system is directed against the restraint of Nature; first, the Persian, whose aim is conquest; second, the Egyptian, whose aim is preparation for death and the immortal life; third, the Phœnician and the conquest of the ocean (p. 192). § 182. The individual system with the Greek aims at freedom and its expression in the work of art. § 183. The æsthetic (Greek) aim is followed by the practical (Roman) aim, which seeks individuality in its essential form of rights under equal laws; the

German tribes possessed a morbid love of individuality for its own sake (p. 194).

CHAPTER II. First Group—the System of Passive Education. § 184. The rational basis of passive education, the desire to free man from the thralldom of Nature by mutual social help; its defect lies in the fact that it produces a new thralldom to social order, which, however, is better than the former thralldom to Nature (p. 196). § 185. *Family education*, in its purest form in China (p. 196). § 186. The family feeling *(pietas)* demanding obedience to paternal authority and the protection and guidance of the younger by the elder (p. 197). § 187. Family education consists in learning the network of usages or etiquette; punishment corrective only; endless number of maxims of obedience; Hegel's description of the Chinese (p. 198); the Chinese alphabet; Chinese schools and fourfold system of examinations; effect of exclusive cultivation of the memory in producing a conservative people (p. 199). § 188. Chinese reading and writing (p. 200). § 189. *Caste education* in India; the station determined by birth and not by education (p. 200). § 190. Education consists in learning the ceremonies due from one caste to the others (p. 201); examples of this (p. 202). § 191. Literature of India; fables and proverbs; the Hitopadesa (p. 202). § 192. *Monkish education* in Thibet; its reaction against Nature, against the family, and against civil society and industry (p. 203). § 193. Division into monks and laity (p. 204). § 194. The Chinese Buddhism and Indian hermit system form a natural transition to the cloister system of Thibet (p. 204); the defect of quietism; contrast of Lamaism and Christian monasticism; *nirvana*; selfishness *versus* selfhood; the Sankhya doctrine of India the root of Buddhist theology (p. 205).

CHAPTER III.—Second Group—the System of Active Education. § 195. Active education subordinates family, caste, and cloister to an objective purpose of conquest—military as in Persia, future life as in Egypt, industrial as in Phœnicia (p. 206). § 196. *Military education* for the purpose of establishing an absolute, unlimited empire by subjugation of all neighboring nations; history of Persia (p. 207), the absolute limit of Persian conquest found in Grecian individuality (p. 208). § 197. Persian education in truth-speaking, in riding horseback, and in the use of the bow and arrow; its contrast with education in India and Thibet (p. 208); explanation of truth-speaking as indicating a sense of the reality of finite things—the Hindoo believed finite things to be a dream-product; the uses of social order, its sacredness to the Chinese and Hindoos; its better appreciation by the Persians and active peoples (p. 209). § 198. Herbeds, Mobeds, Destur-mobeds among the Magi; the Persian deities Ormuzd and Ahriman at war with each other (p. 210). § 199. *Priestly education* of Egypt for the sake of preparing man in this life for the next; how the Persian meets death; in Egypt the death-court the supreme tribunal (p. 211); Osiris and Amenti (p. 212). § 200. School studies; aim in life; Chinese, Hindoo, Buddhist, Persian, and Egyptian contrasted (p. 212); Egyptian science; engineering; surveying, why so important; hieroglyphics; method of teaching arithmetic; cost of rearing a child up to manhood only four dollars (p. 213). § 201. *Industrial education* of Phœnicia resembles in its aim that of the other active (i. e., restless) peoples; manufacture of articles of luxury; commerce; Phœnician quarter in foreign cities; education in deceit, and in indifference toward family and native land; love of gain; extent of Phœnician commerce and manufactures; the alphabet (p. 214). § 202. Branches of study; sacrifice of first-born to Moloch produced filial indifference necessary to a nation of sailors (p. 215).

CHAPTER IV.—Third Group—the System of Individual Education. § 203. Individuality contains both passivity and activity; it desires *to be* rather than *to have;* its three principles—beauty (Greek), legal rights (Roman), dæmonic love of individuality (German tribes) (p. 216); characterization of these principles (p. 217); Norse sea-kings, knights-errant, "cow-boys" (p. 218). § 204. *Æsthetic education.* Gracefulness, the expression of freedom in the control of the limbs, constitutes the essence of Greek beauty (p. 218). § 205. At first athletic games formed the chief education in Greece; then politics and poetry (p. 218); an account of the games; cultivation of the sense of the beautiful in the human form; followed by a race of artists who fixed in stone the ideal types of gracefulness (p. 220). § 206. Composite races of Greece; Dorians, Æolians, Ionians; gymnastics, music, poetry; Athens the supreme center of Greek individuality (p. 221). § 207. Education in the heroic age; epic histories and adventures (p. 221); Hercules, Melkarth, Izdubar, Mar-duk, Babel (p. 222). § 208. Gymnastics, music, grammatics (p. 222). § 209. Objects aimed at in gymnastics (p. 222). § 210. Music expressed to the ear what gracefulness did to the eye—a sense of rhythm and self-control (p. 222); rhythm explained; the nine muses; Hegel's description of the Greek spirit; Greek faculty of interpreting the sounds and movements in Nature (p. 223). § 211 The cithern; the flute at Thebes (p. 223); strange theory of Aristotle in regard to the immoral effect of flute-music (p. 224). § 212. Grammar or literary culture; Iliad, Odyssey, Æsop, and tragic poets (p. 224). § 213. The Peloponnesian war destroyed the Greek worship of the beautiful (p. 224); sophists; Diogenes the Cynic; Socrates and his teaching of conscious investigation of motives; the oracle or external omen *versus* conscience (p. 225). § 214. Socrates' doctrine that virtue can be taught; Plato's Dorianism; Aristotle's modern views (p. 226). § 215. Dissolution of the Greek principle in Stoicism and Epicureanism (p. 227). § 216. Educational significance of Stoicism and Epicureanism to be found in the fact that they both depend on a careful discipline of the intellect and will, whereas early Greek life was spontaneous—not labor, but play (p. 228); Marcus Aurelius (p. 229).

CHAPTER V.—*Practical Education.* § 217. The Roman makes usefulness rather than beauty his principle, and the ideal of the useful is to him the political power of the State which makes possible to the citizen all the good things—life itself, and all the enjoyments of life (p. 229); discussion of the peculiarity of the Roman character; its history; outlaws living on a border-land; compact; the political bond the highest religion; private right of property and the network of laws that protect it; essential dualism in the Roman consciousness (p. 230). § 218. Æsthetic culture, which was religion to the Greeks, was to the Romans mere amusement; three epochs in Roman education (p. 231). § 219. The first epoch, juristic and military (p. 231); laws of the twelve tables; fugitives to the Roman hills; Latin words expressing self-control and severe self-criticism (p. 232); ancestor-worship in Rome; Christianity adapted to solve the contradiction of the Roman mind (p. 233). § 220. Education of woman in Rome contrasted with that in Greece (p. 233). § 221. Education by the mother; by a jurist; in the army; stress laid on implicit obedience; schools called *ludi;* love of moderation (p. 234); Shakespeare's "Coriolanus" (p. 235). § 222. Influence of Greece after the conquest; æsthetic education supplants the old Roman education; study of Greek language and rhetoric (p. 235); Greek philosophy; Cicero, Seneca, Boëthius: use of rhetoric; Apollonius of Rhodes (p. 236). § 223. Literary trifling and the study of art for amusement; *belles-lettres; salons;* Sallust, Pliny, Nero (p. 237). § 224. Wearied of amusement in art, the Roman betook himself to mysticism and secret rites borrowed from Persian and Egyptian mysteries (p. 238).

§ 225. Grades of initiation in the mysteries; Mithras, Isis, Pythagoreanism; Apollonius of Tyana; the Illuminati (p. 239). § 226. *Abstract individual education.* The individualism of the Germanic tribes called *abstract* because pure and simple; its characteristics; why called *dæmonic* (p. 240); Berserker rage; tragedy of Brunhild in the old Norse Edda (p. 241).

Chapter VI.—The System of Theocratic Education. § 227. The Roman idea of the *genus humanum;* same idea reached by the Hebrew prophets in the doctrine of a Messiah recognized as God by all nations; the Jewish view of Nature as entirely distinct from God; God a pure, spiritual personality (p. 249); Jewish proselytes; in what the Jewish and Roman ideas are identical (p. 243). § 228. Emancipation from idolatry and superstition through the worship of God as absolutely above Nature; the ceremonial law as God's direct will and not as a natural law; the decalogue (p. 244). § 229. Patriarchal element, hereditary people of God; hierarchical element, observance of ceremonial law; cultivation of the memory (p. 245). § 230. A progress from the external to the internal and from lower to higher (p. 245). § 231. At first the inducement of external prosperity and the threat of punishment for disobedience; then the insight into the fact that the law contains its own reward; Jesus Sirach, Plato's "Republic" and "Laws" (p. 246). § 232. In the law was revealed an ideal standard of conduct by which each one could criticise his own life; the belief that the one true religion will prevail everywhere ultimately (p. 248). § 233. The Prince of Peace; not beautiful, not great in battle, but holy; this ideal the highest of all ideals (p. 249).

Chapter VII.—The System of Humanitarian Education. § 234. The systems of national and theocratic education unite in that of humanitarian education (p. 250); this looks upon all men as having the same ultimate possibilities; the goal to be reached is the brotherhood of all men and the realization of the consciousness of freedom in each. Its ideal is the foundation of such institutions as secure the common good of all without suppressing the individuality of each. The best institution enables each of its members to participate to the greatest degree in the good of all, and it encourages self-activity in the highest degree (p. 251). § 235 and § 236. The epochs of humanity-education are three—monkish, chivalric, citizen, corresponding to the predominance of the Greek, Roman, and Protestant Christianity (p. 253). § 237. *The epoch of monkish education;* within the Greek Church the principle of renunciation of the world took strongest hold, and produced the hermit phases of Christianity, together with the first phase of monasticism (p. 253); St. Francis and St. Dominic make essential changes in monasticism (p. 254). § 238. The one-sidedness of monasticism; its tendency toward Oriental quietism (p. 254). § 239. Its tendency to reproduce the historic past rather than to realize an ideal in the present (p. 254). § 240. The three vows of poverty, chastity, obedience, signify the rejection of the institutions of civilization—civil society, the family, the state; relation of Lamaism to Christian monasticism; Abbé Huc (p. 255); explanation of the effect of the three vows (p. 256). § 241. Monkish discipline—fasts, vigils, penances (p. 256); espionage (p. 257). § 242. The withdrawal of the religious element into cloisters leaves the secular world to barbarism; the Roman Church corrects this defect (p. 257). § 243. *The epoch of chivalric education.* § 243. By the principle of sanctity in works, the Roman Church brings back religion into the secular, and chivalric education arises (p. 258). § 244. Industry was admitted side by side with religious ceremonial in the Roman Church; Tauler's "Imitation of the Life of Christ" (p. 258). § 245. The education of chivalry in the practice of arms, in knightly etiquette, and poetry (p. 259). § 246. Chivalry goes to the opposite extreme of monkish education in its placing unbounded value on individuality; eccentricity of knight-errantry (p. 260). § 247. Downfall of chivalry (p. 260); the Crusades; free cities; free citizenship (p. 261).

Chapter VIII.—*The Epoch of Education fitting one for Civil Life.* § 248. The growth of cities and free citizenship finds especial recognition in Protestantism, whose most important feature is the recognition of secularism (p. 262). § 249. The phases of development three—citizen education in the two forms of pietism and Jesuitism, a reaction in favor of classics and history on the one hand and toward the study of natural science on the other, the reconciliation of these in the education of the future (p. 262). § 250. *Civil education as such* overcomes the one-sidedness of chivalric and monkish education (p. 263); sensuality and love of display (p. 264). § 251. Utility becomes a very important principle (p. 265). § 252. Founding of schools for citizens' children; defects of educational methods; Melanchthon, Amos Comenius, Sturm, Roman law, and medicine at Bologna and Salerno; Protestant universities (p. 266). § 253. The citizen class is recognized as one of the three estates; French the language of courts; unscrupulous, worldly-wise maxims; self-estrangement of the nobles (p. 268). § 254. Two religious systems—Jesuitic and pietistic (p. 269). § 255. *Jesuitic education* characterized; Claudius of Aquaviva; dialectics; rhetoric; physics; morals; declamation; diplomatic conduct (p. 270); obedience; discipline; number of schools; emulation; supervision (p. 271). § 256. *Pietism* as the counterpart of Jesuitism—its tendency toward quietism; its estrangement from the world; its negative dependence on works (p. 272); its espionage; its attitude toward Nature, history, and philosophy; the catechism, the Bible and hymn-book; the feeling of abandonment by God (p. 273); Spener and Francke; Quakers and Puritans; the truth of pietism; the truth of Jesuitism (p. 274).

CHAPTER IX.—*The Ideal of Culture.* § 257. Civil education rested on the fourfold basis of (*a*) marriage and the family, (*b*) labor and enjoyment of its products, (*c*) equality of all before the law, (*d*) the duty of acting according to conscience; a counter-reaction now set in against Jesuitism and pietism (p. 275); this was the study of Latin and Greek and the study of natural science (p. 276). § 258. *The humanist ideal* was supposed to be attained through the study of Latin and Greek (p. 276); the uselessness and remoteness of these studies gave the mind an ideal drift; the true reason for the study of Latin and Greek—self-estrangement (p. 277); Trotzendorf and Sturm, the founders of academic methods that still prevail; discipline of mind (p. 278). § 259. The philanthropic ideal was found in the study of natural science and of useful knowledge (p. 279); it spared no pains to make the pupil's work interesting; it sought cosmopolitanism, and found its ideal realized in the state of Nature—the savage in America or Otaheite (p. 280); Rousseau; the *Philanthropina* of Basedow; the French Revolution; Pestalozzi (p. 281); Fichte; the dangers of humanism; the "moderns" (p. 282); self-estrangement studies; the imaginary "natural man" of Rousseau (p. 283); Friedrich Froebel (p. 284). § 260. *Free education* or education of all classes of society for free citizenship (p. 284); moral culture; the consciousness of the essential equality of all men (p. 285); the education by means of the newspaper; modern literature; universal toleration; fraternal interest of each in all; commerce uniting all nations; facilities of rapid transit, rapid communication, and the printed page, hasten forward the participation of each in the life of the whole race (p. 286).

THE PHILOSOPHY OF EDUCATION

INTRODUCTION.

§ 1. The science of education can not be deduced from a simple principle with such strictness as logic, ethics, and like sciences. It is rather a mixed science, which has its presuppositions in many others. In this respect it resembles medicine, with which it has this also in common, that it must make a distinction between a sound and an unhealthy system of education, and must devise means to prevent or to cure the latter. It may, therefore, have, like medicine, the three departments of physiology, pathology, and therapeutics.

[* The science of education is not a complete, independent science by itself. It borrows the results of other sciences, e. g., it presupposes psychology, physiology, æsthetics, and the science of rights (treating of the institutions of the family and civil society, as well as of the state); it presupposes also the science of anthropology, in which is treated the relation of the human mind to nature. Nature conditions the development of the individual human being. But the history of the individual and the history of the race present to us a record of continual emancipation from nature, and continual growth into freedom, i. e., into ability on the part of man to know himself and to realize himself in the world by making the matter and forces of the

* The [ ] include an analysis of, and commentary on, the text.—Editor.

world his instruments and tools. Anthropology shows us how man as a natural being—i. e., as having a body—is limited. There is climate, involving heat and cold and moisture, the seasons of the year, etc.; there is organic growth, involving birth, growth, reproduction, and decay; there is race, involving the limitations of heredity; there is the telluric life of the planet and the circulation of the forces of the solar system, whence arise the processes of sleeping, waking, dreaming, and kindred phenomena; there is the emotional nature of man, involving his feelings, passions, instincts, and desires; then there are the five senses, and their conditions. Next, there is the science of phenomenology, treating of the steps by which mind rises from the stage of mere feeling and sense-perception to that of self-consciousness, i. e., to a recognition of mind as true substance, and of matter as mere phenomenon created by Mind (God). Then follows psychology, including the treatment of the stages of activity of mind, as so-called "faculties" of the mind, e. g., attention, sense-perception, imagination, conception, understanding, judgment, reason, and the like. Psychology is generally made (by English writers) to include, also, what is here called anthropology and phenomenology. After psychology, there is the science of ethics, or of morals and customs; then, the science of rights, already mentioned; then, theology, or the science of religion; and, after all these, there is philosophy, or the science of science. Now, it is clear that the science of education treats of the process of development, by and through which man, as a mere animal, becomes spirit, or self-conscious mind; hence, it presupposes all the sciences named, and will be defective if it ignores nature or mind, or any stage or process of either, especially anthropology, phenomenology, psychology, ethics, rights, æsthetics, religion, or philosophy.

Here is a conspectus showing the systematic classification and arrangement of the topics necessary to a full treatment of man as a spiritual being, according to Rosenkranz (who follows Hegel):

PART I.—ANTHROPOLOGY.

A. The soul in its unity with the body.

I. Natural qualities that affect mental development.

(1) Telluric influences of locality, climate, seasons, etc.

(2) Race peculiarities.

(3) Individual endowments of temperament, talents, idiosyncrasy.

II. Natural processes that arise in the human organism, and produce various shades and varieties of character.

(1) Difference of sex.

(2) Age: infancy, youth, maturity, old age.

(3) Alternation of sleeping and waking.

III. Feeling.

(1) Feeling as distinction of the soul into subject and object (pleasure and pain).

(2) External and internal feeling or (a) *sensations* of touch, taste, smell, hearing, seeing, and (b) *emotions* of love, hate, joy, sorrow, fear, hope, envy, etc.

(3) Feeling of personality or individual identity in contradistinction to sensations and emotions.

β. The soul in its struggle against its union with the body:

I. Dreams.

(1) Ordinary dreams that occur in sleep.

(2) Waking dreams that take the form of (a) presentiments, (b) hallucinations, (c) "second-sight," so called.

(3) Hypnotism: (a) somnambulism, (b) "animal magnetism" or "magnetic sleep," (c) clairvoyance.

II. Sanity and insanity.

(1) In what sanity consists.

(2) Derangement: (a) idiocy and feeble-mindedness, (b) lunacy, (c) raving madness.

(3) Cure of insanity.

III. Habit.

(1) How the soul makes new and strange things familiar and natural by repetition.

(2) By habit the soul makes a second nature in place of its animal nature, controlling its body in accordance with customs, fashions, and ethical laws.

(3) The body obedient to the soul becomes a symbol.

C. The symbolical manifestation of the soul by means of its body.

I. Mimicry and gestures (conventional mimicry of different nations).

II. Physiognomy and facial expression.

III. The voice.

PART II.—PHENOMENOLOGY OF THE SOUL

(or the history of consciousness and its views of the world).

A. Consciousness.
  I. Sensuous certitude.
  II. Perception.
  III. Understanding (the discovery of laws of nature and the announcement of ethical laws for itself).
B. Self-consciousness.
  I. The non-personal, or that which is devoid of self.
  II. The ego.
  III. The ego related to other egos.
C. Rational self-consciousness (or that view of the world that recognizes it as a manifestation of reason).

PART III.—PSYCHOLOGY.

A. Theoretical mind (or the intellect).
  I. Sense-perception.
  II. Representation (or mental picturing).
    (1) Recollection.
    (2) Imagination and fancy.
    (3) Memory.
  III. Thinking.
    (1) Understanding.
    (2) Reflection.
    (3) Speculative thinking.
B. Practical mind (or the will).
  I. Practical feeling (or the emotions that lead to action of the will).
  II. The species of practical feeling.
    (1) Appetite (or desire for present objects of sense-perception).
    (2) Inclination or propensity (desire for absent objects).
    (3) Passion (or desire that absorbs the entire thought and will).
  III. Happiness as the result of regulated impulses and their gratification.

Part IV.—Ethics.

A. The good (established form of civilization).

I. Will realized in the form of law.

II. Caprice and arbitrariness (its sphere).

III. Freedom.

(1) Self-legislation (autonomy).

(2) Self-rule (autocracy).

(3) Independence (autarky).

B. Morality.

I. Duty.

(1) The deed of the individual.

(a) Free-will (voluntary and involuntary action).

(b) The purpose proposed to be accomplished by the deed.

(c) The ethical intention of the deed.

(2) Duty.

(a) Division into duties toward one's self and toward society.

(b) Collision of duties.

(c) Relation of duties to ability to perform them.

II. Virtue.

(a) System of virtues (physical, intellectual, and practical).*

(b) Self-discipline.

(c) Character.

III. Conscience.

C. Ethical institutions, or science of rights.

I. Rights of the individual.

(1) Natural rights.

(a) Personal freedom.

(b) Property.

(c) Contract.

(2) Wrong.

(3) Punishment.

II. Particular rights (i. e., those that appertain to institutions).

(1) The family.

(2) Civil society and the community.

(a) The nature of society.

---

* "Practical" used in the Aristotelian sense of *belonging to the will.*

(b) Its functions in detail.
- (*a*) Human wants (food, clothing, shelter, etc.), and the division of labor, in order to supply them.
- (*b*) Courts of law, civil and criminal.
- (*c*) Civil and municipal authority (having charge of public peace and order, sanitary regulations, public works for the common benefit, such as highways, water-works, police, poor-house, jail, markets, tax-levies, etc.).

(c) The commonwealth.

(3) The state.
- (a) The legislative power.
- (b) The administrative power.
- (c) The supreme executive power.

III. International relations and the history of nations.

(1) The national state.

(a) The states of the passive peoples.
- (*a*) Patriarchal state (China).
- (*b*) Caste state (India).
- (*c*) Cloister state (Thibet).

(b) The states of active peoples.
- (*a*) Warrior state (Persia).
- (*b*) Priestly-agricultural state (Egypt).
- (*c*) Manufacturing and commercial state (Phœnicia).

(c) The states of free individuality.
- (*a*) Æsthetic individuality (Greece).
- (*b*) Practical (will-power) individuality (Rome).
- (*c*) Chivalric individuality (the German or "Holy Roman" Empire).

(2) The theocratic state.

(a) Jewish theocracy.
- (*a*) Mosaic rule.
- (*b*) Talmudic rule.

(b) Mohammedan state.

(3) Humanitarian state.

Part V.—Æsthetic Art.

A. The beautiful.
  I. The nature of the beautiful.
  II. The ugly.
  III. The comic.
B. Art.
  I. The ideal.
  II. Style.
  III. The work of art.
C. The system of fine arts.
  I. Plastic arts and those that offer visible shapes.
    (a) Architecture.
    (b) Sculpture.
    (c) Painting.
  II. Music.
  III. Poetry.
    (a) Epic.
    (b) Lyric.
    (c) Dramatic.

Part VI.—Religion.

A. The nature of religion.
  I. Subjective process (regeneration).
    (a) Unconscious unity with God.
    (b) The fall, and consciousness of sin.
    (c) The atonement and reconciliation.
  II. Objective process (worship).
    (a) Prayer.
    (b) Ceremonial.
    (c) Sacrifice.
  III. Absolute process (the Church).
    (a) The Church educates the individual by awakening his consciousness of sin and leading him to regeneration.
    (b) The Church organizes worship and provides times, places, and a consecrated priesthood.
    (c) The Church organizes a universal missionary movement to extend its view of the divine world-order to all men.

B. Religious phenomenology.
  I. Religions of mere emotion.
    (1) Fetichism.
    (2) Worship of elements.
    (3) Worship of plants and animals.
  II. Religions of imagination.
    (1) Cosmogonies.
    (2) Ethical-heroic.
    (3) Allegorical.
  III. Religions of pure thought.
C. Historic systems.
  I. Religion of absolute substance (the heathen religions).
  II. Religion of absolute subjectivity (Jewish).
  III. Religion of absolute spirituality (Christianity—which holds that the Absolute is Divine-human).

PART VII.—SCIENCE.

A. Sciences of nature.
  I. Matter—mechanics.
  II. Force—dynamics.
    (1) Gravitation.
    (2) Cohesion.
    (3) Reaction against cohesion.
      (a) Sound—acoustics.
      (b) Heat.
      (c) Light.
    (4) Magnetic polarity.
    (5) Electric polarity.
    (6) Chemical polarity.
    (7) Meteorological process.
      (a) Process of the atmosphere—winds, temperature, zones, etc.
      (b) Process of the water.
      (c) Fire process.
  III. Life—organics.
    (1) Geology.
      (a) Mineralogy.
      (b) Stratification.

(c) Configuration of the surface of the earth.
(*a*) The factors: mountains, rivers, sea.
(*b*) The formations: insular, continental, and peninsular.
(2) Vegetation—botany.
(3) Animal—zoölogy.
(a) Structure of animal form.
(b) Vital process.
(c) Classification of animals.

B. Sciences of spiritual individuality.
I. Anthropology.
II. Phenomenology.
III. Psychology.
IV. Ethics.
(1) The will.
(2) Morality.
(3) Institutions of civilization.
V. Æsthetic art.
VI. Religion.
VII. Philosophy.]

§ 2. Since education is capable of no such exact definitions of its principle and no such logical treatment as other sciences, the treatises written upon it abound more in shallowness than any other literature. Short-sightedness and arrogance find in it a most congenial atmosphere, and uncritical methods and declamatory bombast flourish as nowhere else. The literature of religious tracts might be considered to rival that of the science of education in its superficiality and assurance, if it did not for the most part seem itself to belong, through the fact that it attempts to influence human conduct, to the science of education. But teachers as persons should be treated in these their weaknesses and failures with the utmost consideration, because with most of them the endeavor to contribute their mite for the improvement of education arises from pure motives, and the work of teaching tends to foster the habit of administering reproof and giving advice.

[The scope of the science of education being so broad, and its presuppositions so vast, its limits are not well defined, and its treatises are very apt to lack logical sequence and conclusion; and, indeed, frequently to be mere collections of unjustified and unexplained assumptions, dogmatically set forth. Hence the low repute of educational literature as a whole.]

§ 3. The charlatanism of educational literature is also increased by the fact that schools have become profitable undertakings, and the competition in this business tends to encourage the advertising of one's own merits.

When "Boz" in his "Nicholas Nickleby" exposed the shocking doings of an English boarding-school, many teachers of such schools were, as he assures us, so accurately described that they openly complained he had aimed his caricatures directly at them.

[Moreover, education furnishes a special vocation, that of teaching. (All vocations are specializing—being cut off, as it were, from the total life of man. The "division of labor" requires that each individual shall concentrate his endeavors on his own specialty and be a *part* of the whole.)]

§ 4. In the system of the sciences, the science of education belongs to the philosophy of spirit—and in this, to the department of practical philosophy, the problem of which is the comprehension of the essence of freedom; for education is the conscious influence of one will upon another, so as to produce in it a conformity to an ideal which it sets before it. The idea of subjective spirit, as well as that of art, science, and religion, forms an essential presupposition for the science of education, but does not contain its principle. In a complete exposition of practical philosophy (ethics), the science of education may be distributed under each of its several heads. But the point at which the science of education branches off in practical philosophy is the idea of the family, inasmuch as here the distinctions of age and degrees of maturity are taken account of as arising from nature, and the claim of children upon their parents for education makes itself manifest. All other phases of education, in order to succeed, must presuppose a true family life. They may extend and complement the school, but can not be its original foundation.

In this systematic exposition of education, we must not allow ourselves to be led into error by those theories which do not recognize family nurture as an essential educative influence, but demand that children shall be removed from their parents at an early age, and brought up in institutions provided for infants. The Platonic philosophy is the most respectable representative of this class. Modern writers who testify their great pleasure at seeing the world full of children, but who would dispense with the loving care of the family in their education, offer us only a weak and impractical imitation of the Platonic "Republic."

[The science of education, as a special science, belongs to the collection of sciences (already described, in commenting on § 1) included under the philosophy of spiritual being or Mind, and more particularly to that part of it which relates to the will (ethics and science of rights, rather than to the part relating to the intellect and feeling, as anthropology, phenomenology, psychology, æsthetics, and religion. "Subjective spirit" includes anthropology, phenomenology, and psychology. "Theoretical" relates to the *intellect*, "practical" relates to the *will*, in this philosophy). The province of practical philosophy is the investigation of the nature of freedom, and the process of securing it by self-emancipation from nature. The science of education presupposes the conscious exertion of influence on the part of the will of the teacher upon the will of the pupil, with a purpose in view —that of inducing the pupil to form certain prescribed habits, and adopt prescribed views and habits. According to this definition, the unconscious influences which are so powerful in forming human character are not included under the term "education" (*Erziehung*) as here used. The entire science of man (as above shown) is presupposed by the science of education, and must be kept constantly in view as a guiding light. The institution of the *family* (treated in practical philosophy) is the starting-point of education, and, without this institution properly realized, education would find no solid foundation. The right to be educated on the part of children and the duty to educate on the part of parents are reciprocal; and there is no family life so poor and rudimentary that it does not furnish the most important elements of education—no matter what the subsequent influence of the school, the vocation, and the state.]

§ 5. Much confusion also arises from the fact that many do not clearly enough draw the distinction between education as a science and education as an art. As a science, it busies itself with developing *a priori* the idea of education in the universality and necessity of that idea, but as an art it is the concrete special realization of this abstract idea in any given case. And, in any such given case, the peculiarities of the person who is to be educated and, in fact, all the existing circumstances necessitate an adaptation of the universal aims and ends, that can not be provided for beforehand, but must rather test the ready tact of the educator who knows how to take advantage of the existing conditions to fulfill his desired end. Just here it is that the educator may show himself inventive and creative, and that pedagogic talent can distinguish itself. The word "art" is here used in the same way as it is used when we say, the art of war, the art of government, etc.; and rightly, for we are talking about the possibility of the realization of the idea or theory.

The educator must adapt himself to the pupil, but not to such a degree as to imply that the pupil is incapable of change; on the contrary, he must be sure that the pupil shall learn through his experience the independence of the object studied, which remains uninfluenced by his variable personal moods, and the adaptation on the teacher's part must never compromise this independence.

[The science of education distinguished from the art of education: the former containing the abstract general treatment, and the latter taking into consideration all the conditions of concrete individuality, e. g., the peculiarities of the teacher and the pupil, all the local circumstances, and the power of adaptation known as "tact."]

§ 6. If conditions which are local, temporal, and individual, are fixed as constant rules, and carried beyond their proper limits, unavoidable error arises. The formulæ of teaching are admirable material upon which to apply the science, but are not the science itself.

[The special conditions and peculiarities considered in education as an art may be formulated and reduced to system, but they should not be introduced as a part of the *science* of education.]

§ 7. The science of education must (1) unfold the general idea of education; (2) must exhibit the particular phases into which the general work of education is divided; and (3) must describe the particular standpoint upon which the general idea realizes or will realize itself in its special processes at any particular time.

[The science of education has three parts: First, it considers the idea and nature of education, and arrives at its true definition; second, it presents and describes the special provinces into which the entire field of education is divided; third, it considers the historical evolution of education by the human race, and the individual systems of education that have arisen, flourished, and decayed, and their special functions in the life of man.]

§ 8. The treatment of the first part is logically too evident to offer any difficulty. It would not do to substitute for it the history of education, because history uses and hence presupposes all the ideas that are treated of in the general and particular divisions of the system.

(Reference to G. Thaulow's pamphlet on "Pedagogics as a Philosophical Science." Berlin, 1845.)

[The scope of the first part is easy to define. The history of education, of course, contains all the ideas and definitions of the nature of education; but it must not for that reason be substituted for the scientific investigation of the nature of education, which alone should constitute this first part (and the history of education be reserved for the third part).]

§ 9. The second division unfolds the subject of the physical, intellectual, and practical culture of the human race, and constitutes the main part of all books on the science of education. Here arises the greatest difficulty as to the limitations, partly in relation to the amount of explanation to be given to the ideas that are borrowed from other sciences, partly in relation to the degree of amplification allowed to the details. Here is the field of the widest possible differences. If, e. g., one studies out the idea of the school with reference to the different species which may arise, it is evident that he can extend his treatise indefinitely; he may, for example, go into the consideration of technological schools of all kinds, for mining, navigation, war, art, etc.

[The second part includes a discussion of the threefold nature of man as body, intellect, and will. The difficulty in this part of the science is very great, because of its dependence upon other sciences (e. g., upon physiology, anthropology, etc.), and because of the temptation to go into details (e. g., in the practical department, to consider the endless varieties of schools for arts and trades).]

§ 10. The third division distinguishes between the different standpoints which are possible in the working out of the conception of education in its special elements, and which therefore produce different systems of education wherein the general and the particular are united or realized in different ways. In every system (historically realized) the general principles that belong to the idea of education (treated under the first division), and the different phases of physical, intellectual, and practical culture of man (treated under the second division), must be found. But the mode of treatment is decided by the historical standpoint which gives reality in a special form to the system of education. Thus it becomes possible to discover the essential contents of the history of education from its idea, since this can furnish only a limited number of systems.

The lower standpoint always merges into the higher, and in so doing first attains its full meaning, e. g.: Education for the sake of the nation is set aside for higher standpoints, e. g., that of Christianity; but we must not suppose that the "national phase" of education was counted as naught from the Christian standpoint, but rather that now, being assigned its proper limits, it can unfold its true idea. This is seen to be the case in the fact that the national individualities become indestructible by being incorporated into Christianity—a fact that condemns the abstract seizing of such relations.

[The third part contains the exposition of the various national standpoints furnished (in the history of the world) for the bases of particular systems of education. In each of these systems will be found the general idea underlying all education, but it will be found existing under special modifications which have arisen through its application to the physical, intellectual, and ethical conditions of the people. But we can deduce the essential features of the different systems that may appear in history, for there are only a limited number of systems possible. Each lower form finds itself complemented in some higher form, and its function and purpose then become manifest. The systems of "national" education (i. e., Asiatic systems, in which the individuality of each person is swallowed up in the substantiality of the national idea—just as the individual waves get lost in the ocean on whose surface they arise) find their complete explanation in the systems of education that arise in Christianity (the preservation of human life being the object of the nation, it follows that, when realized abstractly or exclusively, it absorbs and annuls the mental independence of its subjects, and thus contradicts itself by destroying the essence of what it undertakes to preserve, i. e., human life, which demands freedom and enlightenment; but within Christianity the principle of the state is found so modified that it is consistent with the infinite, untrammeled development of the individual, intellectually and morally, and thus not only life is saved, but spiritual, free life is attainable for each and for all).]

§ 11. The last system must be that of the present, and since this is certainly, on one hand, the result of all the past which still dwells in it, while, on the other hand, engaged in preparing for the future, education demands the unity of the general and particular principle as its ideal, so that looked at in this way the science of education at its end returns to its beginning. The first and second divisions already contain the idea of the system necessary for the present.

[The history of pedagogy ends with the present system as the latest one. As science sees the future ideally contained in the present, it is bound to comprehend the latest system as a realization (though imperfect) of the ideal system of education. Hence, the system, as scientifically treated in the first part of our work, is the system with which the third part of our work ends.]

FIRST PART.

THE GENERAL IDEA OF EDUCATION.

FIRST PART.

THE GENERAL IDEA OF EDUCATION.

§ 12. The idea of the science of education in general must distinguish—

(1) The nature of education in general;
(2) Its form;
(3) Its limits.

[The nature of education, its form, its limits, are now to be investigated. (§§ 13–50.)]

CHAPTER I.

THE NATURE OF EDUCATION.

§ 13. The nature of education is determined by the nature of mind—that it can develop what it is in itself only by its own activity. Mind is in itself free; but, if it does not actualize this possibility, it is in no true sense free, either for itself or for another. Education is the influencing of man by man, and it has for its end to lead him to actualize himself through his own efforts. The attainment of perfect manhood as the actualization of the freedom essential to mind constitutes the nature of education in general.

The completely isolated man does not become man. Solitary human beings who have been found in forests, like the wild girl of the forest of Ardennes, sufficiently prove the fact that the truly human qualities in man can not be developed without reciprocal action with human beings. Caspar Hauser, in his subterranean prison, is an illustration of what man would be by himself. The first cry of the child expresses in its appeals to others this helplessness of man's spiritual being on its first advent in nature.

[The nature of education determined by the nature of Mind or Spirit, whose activity is always devoted to realizing for itself what it is potentially—to becoming conscious of its possibilities, and to getting them under the control of its will. Mind is potentially free. Education is the means by which man seeks to realize in man his possibilities (to develop the possibilities of the race in each individual). Hence, education has freedom for its object.]

§ 14. Man, therefore, is the only fit subject for education. We often speak, it is true, of the education of plants and animals; but, even when we do so, we apply other expressions, as "raising," "breaking," "breeding" and "training," in order to distinguish it from the education of man. "Training" consists in producing in an animal, either by pain or pleasure of the senses, an activity of which, it is true, he is capable, but which he never would have developed if left to himself. On the other hand, it is the nature of education only to assist in the producing of that which the subject would strive most earnestly to develop for himself if he had a clear idea of himself. We speak of raising trees and animals, but not of raising men; and it is only a planter who looks to his slaves for an increase in their number.

The education of men is quite often enough, unfortunately, only a "breaking," and here and there still may be found examples where one tries to teach mechanically, not through the almighty power of the creative Logos, but through the powerless and fruitless appeal to physical pain.

[Man is the only being capable of education, in the sense above defined, because the only conscious being. He must know himself ideally, and then realize his ideal self, in order to become actually free. The animals and plants may be *trained*, or *cultivated*, but, as devoid of self-consciousness (even the highest animals not getting above impressions, not reaching ideas, not seizing general or abstract thoughts), they are not realized for *themselves*, but only for us. (That is, they do not know their ideal as we do.)]

§ 15. The idea of education may be more or less comprehensive. We use it in the widest sense when we speak of the education of the race, for we understand by this expression the connection which the situations and undertakings of different nations have to each other, as steps toward self-conscious freedom. In this the world-spirit is the teacher.

[Education, taken in its widest compass, is the education of the human race by Divine Providence. Here education (*Erziehung*) is recognized to include much more than the "conscious" exertion of influence as defined in § 4.]

§ 16. In a more restricted sense we mean by education the shaping of the individual life by the laws of nature, the rhythm of national customs, and the might of destiny; since, in these, each one finds limits set to his arbitrary will. These mold him into a man often without his knowledge. For he can not act in opposition to nature, nor offend the ethical sense of the people among whom he dwells, nor despise the leading of destiny without discovering through experience that upon the Nemesis of these substantial elements his subjective power can dash itself only to be shattered. If he perversely and persistently rejects all our admonitions, we leave him, as a last resort, to destiny, whose iron rule must educate him, and reveal to him the God whom he has ignored.

It is, of course, sometimes not only possible, but necessary for one, moved by the highest sense of morality, to act in opposition to the laws of nature, to offend the ethical sense of the people that surround him, and to brave the blows of destiny; we are not, however, now speaking of a sublime reformer or martyr, but of the perverse, the frivolous, and the conceited.

[In a narrow sense, education is applied to the shaping of the individual by his environment, so that his caprice and arbitrariness shall give place to rational habits and views, in harmony with nature and ethical customs. He must not abuse nature, nor slight the ethical code of his people, nor despise the gifts of Providence (whether for weal or woe), unless he is willing to be crushed in the collision with these more substantial elements.]

§ 17. In the narrowest sense, which, however, is the usual one, we mean by education the influence which one individual exerts on another in order to develop the latter in some conscious and methodical way, either generally or with reference to some special aim. The teacher must, therefore, be relatively finished in his own education, and the pupil must possess complete confidence in him. If authority be wanting on the one side, or respect and obedience on the other, this ethical basis of development will be lacking, and it can not be replaced by talent, knowledge, skill, or prudence.

Education takes on this form only under the culture which has been developed through the influence of town life. Up to that time we have the *naïve* period of education, which is limited to the general powers of nature, of national customs, and of destiny, and which lasts for a long time among the rural populations. But in the city a greater complication of the environment owing to the uncertainty of the results of reflection (one's environment being chiefly human and given to reflection, and not so simple as the rural environment of plants and animals), the specializing of individuality, through the need of the possession of many arts and trades (and consequent division of labor), these render it impossible for men longer to be ruled by mere custom. The Telemachus of Fénelon was educated to rule himself by means of reflection; the actual Telemachus in the heroic age lived simply according to custom.

[In the narrowest but most usual application of the term, we understand by "education" the influence of the individual upon the individual, exerted with the object of developing his powers in a conscious and methodical manner, either generally or in special directions, the educator being relatively mature, and exercising authority over the relatively immature pupil. Without authority on the one hand and obedience on the other, education would lack its ethical basis—a neglect of the will-training could not be compensated for by any amount of knowledge or smartness.]

§ 18. The general problem of education is the development of the theoretical and practical reason in the individual. If we say that to educate one means to fashion him into morality, we do not make our definition sufficiently comprehensive, because we say nothing of intelligence, and thus confound education and ethics. A man is not merely a human being in general, but, as a rational, conscious subject, he is a peculiar individual, and different from all others of the race.

[The general province of education includes the development of the individual into the theoretical and practical reason immanent in him. The definition which limits education to the development of the individual into ethical customs (obedience to morality, social conventionalities, and the laws of the state—Hegel's definition is here referred to: "The object of education is to make men ethical") is not comprehensive enough, because it ignores the side of the *intellect*, and takes note only of the *will*. The individual should not only be man in general (as he is through the adoption of moral and ethical forms—which are *general* forms, customs, or laws, and thus the forms imposed by the *will* of the *race*), but he should also be a self-conscious subject, a particular individual (man, through his intellect, exists for himself as an individual, while through his general habits and customs he loses his individuality and spontaneity).]

§ 19. Education must lead the pupil, by a connected series of efforts previously foreseen and arranged by the teacher, to a definite end; but the particular form which this shall take must be determined by the individuality of the pupil and the other conditions. Intermittent effort, sudden and violent influences, may accomplish much, but only *systematic* work can advance and fashion him in conformity with his nature; and, if this is lacking, it does not belong to education, for this includes in itself the idea of an end, and that of the technical means for its attainment.

[Education has a definite object in view, and it proceeds by grades of progress toward it. The systematic tendency is essential to all education, properly so called.]

§ 20. But as culture comes to mean more and more, there becomes necessary a division of labor in teaching on account of technical qualifications and special information demanded, because as the arts and sciences are continually increasing in number one can become learned in any one branch only by devoting himself exclusively to it, and hence becoming a specialist. A difficulty hence arises, which is also one for the pupil, of preserving, in spite of this unavoidable one-sidedness, the unity and wholeness which are necessary to humanity.

The *naïve* dignity of the happy savage and the good-natured simplicity of country people appear to very great advantage when contrasted with the narrowness of a special trade, and the endless curtailing of the wholeness of man by the pruning processes of city life. Thus the often-abused savage has his hut, his family, his cocoa-tree, his weapons, his passions; he fishes, hunts, plays, fights, adorns himself, and enjoys the consciousness that he is the center of a whole, while a modern citizen is often reduced by culture to a mere shred of humanity.

[Division of labor has become requisite in the higher spheres of teaching. The growing multiplicity of branches of knowledge creates the necessity for the specialist as teacher. With this tendency to specialties it becomes more and more difficult to preserve what is so essential to the pupil—his rounded human culture and symmetry of development. The citizen of modern civilization sometimes appears to be an artificial product by the side of the versatility of the savage man.]

§ 21. As it becomes necessary to divide the work of instruction, a difference between general and special schools arises, also, from the needs of growing culture. The former give to the pupil with various degrees of completeness all the sciences and arts reckoned as belonging to "general education," and which were included by the Greeks under the general name of Encyclopædia. The latter are known as special schools, suited to particular needs or talents.

The isolation of country life renders it often necessary, or at least desirable, that one man should develop culture symmetrically in very different directions. The poor tutor is required not only to instruct in all the sciences, he must also speak French, and be able to play the piano.

[From this necessity of the division of labor in modern times there arises the demand for two kinds of educational institutions—those devoted to general education (common schools, colleges, etc.), and special schools (for agriculture, medicine, mechanic arts, etc.)].

§ 22. For any person, his actual education compared with its infinite possibilities remains only an approximation, and it can be considered as only relatively finished in particular directions. Education is impossible to him who is born an idiot, since the want of the power of generalizing and of ideality of conscious personality leaves to such an unfortunate only the possibility of a mechanical training.

Sägert, the teacher of the deaf-mutes in Berlin, has made laudable efforts to educate idiots, but the account, as given in his publication, "Cure of Idiots by an Intellectual Method," Berlin, 1840, shows that the results obtained were only external; and, though we do not desire to be understood as denying to this class the possession of a mind *in potentia*, it appears in them to be confined by disease to an embryonic state.

[The infinite possibility of culture for the individual leaves, of course, his actual accomplishment a mere approximation to a complete education. Born idiots are excluded from the possibility of education, because the lack of universal ideas in their consciousness precludes to that class of unfortunates anything beyond a mere mechanical training.]

CHAPTER II.

THE FORM OF EDUCATION.

§ 23. The general form of education is determined by the nature of the mind: mind has reality only in so far as it produces it for itself. The mind is (1) immediate (or potential); but (2) it must estrange itself from itself, as it were, so that it may place itself over against itself as a special object of attention; (3) this estrangement is finally removed through a further acquaintance with the object—it feels itself at home in that on which it looks, and returns again enriched to the form of immediateness (to unity with itself). That which at first appeared to be another than itself is now seen to be itself.

Education can not create; it can only help to develop to reality what was already a possibility; it can only help to bring forth to light the hidden life.

[Spirit, or mind, makes its own nature; it *is* what it produces —a self-result. That is to say: it produces its ideas through self-activity, and only in proportion to its stock of ideas—their number and importance—can mind be said to be realized. Ideas form its "nature," and they are made by the self-activity of mind. From this follows the *form* of education. It commences with (1) undeveloped mind—that of the infant—wherein nearly all is potential, and but little is actualized; (2) its first stage of development is self-estrangement—it is absorbed in the observation of objects around it; (3) but it discovers laws and principles (universality) in external nature, and finally identifies them with reason—it comes to recognize itself in nature—to recognize conscious mind as the creator and preserver of the external world —and thus spirit becomes at home in nature. Education does not create, but it emancipates. It does not make self-activity, but it influences it to develop itself. "Self-estrangement" as here used is perhaps the most important idea in the philosophy of education. Rosenkranz and others have borrowed it from Hegel, who first used it in his "Phenomenology of Spirit" (p. 353) in explaining the revolutionary reaction against established authority and traditional faith as it had been manifested in the French Revolution. The explanation of the effect of the study of classics, pure mathematics, the effect of foreign travel, of the isolated life of students at universities, of wearing special garbs that distinguish one's order from the rest of the community, in short, of any study of strange and far-off phases of the world—the explanation is to be found in the principle of self-estrangement, and its annulment by changing what was foreign into what is familiar.]

§ 24. All culture, whatever may be its special purport, must pass through these two stages—of estrangement, and its removal. Culture must intensify the distinction between the subject and the object, or that of immediateness, though it has again to absorb this distinction into itself; in this way the union of the two may be more complete and lasting. The subject recognizes, then, all the more certainly that what at first appeared to it as a foreign existence belongs to it potentially as its own possession, and that it comes into actual possession of it by means of culture.

Plato, as is known, calls the feeling with which knowledge must begin, wonder; but this can serve as a beginning only, for wonder itself can only express the tension between the subject and the object upon their first presentation to each other—a tension which would be impossible if they were not in themselves identical. Children have a longing for the far-off, the strange, and the wonderful, as if they hoped to find in these an explanation of themselves. They want the object to be a genuine object. That to which they are accustomed, which they see around them every day, seems to have no longer any objective energy for them; but an alarm of fire, banditti life, wild animals, gray old ruins, Robinsons' adventures on far-off happy islands, etc.—everything high colored and glaring—leads them irresistibly on. The necessity of the mind's making itself foreign to itself is that which makes children prefer to hear of the adventurous journeys of Sindbad rather than news of their own city or the history of their nation. On the part of youth this same necessity manifests itself in their desire of traveling.

[This process of self-estrangement and its removal belongs to all culture. The mind must fix its attention upon what is foreign to it, and penetrate its disguise. It will discover its own substance under the seeming alien being. That is to say, it will discover the rational laws that underlie the strange and foreign being, and thereby come to recognize reason or itself. Wonder is the accompaniment of this stage of estrangement. The love of travel and adventure arises from this basis. Culture endeavors first to develop the contrast of the strange to the familiar, but it does this in order to annul it and make the alien into the well-known. Thus it enlarges the individual by making him more inclusive, by making him contain his environment.]

§ 25. This activity of the mind in concentrating itself consciously upon an object with the purpose of making it one's own, or of producing it, is *work*. But when the mind gives itself up to its objects as chance may present them, or through arbitrariness, careless as to whether they have any result, such activity is *play*. Work is laid out for the pupil by his teacher authoritatively, but in his play he is left to himself.

[Labor is distinguished from play: The former concentrates its energies on some object, with the purpose of making it conform to its will and purpose; play occupies itself with its object according to its caprice and arbitrariness, and has no care for the results or products of its activity; work is prescribed by authority, while play is necessarily spontaneous.]

§ 26. Thus work and play must be sharply distinguished from each other. If one does not insist on respect for work as an important and substantial activity, he not only spoils play for his pupil (for this loses all its attraction when deprived of the antithesis of an earnest, set task), but he undermines his respect for real existence. On the other hand, if he does not give him space, time, and opportunity, for play, he prevents the peculiarities of his pupil from developing freely through the exercise of his creative ingenuity. Play sends the pupil back refreshed to his work, since in play he forgets himself in his own way, while in work he is required to forget himself in a manner prescribed for him by another.

Play is of great importance in helping one to discover the true individualities of children, because in play they may betray thoughtlessly their inclinations. The antithesis of work and play runs through the entire life. Children anticipate in their play the earnest work of after-life; thus the little girl plays with her doll, and the boy pretends he is a soldier and in battle.

[Work and play: the distinction between them. In play the child feels that he has entire control over the object with which he is dealing, both in respect to its existence and the object for which it exists. His arbitrary will may change both with perfect impunity, since all depends upon his caprice; he exercises his powers in play according to his natural proclivities, and therein finds scope to develop his own individuality. In work, on the contrary, he must have respect for the object with which he deals. It must be held sacred against his caprice, must not be destroyed nor injured in any way, and its purpose must likewise be respected. His own personal inclinations must be entirely subordinated, and the business that he is at work upon must be carried forward in accordance with its own ends and aims, and without reference to his own feelings in the matter. Thus work teaches the pupil the lesson of self-sacrifice (the right of superiority which the general interest possesses over the particular), while play develops his personal idiosyncrasy.]

§ 27. Work should never be treated as if it were play, nor play as if it were work. In general, the practice of the arts and the study of the sciences stand in this relation to each other: the accumulation of stores of knowledge is the recreation of the mind which is engaged in independent creation, and the practice of arts fills the same office to those whose work is to collect knowledge.

[Without play, the child would become more and more a machine, and lose all freshness and spontaneity—all originality. Without work, he would develop into a monster of caprice and arbitrariness. From the fact that man must learn to combine with man, in order that the individual may avail himself of the experience and labors of his fellow-men, self-sacrifice for the sake of combination is the great lesson of life. But as this should be *voluntary* self-sacrifice, education must train the child equally in the two directions of spontaneity and obedience. The educated man finds recreation in change of work.]

§ 28. Education seeks to transform every particular condition so that it shall no longer seem strange to the mind or in any wise foreign to its own nature. This identity of the feeling of self with the special character of anything done or endured by it, we call habit (Gewohnheit = customary activity, habitual conduct or behavior. Character is a "bundle of habits"). It conditions formally all progress; for that which is not yet become habit, but which we perform with design and an exercise of our will, is not yet a part of ourselves.

[Education seeks to assimilate its object—to make what was alien and strange to the pupil into something familiar and habitual to him. The pupil is to attack, one after the other, the foreign realms in the world of nature and man, and conquer them for his own, so that he can be "at home" in them. It is the necessary condition of all growth, all culture, that one widens his own individuality by this conquest of new provinces alien to him. By this the individual transcends the narrow limits of particularity and becomes generic—the individual becomes the species. A good definition of education is this: It is the process by which the individual man elevates himself to the species.]

§ 29. (1) Habit may be, in the first place, indifferent as to the subject-matter to which it relates. But that which is to be considered as indifferent or neutral can not be defined in the abstract, but only in the concrete, because anything that is indifferent as to whether it shall act on this particular man, or in this special situation, is capable of another or even of the opposite meaning for another man or even for the same man in other circumstances. Here, then, appeal must be made to the individual conscience in order to be able from the depths of individuality to decide what we can permit to ourselves and what we must deny ourselves. The aim of education must be to arouse in the pupil this spiritual and ethical sensitiveness which does not look upon anything as merely indifferent, but rather knows how to seize in everything, even in the seemingly unimportant, its universal human significance. But, in relation to the highest interests, he must learn that what concerns his own immediate personality is entirely indifferent, and must be subordinated to them.

[Therefore, the first requirement in education is that the pupil shall acquire the habit of subordinating his likes and dislikes to the attainment of a rational object. It is necessary that he shall acquire this indifference to his own pleasure, even by employing his powers on that which does not appeal to his interest in the remotest degree. Habit is "formal," i. e., it is an empty form that will fit any sort of activity or passivity. Habit can make anything a second nature.]

§ 30. The indifference of habit to its subject-matter disappears when external considerations of usefulness or hurtfulness (advantage or disadvantage) come into view. Whatever tends as a means to the realization of an end is useful, but that is hurtful which, by contradicting it, hinders or destroys it. Usefulness and hurtfulness being then only relative terms, a habit which is useful for one man in one case may be hurtful for another man, or even for the same man, under different circumstances. Education must, therefore, accustom the youth to judge as to the expediency or inexpediency of any action by its relation to the essential vocation of his life, so that he shall avoid that which does not promote its success.

[Habit soon makes us familiar with subjects which seem remote from our personal interest, and they become agreeable to us. The objects, too, assume a new interest upon nearer approach, as being useful or injurious to us. That is useful which serves us as a means for the realization of a rational purpose; injurious, if it hinders such realization. It happens that objects are useful in one respect and injurious in another, and *vice versa*. Education must make the pupil capable of deciding on the usefulness of an object by reference to its effect on his permanent vocation in life.

§ 31. But the *absolute* distinction for the subject-matter of habit is the moral distinction between the good and the bad. For from this standpoint alone can we finally decide what is allowable and what is forbidden, what is useful and what is hurtful.

[But *good and evil* are the ethical distinctions which furnish the absolute standard to which to refer the question of the usefulness of objects and actions.]

§ 32. (2) As relates to form (in contradistinction to subject-matter), habit may be either passive or active. The passive is that which teaches us to bear the vicissitudes of nature as well as of life with such composure that we shall hold our ground against them, being always equal to ourselves, and that we shall not allow our power of acting to be paralyzed through any mutations of fortune. Passive habit is not to be confounded with obtuseness in receiving impressions, a blank abstraction from the affair in hand, which at bottom is nothing more than a selfishness which desires to be left undisturbed; it is simply composure of mind in view of changes over which we have no control. While we vividly experience joy and sorrow, pain and pleasure—inwoven as these are with the change of seasons, of the weather, or with the alternation of life and death, of happiness and misery—we ought nevertheless to harden ourselves against them, so that at the same time, in our consciousness of the supreme worth of the soul, we shall build up the inaccessible stronghold of freedom in ourselves.

Active habit (or behavior) is found realized in a wide range of activity which appears in manifold forms, such as skill, dexterity, readiness of information, etc. It is a steeling of the internal for action upon the external, as the passive is a steeling of the internal against the influences of the external.

[Habit is (a) *passive* or (b) *active*. The passive habit is that which gives us the power to retain our equipoise of mind in the midst of a world of changes (pleasure and pain, grief and joy, etc.). The active habit gives us skill, presence of mind, tact in emergencies, etc.]

§ 33. (3) Habit (i. e., fixed principles of behavior, active and passive) is the general form which culture (or the outcome of education) takes. For, since it reduces a condition or an activity within ourselves to an instinctive use and wont (to a second nature), it is necessary for any thorough education. But as, according to its content (or subject-matter to which it relates), it may be either proper or improper (§ 29), advantageous or disadvantageous (§ 30), good or bad (§ 31), and according to its form may be the assimilation of the external by the internal, or the impress of the internal upon the external (§ 32), education must procure for the pupil the power of being able to free himself from one habit and to adopt another. Through his freedom he must be able not only to renounce any habit formed, but to form a new one; and he must so govern his system of habits that it shall exhibit a constant progress of development into greater freedom. We must discipline ourselves constantly to form and to break habits, as a means toward the ever-developing realization of the good in us.

We must characterize those habits as corrupting which relate only to our convenience or our enjoyment. They are often not blamable in themselves, but there lies in them a hidden danger that they may allure us into luxury or effeminacy. It is a false and mechanical way of looking at the mind to suppose that a habit which has been formed by a certain number of repetitions can be broken by an equal number of denials. We can never renounce a habit, which we decide to be pernicious, except through clearness of judgment and firmness of will.

[Education deals altogether with the formation of habits. For it aims to make some condition or form of activity into a second nature for the pupil. But this involves, also, the breaking up of previous habits. This power to break up habits, as well as to form them, is necessary to the freedom of the individual.]

§ 34. Education comprehends, therefore, the reciprocal action of the opposites: authority and obedience; rationality and individuality; work and play; habit and spontaneity. If these are reconciled in a normal manner, the youth is now free from the tension of these opposites. But a failure in education in this particular is very possible through the freedom of the pupil, through special circumstances, or through the errors of the educator himself. And for this very reason any theory of education must take into account in the beginning this negative possibility. It must consider beforehand the dangers which threaten the pupil, in all possible ways even before they surround him, and fortify him against them. Intentionally to expose him to temptation in order to prove his strength, is devilish; and, on the other hand, to guard him against the possible chance of dangerous temptation, to wrap him in cotton (as the proverb says), is womanish, ridiculous, fruitless, and much more dangerous; for temptation comes not alone from without, but quite as often from within, and secret inclination seeks and creates for itself the opportunity for its gratification, often perhaps an unnatural one. The truly preventive activity consists not in an abstract seclusion from the world, all of whose elements are innate in each individual, but in the activity of instruction and discipline, modified according to age and culture.

The method that aims to deprive the youth of all free and individual intercourse with the world only leads to continual espionage, and the consciousness that he is watched destroys in him all elasticity of spirit, all confidence, all originality. The police shadow of control undermines all self-reliance, and systematically accustoms him to dependence. The tragi-comic story of Peter Schlemihl * shows, it is true, that one can not lose his own shadow without falling into the saddest fatalities; but the shadow of a constant companion, as in the pedagogical system of the Jesuits, undermines all naturalness and ease of mind. And if one endeavors too strictly to guard against that which is ill-mannered and forbidden, the intelligence of the pupils reacts in deceit against such efforts, till the educators are amazed that such crimes as often come to light can have arisen under such careful control.

[Education deals with these complementary relations (antitheses): (a) authority and obedience; (b) rationality (*general* forms) and individuality; (c) work and play; (d) habit (general custom) and spontaneity. The development and reconciliation of these opposite sides in the pupil's character, so that they become his second nature, remove the phase of constraint which at first accompanies the formal inculcation of rules, and the performance of prescribed tasks. The freedom of the pupil is the ultimate object to be kept in view, but a too early use of freedom may work injury to the pupil. To remove a pupil from all temptation would be to remove possibilities of growth in strength to resist it; on the other hand, to expose him needlessly to temptation is fiendish. The cure of vicious tendencies is best accomplished by strict discipline in such habits as strengthen the pupil against them.]

§ 35. If there should appear in the youth any decided moral deformity which is opposed to the ideal of his education, the instructor must at once make inquiry as to the history of its origin, because the negative and the positive are very closely connected, and, what appears to be negligence, rudeness, immorality, foolish-

* See F. H. Hedge's "Prose Writers of Germany," for a translation of Adalbert von Chamisso's "Wonderful History of Peter Schlemihl."

ness, or oddity, may arise from some real needs of the youth which in their development have only taken a wrong direction.

[Deformities of character in the pupil should be carefully traced back to their origin, so that they may be explained by their history. Only by comprehending the historic growth of an organic defect are we able to prescribe the best remedies. Such deformities are often mere symptoms of deeper evils.]

§ 36. If it should appear on such examination that the negative action was only a product of willful ignorance, of caprice, or of arbitrariness on the part of the youth, then this calls for a simple prohibition on the part of the educator, no reason being assigned. His mere authority must be sufficient to the pupil in such a case. Only when this has happened more than once, and the youth is old enough to understand, should the prohibition be accompanied with a brief statement of the reason therefor.

This should be brief, because the explanation must retain its disciplinary character, and must not become extended into a doctrinal essay, for in such a case the youth easily forgets that it was his own misbehavior which was the occasion of the explanation. The statement of the reason must be honest, and it must present to the youth the point most easy for him to seize. False reasons are morally blamable in themselves, and they tend only to confuse. It is a great mistake to unfold to the youth the broadening consequences which his act may bring. These possibilities seem to him too uncertain to affect him much. The severe lecture wearies him, especially if it be stereotyped, as is apt to be the case with fault-finding and talkative instructors. But more unfortunate is it if the painting of the gloomy background to which the consequences of the wrong-doing of the youth may lead, should fill his feelings and imagination prematurely with gloomy fancies, because then the representation has led him one step toward a state of wretchedness which in the future man may become fearful depression and degradation.

[If the negative behavior of the pupil (his bad behavior) results from ignorance due to his own neglect, or to his willfulness, it should be met directly by an act of authority on the part of the teacher (and without an appeal to reason). An appeal should be made to the understanding of the pupil only when he is somewhat mature, or shows by his repetition of the offense that his proclivity is deep-seated, and requires an array of all good influences to re-enforce his feeble resolutions to amend.]

§ 37. If the censure is accompanied with a threat of punishment, then we have the kind of reproof which in daily life we call "scolding"; but, if a reprimand is given, the pupil must be made to feel that it is in earnest.

[Reproof, accompanied by threats of punishment, is apt to degenerate into scolding.]

§ 38. Only when all other efforts have failed is punishment, which is the real negation of the error, the transgression, or the vice, justifiable. Punishment intentionally inflicts pain on the pupil, and its object is, by means of this sensation, to bring him to reason, a result which neither our simple prohibition, our explanation, nor our threat of punishment, has been able to reach. But the punishment, as such, must not refer to the subjective totality of the youth, i. e., to his disposition in general, but only to the act which, as result, is a manifestation of that disposition. It nevertheless acts on the disposition, but mediately through pain; it does not touch directly the inner being; and this (return of the deed upon the doer) is not only demanded by justice, but is even rendered necessary on account of the sophistry that is inherent in human nature, which assigns to a deed many motives (and takes refuge against blame by alleging good motives).

[After the failure of other means, punishment should be resorted to. Inasmuch as the punishment should be for the purpose of making the pupil realize that it is the consequence of his deed returning on himself, it should always be administered for some particular act of his, and this should be specified. The "overt act" is the only thing which a man can be held accountable for in a court of justice; although it is true that the harboring of evil thoughts or intentions is a sin, yet it is not a crime until realized in an overt act. It is a mistake to punish for "general naughtiness," or for evil intent, or for the "subjective totality" as Rosenkranz calls it. Any particular deed is one of a thousand possible deeds—the intention or disposition contains the totality of all these possible deeds, but they belong to the pupil as his exclusive property for which he is not responsible to his fellow human beings until he by an act of the will makes one of the possible deeds actual.]

§ 39. Punishment as an educational means is nevertheless essentially corrective, since, by leading the youth to a proper estimation of his fault and a positive change in his behavior, it seeks to improve him. At the same time, it stands as a sad indication of the insufficiency of the means previously used. The youth should not be frightened from the commission of a misdemeanor or from the repetition of his negative deed through fear of punishment—a system which leads always to terrorism; but, although this effect may be incidental, the punishment should, before all things, impress upon him the recognition of the fact that the negative is not allowed to prevail without limitation, but rather that the good and the true have the absolute power in this world, and that they are never without the means of overcoming anything that contradicts them.

In the statute-laws, punishment has a different office. It must first of all satisfy justice, and only after this is done can it attempt to improve the guilty. If a government should proceed on the same basis as the educator, it would mistake its task, because it has to deal with adults, whom it elevates to the honorable position of responsibility for their own acts. The state must not go back to the genesis of a negative deed in the disposition, or the motives, or the circumstances. It must assign to a secondary rank of importance the biographical factor which contains the origin of the deed and the circumstances of a mitigating character, and it must consider first of all the deed in itself. It is quite otherwise with the educator; for he deals with human beings who are relatively undeveloped, and who are only growing toward responsibility. So long as they are still under the care of a teacher, the responsibility of their deed belongs in part to him. If we confound these two standpoints on which punishment is administered, that of the state and that of education, we work much evil.

[Corrective punishment seeks solely the improvement of the delinquent; retributive punishment under statute laws seeks only the return of the deed upon the doer; i. e., to satisfy the claims of justice. Hegel, in his "Philosophy of History," in speaking of state punishments in China, drew this distinction and pointed out its significance.]

§ 40. Punishment as a negation of a negation, considered as an educational means, can not be determined, as to its application, by mere reference to the deed, but must always be modified by the peculiarities of the individual offender and by the other circumstances. Its administration calls for the exercise of the ingenuity and tact of the educator.

[Punishment should be regulated, not by abstract rules, but in view of the particular case and its attending circumstances, for the reason that it is for correction and not for retribution. Retributive punishment need only consider the magnitude of the offense.]

§ 41. Generally speaking, we must take into consideration the sex and the age: (1) some kind of corporal punishment is most suitable for children, (2) isolation for older boys and girls, and (3) punishment based on the sense of honor for young men and women.

[Sex and age of pupil should be regarded in prescribing the mode and degree of punishment. Corporal punishment is best for pupils who are very immature in mind; when they are more developed they may be punished by any imposed restraint upon their free-wills which will isolate them from the ordinary routine followed by their fellow-pupils. (Deprivation of the right to do as others do is a wholesome species of punishment for those old or mature enough to feel its effects, for it tends to secure respect for the regular tasks by elevating them to the rank of rights and privileges.) For young men and women, the punishment should be of a kind that is based on a sense of honor. This distinction by Rosenkranz is very important. It is based on Hegel's distinction alluded to above (§ 39) of *corrective* from *retributive* punishment. In cities, suspension of the pupil from school, and his transfer to another school on restoration, is one of the most effective means ever devised for developing in the pupil a self-control that secures good behavior without resort to corporal punishment.*

§ 42. (1) Corporal punishment is the production of physical pain, generally by whipping, and this kind of punishment, provided always that it is not too often administered or with undue severity, is the kindest method of dealing with willful defiance, with obstinate carelessness, or with a really perverted will, so long or so often as the higher perception is closed against appeal. The imposing of other physical punishment, e. g., that of depriving the pupil of food, partakes of cruelty. The view which sees in the rod the panacea † for all the teacher's embarrassments is reprehensible, but equally so is the false sentimentality which assumes that the dignity of humanity is affected by a blow given to a

---

* "Report of St. Louis Public Schools for 1873–'74," pp. 200–202.

† "Although Orbilism is reprehensible," says Rosenkranz, referring to the flogging schoolmaster of Horace: "Memini quæ plagosum mihi parvo Orbilium dictare" (sc. Carmina). Hor. Ep., 2, 1, 71.

child, and confounds self-conscious humanity with child-humanity, to which a blow is the most natural form of reaction, when all other forms of influence have failed.

The fully-grown man ought never to be whipped, because this kind of punishment reduces him to the level of the child, and, when it becomes barbarous, to that of a brute animal, and so is absolutely degrading to him. In the English schools the rod is much used. If a pupil of the first class be put back into the second at Eton, he, although before exempt from flogging, becomes liable to it. But however necessary this system of flogging may be in the discipline of the schools of the English aristocracy, flogging in the English army is a shameful thing for the free people of Great Britain.

[Corporal punishment should be properly administered by means of the rod, subduing willful defiance by the application of force.]

§ 43. (2) By isolation we remove the offender temporarily and locally from the society of his fellows. The boy or girl left alone, in abstract independence, cut off from all companionship, suffers from a sense of helplessness. The time passes heavily, and soon he is very anxious to be allowed to return to the company of parents, brothers and sisters, teachers, and fellow-pupils.

To leave a child entirely to himself without any supervision, even if one shuts him up in a dark room, is as mistaken a practice as to leave a few together without supervision, as is sometimes done when they are kept after school; in such situations they give the freest rein to their childish wantonness and commit the wildest pranks.

[Isolation makes the pupil realize a sense of his dependence upon human society, and of his need for the constant expression of this dependence by co-operation in the common tasks. Pupils should not be shut up in a dark room, nor removed from the personal supervision of the teacher. (To shut up two or more in a room without supervision is not isolation, but association; only it is association for mischief, and not for study.) (All good behavior that is not founded on fear must take its rise in a sense of honor. Corporal punishment degrades the man or the youth who has arrived at a sense of honor. In communities where children acquire this sense at a very early age, corporal punishment should be dispensed with altogether, and punishments resorted to that develop a sense of responsibility by causing the culprit to feel the effect of his deeds in depriving him of privileges common to all good pupils.)]

§ 44. (3) This way of isolating a child does not properly touch his sense of honor, and is soon forgotten, because it relates to only one side of his conduct. It is quite different from punishment based on the sense of honor, which, in a formal manner, shuts the youth out from social participation because he has attacked the principle which holds society together, and for this reason can no longer be subsumed under its generality (i. e., allowed to participate in the society of his fellows). Honor is the recognition of one individual by others as their equal. Through his transgression, or it may be his misdemeanor, he has simply lost his equality with them, and in so far has separated himself from them, so that his banishment from their society is only the outward expression of the real isolation which he himself has brought to pass in his inner nature, and which he by means of his negative act only betrayed to the outer world. Since the punishment founded on the sense of honor affects the whole ethical man and makes a lasting impression upon his memory, extreme caution is necessary in its application lest a permanent injury be inflicted upon the character. The idea of his perpetual continuance in disgrace, destroys in a man all aspiration for improvement.

Within the family this feeling of honor can not be so actively developed, because every member of it is bound to every other immediately by natural ties, and hence is equal to every other. Within its sacred circle, he who has isolated himself is still beloved, though it may be through tears. However bad may be the deed he has committed, he is never given up, but the deepest sympathy is felt for him because he is still brother, father, etc. But first in the relation of one family with another, and still more in the relation of an individual with any institution which is founded not on natural ties, but is set over against him as an entirely independent existence, this feeling of honor appears. In the school, and in the matter of ranks and honors in a school, this is very important.

[Punishment based on the sense of honor may or may not be based on isolation. It implies a degree of maturity on the part of the pupil. Through his offense the pupil has destroyed his equality with his fellows, and has in reality, in his inmost nature, isolated himself from them. Corporal punishment is external, but it may be accompanied with a keen sense of dishonor. Isolation also may, to a pupil who is sensitive to honor, be a severe blow to self-respect. But a punishment founded entirely on the sense of honor would be wholly internal, and have no external discomfort attached to it. He who "attacks the principle that holds society together," by doing things that tend to destroy that social union, should be excluded from it or "not subsumed under its generality." Social union is a common bond, a general condition, or a participation. Regularity, punctuality, silence, attention, and industry, are indispensable for the associated effort of the school, and the pupil who persistently violates these conditions should be isolated from the school.]

§ 45. It is important to consider well this gradation of punishment—which, starting with physical pain, which appeals to the senses, passes through the external teleology (appeal to external motives) of temporary isolation up to the idealism (appeal to one's ideal) of the sense of honor—both in relation to the different ages at which they are appropriate and to the training which they bring with them. Every punishment must be considered merely as a means to some end, and, in so far, as transitory. The pupil must always be deeply conscious that it is very painful to his instructor to be obliged to punish him. This pathos of another's solicitude for his cure, which he perceives in the mien, in the tone of the voice, in the hesitation with which the punishment is administered, will become a purifying fire for his soul.

[The necessity of carefully adapting the punishment to the age and maturity of the pupil renders it the most difficult part of the teacher's duties. It is essential that the air and manner of the teacher who punishes should be that of one who acts from a sense of painful duty, and not from any delight in being the cause of suffering. Not personal likes and dislikes, but the rational necessity which is over teacher and pupil alike, causes the infliction of pain on the pupil.]

CHAPTER III.

THE LIMITS OF EDUCATION.

§ 46. As respects its form, education reaches its limits with the idea of punishment, because this is the effort to conquer the negative reality (i. e., the resistance which it meets in the pupil's opposition) and to make it conformable to its positive idea. But the general limits of education are found in the idea of its function, which is to fashion the individual into theoretical and practical rationality. The authority of the educator at last becomes imperceptible, and it passes over into advice and example, and obedience changes from blind conformity to free gratitude and attachment. Individuality wears off its rough edges, and is transfigured into the universality and necessity of reason without losing in this process its personal identity. Work becomes enjoyment, and he finds his play in a change of activity. The youth takes possession of himself, and can be left to himself.

There are two widely differing views with regard to the limits of education. One lays great stress on the weakness of the pupil and the power of the teacher. According to this view, education has for its province the entire formation of the youth. The despotism of this view often manifests itself, where large numbers are to be educated together, and with very undesirable results, because it assumes that the individual pupil is only a specimen of the whole, as if the school were a great factory where each piece of goods is to be stamped exactly like all the rest. Individuality is reduced by the tyranny of such despotism to one uniform level till all originality is destroyed, as in cloisters, barracks, and orphan asylums, where only one individual seems to exist. There is a kind of pedagogy, also, which fancies that one can thrash into or out of the individual pupil what one will. This may be called a superstitious belief in the power of education. The opposite extreme is skeptical, and advances the policy which lets alone and does nothing, urging that individuality is unconquerable, and that often the most careful and far-sighted education fails of reaching its aim in so far as it is opposed to the nature of the youth, and that this individuality has made of no avail all efforts toward the obtaining of any end which was opposed to it. This view of the fruitlessness of all educational efforts engenders an indifference toward it which would leave, as a result, only a sort of vegetation of individuality growing at hap-hazard.

[Punishment is the final topic considered under the head of "Form of Education," and it introduces us to the next topic, "The Limits of Education." In the act of punishment, the teacher abandons the legitimate province of education, which seeks to make the pupil rational or obedient to what is reasonable, as a habit, and from his own free-will. The pupil is punished in order that he may be *made* to conform to the rational, by the application of constraint. Another will is substituted for the pupil's, and good behavior is produced, but not by the pupil's free act. In disobedience and in the occasion for the use of punishment accordingly education encounters its negative limit—the limit that excludes it and refuses to receive it. While education finds a negative limit in punishment, it finds a positive limit in the accomplishment of its legitimate object, which is the emancipation of the pupil from the state of imbecility, as regards mental and moral self-control, into the ability to direct himself rationally. The school has done its work and is no longer needed. When the pupil has acquired the discipline which enables him to direct his studies properly, and to control his inclinations in such a manner as to pursue his work regularly, the teacher is superfluous for him—he becomes his own teacher. There may be two extreme views on this subject—the one tending toward the negative extreme of requiring the teacher to do everything for the pupil, substituting his will for that of the pupil, and the other view tending to the positive extreme, and leaving everything to the pupil, even before his will is trained into habits of self-control, or his mind provided with the necessary elementary branches requisite for the prosecution of further study.]

§ 47. (1) *The first limit of education is a subjective one*, a limit found in the individuality of the youth. This is a definitive (insurmountable) limit. Whatever does not exist in this individuality as a possibility can not be developed from it. Education can only lead and assist; it can not create. What Nature has denied to a man, education can not give him any more than it is able, on the other hand, to annihilate entirely his original gifts, although it is true that his talents may be suppressed, distorted, and measurably destroyed. But the decision of the question in what the real essence of any one's individuality consists can never be made with certainty till he has left behind him his years of development, because it is then only that he first arrives at the consciousness of his entire self; besides, at this time, many superficial acquirements will drop off; and on the other hand, talents, long slumbering and unsuspected, may first make their appearance. Whatever has been forced upon a child in opposition to his individuality, whatever has been only driven into him and has lacked receptivity on his part or a demand for cultivation, remains attached to his being only as an external ornament, a parasitical outgrowth which enfeebles his own proper character.

We must distinguish from that false tendency which arises through a misunderstanding of the limit of individuality, the affectation of children and young persons who often suppose, when they see models finished and complete in grown persons, that they themselves are endowed by Nature with the power to develop into the same. When they see a reality which corresponds to their own possibility, the anticipation of a like or a similar attainment moves them to an imitation of it as a model personality. This may be sometimes carried so far as to be disagreeable or ridiculous, but should not be too strongly censured, because it springs from a positive striving after culture, and needs only proper direction.

[The subjective limit of education (on the negative side) is to be found in the individuality of the pupil—the limit to his natural capacity.]

§ 48. (2) *The second or objective limit of education* lies in the means which can be appropriated for it. That the talent for a certain culture shall be present is certainly the first thing; but the cultivation of this talent is the second, and no less necessary. But how much cultivation can be given to it extensively and intensively depends upon the means used, and these again are conditioned by the material resources of the family to which one belongs. The greater and more valuable the means of culture which are found in a family, the greater is the immediate advantage which the culture of each one has at the start. With regard to many of the arts and sciences this limit of education is of great significance. But the means alone are of no avail. The finest educational apparatus will produce no fruit where corresponding talent is wanting, while on the other hand talent often accomplishes incredible feats with very limited means, and, if the way is only once open, makes of itself a center of attraction which draws to itself with magnetic power the necessary means. The moral culture of each one is, however, fortunately from its very nature, out of the reach of such dependence.

In considering the limit made by individuality we recognize the side of truth in that indifference which considers education entirely superfluous, and in considering the means of culture we find the truth in the other extreme, that of pedagogical despotism, which fancies that it can command whatever culture it chooses for any one without regard to his individuality.

[The objective limit to education lies in the amount of time that the person may devote to his training. It, therefore, depends largely upon wealth, or other fortunate circumstances.]

§ 49. (3) *Finally, the absolute limit of education* is the time when the youth has apprehended the problem which he has to solve, has learned to know the means at his disposal, and has acquired a certain facility in using them. The end and aim of education is the emancipation of the youth. It strives to make him self-dependent, and as soon as he has become so it wishes to retire and leave to him the sole responsibility for his actions. To treat the youth after he has passed this point of time still as a youth, contradicts the very idea of education, which idea finds its fulfillment in the attainment of this state of maturity by the pupil. Since the completion of education cancels the original inequality between the educator and the pupil, nothing is more oppressing, nay, revolting to the latter than to be excluded by a continued state of dependence from the enjoyment of the freedom which he has earned.

The opposite of this extreme, which protracts education beyond its proper time and produces this state of inward revolt, is the undue hastening of the emancipation.—The question whether one is prepared for freedom has been often opened in politics. When any people have gone so far as to ask this question themselves, it is no longer a question whether that people are prepared for it, for without the consciousness of freedom this question would never have occurred to them.

[The absolute limit of education is the positive limit (see § 46), beyond which the youth passes into freedom from the school, as a necessary instrumentality for further culture.]

§ 50. Although teachers must now leave the youth free, the necessity of further culture for him still remains. But it will no longer come directly through them. Their prearranged, pattern-making work is now supplanted by self-education. Each sketches for himself an ideal to which in his life he seeks to approximate every day.

In the work of self-culture one friend can help another by advice and example; but he can not educate, for education presupposes inequality of acquirement and authority.—The necessities of human nature produce societies in which equals seek to influence each other in a pedagogical way, since they establish certain grades or orders based on steps of culture. They presuppose education in the ordinary sense. But they wish to bring about education in a higher sense, and therefore they veil the last form of their ideal in the mystery of secrecy.—To one who lives on contented with himself and without the impulse toward self-culture, unless his unconcern springs from his belonging to a savage state of society, the Germans give the name of Philistine, and he is always repulsive to the student who is intoxicated with an ideal.

[The prearranged pattern-making work of the school is now done, but self-education may and should go on indefinitely, and will go on if the education of the school has really arrived at its "absolute limit"—i. e., has fitted the pupil for self-education. Emancipation from the school does not emancipate one from learning through his fellow-men. Man's spiritual life is one depending upon co-operation with his fellow-men. Each must avail himself of the experience of his fellow-men, and in turn communicate his own experience to the common fund of the race. Thus each lives the life of the whole, and all live for each. School-education gives the pupil the instrumentalities with which to enable him to participate in this fund of experience—this common life of the race. After school-education comes the still more valuable education, which, however, without the school, would be in a great measure impossible.]

SECOND PART.

THE SPECIAL ELEMENTS OF EDUCATION.

SECOND PART.

THE SPECIAL ELEMENTS OF EDUCATION.

INTRODUCTION.

§ 51. EDUCATION in general consists in the development in man of his inborn theoretical and practical rationality; it takes on the form of labor, which changes that state or condition, which appears at first only as a mere thought, into a fixed habit, and transfigures individuality into a worthy humanity. Education ends in that emancipation of the youth which places him on his own feet. The special elements which form the concrete content of all education in general are the life, cognition, and will of man. Without life mind has no phenomenal reality; without cognition, no genuine—i. e., conscious—will; and without will, no self-confirmation of life and of cognition. It is true that these three elements are in real existence inseparable, and continually exhibit their interdependence. But none the less on this account do they themselves prescribe their own succession, and they have a relative and periodical ascendency over each other. In infancy, up to the fifth or sixth year, the purely physical development takes the precedence; childhood is the time of learning, in a proper sense, an act by which the child gains for himself the picture of the world, such as mature minds, through experience and insight, have painted it; and, finally, youth is the transition period to practical activity, to which the self-determination of the will must give the first impulse.

[Education is the development of reason innate in man—theoretical as intellect, practical as will-power. It is a labor that changes an ideal into a real, making what is potential into an actual; transfiguring the "natural" man, so to speak, into a spiritual man. Education forms "habits." It develops ideal human nature into real human nature by means of this formation of habits. (Play differs from labor in this, that it does not seek to transform an ideal into a real, but to make a semblance of contradiction between the ideal and real; it makes a reality *seem* to be what it is not.) There are three special elements in man, each of which needs education: these are life (bodily organism), cognition (knowing faculty or intellect), and will. To some extent there is a succession of periods based on this distinction: (1) the period of nurture, lasting till the sixth year, or during infancy, in which the education of the body is more important than the education of the mind; (2) the period of the school, lasting through childhood—say to fourteen years—in which *general* or intellectual education is most important; (3) the period of youth—from fourteen to eighteen—in which the most important education is the specializing of the practical application of knowledge and strength to particular forms of duty, hence will-education. While these periods are thus distinguished by the relative importance of the three different disciplines, it is essential that no one of these disciplines shall be neglected in any period.]

§ 52. The classification of the special elements of education is hence very simple: (1) the physical, (2) the intellectual, (3) the practical (in the sense of will-education). We sometimes apply to these the words orthobiotics, didactics, and pragmatics.

Æsthetic training constitutes only an element of intellectual education, just as social, moral, and religious training form elements of practical (or will) education. But because these latter elements concern themselves with the action of the individual upon the external world, the name "pragmatics" is appropriate. In this sphere, education (Pädagogik) should coincide with politics, ethics, and religion. But it is distinguished from them through the skill with which it puts into practice the problems of the other two (life and cognition). The scientific arrangement of these ideas must therefore show that the former, as the more abstract, constitutes the condition, and the latter, as the more concrete, the ground of the former, which is presupposed; and in consequence of this it is itself their principle and teleological presupposition, just as in man the will presupposes the cognition, and cognition life; while, at the same time, life, in a deeper sense, must presuppose cognition, and cognition will.

[The classification in pedagogics is based on the distinction of the three elements in man that require education: (1) Physical (correct living = orthobiotics); (2) intellectual (correct perceiving, knowing, and thinking = didactics); (3) practical (correct action, proper habits = pragmatics). Æsthetic training, or the sense for the appreciation and production of the beautiful, falls, in a threefold division, into the second—into theoretic education. Social, moral, and religious training belong to the third division, as they concern the will and its utterance in deeds. "Pragmatics" signifies the doctrine of human deeds, and includes the spheres of ethics, politics, and religion. (There may be defined a fivefold system of education, basing the distinction on the institutions of civilization: (a) Nurture = the education of the family; (b) the school, or education into the conventionalities of intelligence; (c) the art, trade, or profession that forms the vocation in life = the education of civil society; (d) the political education into citizenship, resulting from obedience to laws and participation in making and sustaining them; (e) religious education. These five forms of education depend on (a) the family, (b) the school, (c) civil society, (d) the State, (e) the Church. The school is properly a transition between the family and civil society, and forms the institution of education *par excellence.* Hence, while education, very properly, is defined so as to include all of human life, there is a period specially characterized as "education" which transpires in the school, a special institution that partakes of the character of the family on the one hand, and of civil society on the other. In the school, of course, there should be some attention paid to all spheres of education, but its main business should be the acquisition "of the picture of the world such as mature minds through experience and insight have painted it" (see § 51 near the end), or, in other words, conventional items of information, insights into laws and principles, and the elementary processes of their combination. This makes the "view of the world" which each civilized human being is supposed to possess. It is important to know the exact province of the school, and to see that it is only one of the five forms of education that civilization provides for man. Much of the carping criticism leveled against schools, in times of financial distress or general social depression, is based on the assumption that the province of the school is *all* education instead of a small but very important fraction of it. The school may do its share of correct education, but it can not correct the effects of neglect of family nurture, nor insure its youth against evil that will follow if civil society furnishes no steady employment, no opportunity for settled industry, and the state no training into consciousness of higher manhood by its just laws, and by offering to the citizen a participation in the political process of legislation and administration, carefully guarding its forms so that its politics does not furnish a training in corruption. Nor can the school insure the future of its pupils unless the Church does its part in the education of the individuals of the community.) "The scientific arrangement of these ideas"—i. e., life, intellect, and will—"must show that the former, as more abstract, constitute the conditions"—i. e., life is the condition of intellect, and both intellect and life the conditions of will—while "the latter, as more concrete, are the ground of the former"—i. e., intellect is the ground of life, or, in other words, its final cause, and so will is the ground and final cause of intellect. Intellect contains all that life contains, and much more—namely: While life realizes its totality of species only in many individuals, and each individual is a partial and special half of the species as male or female, the intellect as consciousness is subject and object in one, and each individual intellect is potentially the entire species—each thinking being can think all the thoughts of the greatest thinkers of the race. So, will contains all that intellect contains, and more. For what is potential in intellect (the identity of subject and object of thought) is real in the will. The will makes objective its internal subjective forms, and in its highest ethical activity it becomes conscious freedom.]

CHAPTER I.

PHYSICAL EDUCATION.

§ 53. The art of living rightly is based upon a comprehension of the process of life. Life is the restless dialectic process which ceaselessly transforms the inorganic into the organic, and at the same time produces the inorganic, and separates from itself whatever part of its food has not been assimilated, and that which has become dead and burned out. The organism is healthy when it corresponds to this idea of the dialectic process of a life which moves up and down, inward and outward; of formation and reformation; of organizing and disorganizing. All the rules for physical education, or of hygiene, are derived from this conception.

[The rules of hygiene are derived from an insight into the twofold process of assimilation and elimination which goes on in the living organism with relation to the inorganic substances which it uses.]

§ 54. It follows from this that the change of the relatively inorganic to the organic is going on not only in the organism as a whole, but also in its every organ and in every part of every organ; and that the organic, as soon as it has attained its highest point of energy, is again degraded to the inorganic and thrown out. Every cell has its history. Activity is, therefore, not contradictory to the organism, but favors in it the natural progressive and regressive metamorphosis. This process can go on harmoniously—that is, the organism can be in health—only when not merely the whole organism, but each special organ, is allowed, after its productive activity, the corresponding rest and recreation necessary for its self-renewal. We have this periodicity exemplified in waking and sleeping, also in exhalation and inhalation, excretion and taking in of material. When we have discovered the relative antagonism of the organs and their periodicity, we have found the secret of the perennial renewal of life.

[Perpetual change goes on in the living organism, converting the inorganic into organic tissue and then reconverting it. This alternation is the basis of the demand for the alternation of productive activity with rest and recreation in the whole physical system.]

§ 55. Fatigue makes its appearance when any organ, or the organism in general, is denied time for the return movement into itself and for renovation. It is possible for some one organ, without injury, as if isolated, to exercise a great and long-continued activity, even to the point of fatigue, while the other organs rest; as, e. g., the lungs, in speaking, while the other parts are quiet; on the other hand, it is not well to speak and run at the same time. The idea that one can keep the organism in better condition by inactivity is an error which rests upon a mechanical view of life. Equally false is the idea that health depends upon the quantity and excellence of the food; without the force to assimilate it, it is poison rather than nourishment. *True strength arises only from activity.* [Mention of works on hygiene here is omitted in this translation.]

[Fatigue defined. It may occur with the whole organism or with a part. The idea that total rest is healthy is a misapprehension. The organism requires alternation of rest and activity, which alternation itself is activity because it is change. Hence, "true strength arises only from activity."]

§ 56. Physical education, as it concerns the repairing, the motor, or the nervous activities, is divided into (1) dietetics, (2) gymnastics, (3) sexual education. In real life these activities are scarcely separable, but for the sake of exposition we must consider them apart. In the regular development of the human being, moreover, the repairing system has a relative precedence to the motor system, and the latter to the sexual maturity. But education can treat of these ideas only with reference to the infant, the child, and the youth.

[Physical education treats of (a) the repairing activity or nutrition, (b) the motor or muscular activity, and (c) the nervous activity, as far as they concern children and youth.

CHAPTER II.

(A.) DIETETICS.

§ 57. Dietetics is the art of sustaining the normal repair of the organism. Since this organism is, in the concrete, an individual one, the general principles of dietetics must, in their manner of application, vary with the sex, the age, the temperament, the occupation, and the other conditions of the individual. Education as a science can only go over its general principles, and these can be named briefly. If we attempt to speak of details, we fall easily into triviality. So very important to the whole life of man is the proper care of his physical nature during the first stages of its development, that the science of education must not omit to enumerate the various systems which different people, according to their time, locality, and culture, have made for themselves; many, it is true, embracing some preposterous ideas, but in general never devoid of justification in their time.

[Dietetics defined. Details here are trivial.]

[§§ 58, 59, 60, 61, 62, 63, 64, relating to diet, omitted. The following is a brief summary of the contents: §§ 58, 59, 60, 61, treat of food for infants. § 62, why children need much sleep. § 63 treats of clothing of children.]

§ 64. Cleanliness is a virtue to which children should be accustomed for the sake of their physical well-being, as well as because, in a moral point of view, it is of the greatest significance. Cleanliness will not endure that things shall be deprived of their proper individuality through the elemental chaos. It retains each as distinguished from every other. While it makes necessary to man pure air, cleanliness of surroundings, of clothing, and of his body, it develops in him a sense by which he perceives accurately the particular limits of being in general.

[Cleanliness means "a place for everything and everything in its place." To take a thing out of its proper relations is to "deprive it of its proper individuality," and in an "elemental chaos" everything has lost its proper relations to other things, and has no longer any use or fitness in its existence.]

CHAPTER III.

(B.) GYMNASTICS.

§ 65. Gymnastics is the art of the normal training of the muscular system. The voluntary muscles, which are regulated by the nerves of the brain, in distinction from the involuntary automatic muscles depending on the spinal cord, while they are the means of man's intercourse with the external world, at the same time react upon the automatic muscles in digestion and sensation. Since the movement of the muscular fibers consists in the alternation of contraction and expansion, it follows that gymnastics must bring about a change of movement which shall both contract and expand the muscles.

[*Gymnastics.*—The voluntary and involuntary muscles distinguished: the voluntary muscles form the means of communication with the external world, and also react on the automatic functions of digestion, sensation, etc. Gymnastics seeks to develop the voluntary muscles in a normal manner, and through these indirectly to affect favorably the development of the other bodily systems and processes.]

§ 66. The system of gymnastic exercise of any nation corresponds always to its mode of fighting. So long as this consists in the personal struggle of a hand-to-hand contest, gymnastics will seek to increase as much as possible individual strength and adroitness. As soon as the far-reaching missiles projected from fire-arms become the center of all the operations of war, the individual is lost in a body of men, out of which he emerges only relatively in sharp-shooting, in the charge, in close contests, and in the retreat. Because of this incorporation of the individual in the one great whole, and because of the resulting unimportance of personal daring, gymnastics can never again be what it was in ancient times. Besides this, the subjectiveness of the modern spirit is too great to allow it to devote so much attention to the care of the body, or so much time to the admiration of its beauty, as was given by the Greeks.

The Turner societies and Turner-halls in Germany belong to the period of subjective enthusiasm of the German student population, and had a political significance. At present, they have been brought back to their proper place as an educational means, and they are of great value, especially in large cities. Among the mountains, and in rural districts, special arrangements for bodily exercise are less necessary, for the matter takes care of itself. The situation and the instinct for play help to foster it. In great cities, however, the houses are often destitute of halls or open places where the children can take exercise in their leisure moments. In these cities, therefore, there must be some gymnastic hall where the sense of fellowship may be developed. Gymnastics are not so essential for girls. In its place, dancing is sufficient, and gymnastic exercise should be employed for them only where there exists any special weakness or deformity, when it may be used as a restorative or preservative. They are not to become Amazons. The boy, on the contrary, needs to acquire the feeling of good-fellowship. It is true that the school develops this in a measure, but not fully and simply, because in school the standing of the boy is determined through his intellectual ambition. The college youth will not take much interest in special gymnastics unless he can gain distinction in it. Running, leaping, climbing, and lifting, are too tame for their more mature spirits. They can take a lively interest only in the exercises which have a warlike character. With the Prussians, and some other German states, gymnastic training is provided for in the military training.

[Gymnastics affected by the national military drill. The ancient tribes and nations found special bodily training indispensable to success in war, and even to national preservation. Gunpowder and improved fire-arms have almost rendered gymnastics obsolete—the successful army, other things equal, being the one composed of men thoroughly disciplined in manœuvres, and possessed individually of tact and versatility necessary to manipulate the destructive fire-arms now used. The Greeks (see §§ 204–216) paid so much attention to pure gymnastics because they worshiped the beautiful as the highest manifestation of the divine, and therefore looked upon their own physical perfection as the highest object of life. The favorite exercises with our students are boating, ball-playing, bicycle-riding, etc., rather than boxing, fencing, wrestling, and "exercises which have a warlike character," as Rosenkranz enumerated them in 1840.]

§ 67. The fundamental idea of gymnastics must always be that the spirit shall rule over its body and make this an energetic and docile servant of its will. Strength and adroitness must unite and become confident skill. Strength, carried to its extreme, produces the athlete; adroitness, to its extreme, the acrobat. Education must avoid both. All gigantic strength, as well as acrobatic skill, fit only for display, must be discouraged and so too must be the idea of teaching gymnastics with the motive of utility; e. g., that by swimming one may save his life when he falls into the water, etc. Among other things, utility may also be a consequence; but the principle in general must always be the necessity of the spirit of subjecting its bodily organism to the condition of a perfect instrument, so that it may ever find it equal to the execution of its will.

[Gymnastics, therefore, in modern times must aim chiefly at developing the body for the sake of physical strength and endurance, with a view to the demands of useful industry and mental culture on the bodily health and vigor. Health requires harmonious development; the exercises must develop the parts of the body so as not to produce disproportion. The result of gymnastics is to give the mind control over the body as a whole —the will interpenetrates, as it were, the various organs, and by this means the conscious mind can re-enforce the automatic functions of the body; the will-power can to a certain degree even ward off disease.]

§ 68. Gymnastic exercises form a series from simple to compound. There seems to be so much arbitrariness in plays and games that it is always very agreeable to the mind to find, on nearer inspection, some rational order. The movements are (1) of the lower, (2) of the upper extremities; (3) of the whole body, with relative predominance, now of the upper, now of the lower extremities. We distinguish, therefore, foot, arm, and trunk movements.

[Gymnastic exercises classified: (1) of the lower extremities: (a) walking, (b) running, (c) leaping (including varieties and modifications, such as walking on stilts, skating, dancing, balancing, bicycle-riding, etc.); (2) of the upper extremities: (a) lifting, (b) swinging, (c) throwing (including also the modifications of climbing, carrying, pole and bar exercises, quoits, ball and nine-pin playing, rowing, etc.); (3) of the whole body: (a) swimming, (b) riding, (c) fighting. Foot, arm, and trunk movements. Such games as base-ball, and such athletic exercise as rowing are practiced as whole-body movements.]

§ 69. (1) The first series of foot-movements is the most important, and conditions the carriage of all the rest of the body. They are (*a*) walking; (*b*) running; (*c*) leaping: each of these being capable of modifications, as the high and the low leap, the prolonged and the quick run. Sometimes we give to these different names, according to the means used, as walking on stilts; skating; leaping with a staff, or by means of the hands, as vaulting. Dancing is only the art of the graceful mingling of these movements.

§ 70. (2) The second series includes the arm-movements, and it repeats also the movements of the first series. It includes (*a*) lifting; (*b*) swinging; (*c*) throwing. All pole and bar practice comes under lifting, also climbing and carrying. Under throwing, come quoits, and ball-throwing, and nine-pin playing. All these movements are distinguished from each other, not only quantitatively but also qualitatively, in the position of the stretched and bent muscles; e. g., running is something different from quick walking. [Omission here of notes on books relating to the physiology of exercise.]

§ 71. (3) The third series, or that of movements of the whole body, differs from the preceding two, which prepare the way for it, in this, that it brings the organism into contact with an object, which it has to overcome through its own activity. This object is sometimes an element, sometimes an animal, sometimes a man. Our divisions then are (*a*) swimming; (*b*) riding; (*c*) single combat (fencing, boxing, wrestling, etc.). In swimming, one must conquer the yielding liquid by arm and foot movements. The resistance met on account of currents and waves may be very great, but it is still that of a will-less and passive object. But in riding man has to deal with a self-willed being whose vitality calls forth not only his strength but also his intelligence and courage. The movement is therefore very complicated, and the rider must be able perpetually to individualize his activity according to the circumstances; at the same time, he must give attention not only to the horse, but to the nature of the ground and the entire surroundings. But it is only in the struggle with men that gymnastics reaches its highest point, for in this man offers himself as a living antagonist to man and threatens him with danger. It is no longer the spontaneous activity of an unreasoning existence; it is the resistance and attack of intelligence itself with which he has to deal. Fencing, or single combat, is the truly chivalrous exercise, and this may be combined with horsemanship.

In the single combat there is found also a qualitative gradation, whence we have three systems: (*a*) boxing and wrestling; (*b*) fencing with sticks; and (*c*) rapier and broadsword fencing. In the first, which was cultivated to its highest point among the Greeks, direct immediateness rules. In the boxing of the English, a sailor-like propensity of this nation, fighting with the fists is still retained as a custom. Fencing with a stick is found among the French mechanics, the so-called *compagnons*. Men often use the cane in their contests; it is a sort of refined club. When we use the sword or rapier, the weapon becomes deadly. The Southern Europeans excel in the use of the rapier, the Germans in that of the broadsword. But the art of single combat is much degenerated, and the pistol-duel, through its increasing frequency, proves this degeneration.

NOTE.—The paragraphs § 72–79, relating to sexual education, are designed for parents rather than for teachers, the parent being the natural educator of the family, and sexual education relating to the preservation and continuance of the family. This chapter is accordingly, for the most part, omitted here. It contains judicious reflections, invaluable to parents and guardians.—*Tr.*

CHAPTER IV.

INTELLECTUAL EDUCATION.

§ 80. *Mens sana in corpore sano* is correct as a pedagogical maxim, but false in the judgment of individual cases; because it is possible, on the one hand, to have a healthy mind in an unhealthy body, and, on the other hand, an unhealthy mind in a healthy body. Nevertheless, to strive after the harmony of soul and body is the material condition of all normal activity. The development of intelligence presupposes physical health. Here we are to speak of the science of the art of teaching, technically called "didactics." This had its presupposition on the side of Nature, as was before seen, in physical education, but in the sphere of mind it presupposes psychology and logic. Instruction implies considerations of psychology as well as of logical method.

[Education has to note bodily conditions of the mind, and to prescribe methods of physical training. It has more especially to note also the nature of mind and comprehend the science of psychology, and prescribe the methods of developing the several powers of the mind. It has also to study logic in order to master the proper arrangement of studies and the order of teaching the several topics belonging under each study.]

(a) *The Psychological Presupposition.*

§ 81. In a complete system of philosophy, didactics could refer to the conception of mind which would have there been unfolded in psychology; and it must appear as a defect in scientific method if psychology, or at least the conception of the theoretical mind, has to be treated again within the science of education. We must take something for granted. Psychology, then, will here be consulted no further than is requisite to place on a sure basis the educational function which relates to it.

[Psychology, as a science, is unfolded within the philosophy of spirit as an antecedent presupposition of the science of ethics (which forms the third part of the science of spirit, see analysis and commentary to § 1, pages 4, 5, of this work). Hence the philosophy of education, which belongs to ethics (or social science), presupposes psychology, and in its proper place in an entire system might refer to it as already established. Here, in treating of intellectual education, we must give an outline of psychology.]

§ 82. To education the conception of *attention* is the most important of all those derived from psychology. Mind is essentially self-activity. Nothing exists for it which it does not posit as its own. We hear it often said that outside conditions make an impression on the mind, but this is an error. Mind lets nothing act upon it unless it has rendered itself receptive to it. Without this preparatory self-excitation the object does not really penetrate it, and it passes by the object unconsciously or indifferently. The horizon of perception changes for each person with his peculiarities and culture. Attention is the adjusting of the observer to the object in order to seize it in its unity and diversity. Relatively, the observer allows, for a moment, his relation to all other surroundings to cease, so that he may establish a relation with this one. Without this essentially spontaneous activity, nothing exists for the mind. All result in teaching and learning depends upon the clearness and strength with which distinctions are made, and the saying, *bene qui distinguit bene docet*, applies as well to the pupil.

[The conception of attention—the most important one in pedagogics. Nothing exists for the mind unless the mind gives attention to it—i. e., voluntarily entertains it. Attention is self-activity, not a passivity of the mind. It is the will acting upon the intellect, and hence a combination of intellect and will. Out of the infinitely manifold objects before the senses—each object is capable of endless subdivision, and there is no part so small that it does not possess variety and the possibility of further subdivision—attention selects one special field or province, and refuses to be diverted from it. It neglects all else and returns again and again from the borders of the field of attention and takes note of the relation of the surrounding objects to the object of special attention. It makes it the essential thing, and considers everything else only as related to it.

It is interesting to note how the higher faculties (*so-called* "faculties"—one must not, however, suppose these faculties as isolated "properties" of the mind, existing side by side, like properties of a thing) all originate from the process of attention; they are higher powers or "potencies" of attention. Isaac Newton ascribed his superiority to other men in intellectual power simply to the greater power of attention. Attention appears: *first*, as a mere power of isolating one object from others—a power of concentration upon it to the exclusion of others; *secondly*, it discriminates distinctions within the object or *analyzes* it: thus analysis is continued attention—the second power or potence of attention; *thirdly*, it seizes again upon one of the distinctions found by analysis, and becomes *abstraction;* abstraction might be named the third power or potence of attention; *fourthly*, the attention may be directed to essential relations of the elements found by analysis and abstraction—their essential relations to each other. This is a process of synthetic thought, a grasping-together, a comprehension—a higher activity of mind—a fourth potence of the power of attention. It is the most important matter in psychology, this process of synthesis, through necessary relation. To find that one object of attention, A, involves another, B (i. e., possesses essential relation to it, such that A can not exist without B) is to find a necessary synthesis. It is to discover that instead of A by itself, or B by itself, there is one existence having two phases to it, one phase being A, and the other phase being B. It is a finding of one in place of two, and is a synthetic act of mind. The synthesis is not an arbitrary one. It is a discovery of truth: A and B were really two aspects of one and the same being which we may call A B, but they *seemed* to be independent. The process of attention, up to its fourth power, is thus an ascent of cognition from *seeming* to *being*. The perception of *dependence* ("essential relation" is *dependence*) is the perception of synthesis, and belongs to the activity of *comprehension*. Reflection, as a mental activity (or "faculty"), is the process of discovering relations and dependencies among objects—hence it is a stage of synthesis—belonging to what we call here the "fourth power of attention." The student of educational psychology should follow out this mode of exploring the mind, and define for himself all of the so-called "faculties" and mental acts, in terms of attention. He must note, too, that the act of attention is an act of the mind directed upon itself, the will controlling the intellect, because it *confines* its own activity (i. e., the perception in general) to a special field), i. e., makes it a perception of a special object to the exclusion of others). This synthesis is, as just remarked, the most important theme of psychology—it is also the most wonderful—a veritable fountain of surprise. For the strangest thing to learn in psychology is that the process of reflection (the direction of the mind in upon itself) discovers the truth about the objects or things in the world. The first activity of sense-perception notices objects as independent of each other, as having no essential relations. Reflection, or attention in its higher powers, discovers necessary relations, and forms more adequate ideas of the truth. Isaac Newton saw the sun and planets as one gravitating whole—a *system*—and his knowledge certainly came nearer the truth than did the knowledge of previous astronomers who merely knew the sun and planets in their separate existence. In going into the truth of objects the mind goes into itself at the same time. Psychology points backward to the great fact that reason made both the world and the human intellect.]

§ 83. Attention, depending as it does on the self-determination of the observer, can therefore be improved, and the pupil made attentive, by the educator. Education must accustom him to an exact, rapid, and many-sided attention, so that at the first contact with an object he may grasp it sufficiently and truly, and that it shall not be necessary for him always to be changing his impressions concerning it. The twilight and partialness of intelligence which force a pupil always to new corrections because he has all along failed to give entire attention must not be tolerated.

[Attention (depending as it does upon the voluntary powers of the mind) can be developed or educated. (The fact that the child is capable of exercising his will-power on his intellect is the fundamental fact that makes all intellectual education possible. There is no intellect, strictly speaking, until the will has combined with the perception.) Self-determination or self-activity is the characteristic principle of life or living being. Related to itself it becomes consciousness. By new relations to itself it develops the mental orders or stages of thinking (perception, representation, understanding, reason, as described in the commentary to the preceding section). Aristotle (in his book on the Categories) distinguishes between first and second substances (οὐσίαι) referring to the object of perception (*this* animal or thing) and the object of the intellect (animal or thing as general concept). By the Arabians (Avicenna) this doctrine becomes a psychological doctrine of first and second intention of the mind (*intentio animi*). With the first intention we perceive objects of sense or "primary substances"; with the second intention we perceive universal objects or "second substances." "Intention" here signifies the act of attention or the directing inward of the intellect by the will upon its own processes, so that the process of the "first intention" becomes the object of the "second intention." This wonderful insight is an anticipation of Fichte's modification of the Kantian philosophy. In the "Science of Knowledge" (Wissenschaftslehre) Fichte has laid the basis for the only true psychology by a deduction of the main functions of mind from self-activity as Ego. The intellect and the will are discriminated: the forms of sense-perception (time and space), the categories of the intellect (causality and substantiality), the principles of the will (the moral ideas of duty and virtue).]

§ 84. We learn from psychology that mind does not consist of distinct faculties, but that what we choose to call so are only different activities of the same power. Each one is just as essential as the other, on which account education must grant to each faculty its claim to the same fostering care. Although we construe the axiom *a potiori fit denominatio* quite correctly to mean that man is distinguished from animals by thought, and by will mediated by thought [i. e., will-activity based on rational motives, action directed by moral principles], we must not forget that feeling and imagination are not less necessary to a truly complete human being. The special directions which the activity of cognitive (or theoretical as opposed to practical intelligence or the will) intelligence takes are (1) sense-perception, (2) representation (or imagination), (3) thinking. Dialectically, they pass over into each other; not only does perception grow into representation, and representation into thinking, but thinking goes back into representation, and this again into perception. In the development of the young, the perceptive faculty is most active in the infant, the representative faculty in the child, and the thinking faculty in the youth; and thus we may distinguish an intuitive, an imaginative, and a logical epoch.

Great errors arise from the misapprehension of these different phases and of their dialectic, since the different forms which are suitable to the different grades of youth are mingled. The infant certainly thinks while he perceives, but this thinking is to him unconscious. Or, if he has acquired sense-perceptions, he makes them into mental images, and manifests his freedom in making them the sport of his fancy. This play of fancy must not be taken for mere amusement; it also signifies that he takes care to preserve his intellectual balance, and his power of assimilation while engaged in filling his consciousness with material. Herein the delight of the child for fairy-tales finds its deeper reason. The fairy-tale constantly transcends the limits of common actuality. The abstract "common sense" can not endure this arbitrariness and want of fixed conditions, and thus would prefer that children should read, instead, home-made stories of the "Charitable Ann," of the "Heedless Frederick," of the "Inquisitive Wilhelmine," etc. Above all, it praises Campe's * "Robinson Crusoe," which contains much heterogeneous matter, but nothing improbable. When the maturity of youth necessitates the transition into the earnestness of real life, the drying up of the imagination and the sway of the understanding supervene.

---

* J. H. Campe, the disciple of Basedow, wrote an adaptation of De Foe's work, under the title of "Robinson der Jüngere," with a view to teach how "to live according to Nature." First edition, 1779; fifty-seventh edition, 1859!—*Note by* Ed.

[(Note what has been said above in § 82.) Perception, conception, and thinking are named as the three stages of intellect. Perception (German word, *Anschauen*) here refers simply to the contemplation of objects by the senses. Conception (German word, *Vorstellen*) makes in the mind a picture of the object, but a *general* picture—a representation of the object in its outlines—a representation that will correspond not only to the particular object, but to all objects of the same class. Thinking perceives the essential relations of the object, its dependencies on its environment, and the reciprocal action. Education produces in the pupil the ability to carry back the activity of the higher faculties into the lower ones, as stated in the text. In the presence of perception the mind learns to be able to recall the general representation of the type or class of objects, and compare the object before the senses with the general type or the definition. It enables it also to think in the presence of the object, and to perceive essential relations at the same time that it is occupied with perception and conception. Thus it elevates the lower faculties to thinking perception and to thinking conception. The child delights in fairy-tales because they sport with the fixed conditions of actuality, and present to him a picture of free power over nature and circumstances. Thus they, to some extent, prefigure to him the conquest which his race has accomplished, and is accomplishing—it is made to appear as the exploits of some Aladdin, or Jack the Giant-Killer. To modify, change, or destroy "the limits of common actuality" is the perpetual work of the race. It molds the external world to suit its own ideas. Play is the first education that the child gets to prepare him for this human destiny. The term "dialectic" is a stumbling-block to the reader unacquainted with German philosophy. "Dialectically they pass over into each other"—i. e., in tracing out either of these phases of intellect we discover that it implies each of the others in order to its own completeness and perfection. Perception is increased immensely in power by adding to it conception, which brings the aid of the general image in which are summed up all previous perceptions; thus perception re-enforced by conception is an individual activity re-enforced by the sum total of the race activity, or at least by the sum total of all previous activity of the same individual as well as by what he has learned from his fellows. Thus, too, perception is still more increased by adding to it the thinking activity which perceives necessary relations. Agassiz looks at a new fish from the Amazon River and sees at once its type and its variations—knows at once the great mass of its properties, functions, faculties, habits, and history, simply by its classification under already known genera, species, and sub-classes. This enables him to distinguish at once its variations from the general type and to see the significance of its peculiarities. In the same manner a botanist (Prof. Gray, for example) glances at a tree as he passes it rapidly, from the car-window. He sees its resemblances and its differences, however, in that rapid glance, because he subsumes it under all that he knows—all that is known, in fact, as the aggregate result of all observations for thousands of years. By recognizing its series, class, sub-class, order, sub-order, tribe, genus, species, and variety, he is instantly in possession of information enough to make a library of books on the subject of that one tree. He saw enough, too, in the rapid glance to inform himself of its individual differences, its particular size, age, shape, and condition, in so far as these were peculiar. Contrast this with the information obtained by the sense-perception of an observer endowed with excellent sight but no knowledge of botany. Science, which is the product of conception and thinking, thus re-enforces sense-perception, and "dialectically" the latter demands for its perfection those higher activities, and, *vice versa*, thinking and conception, which deal with the universal or the possibility and the process which creates particular individuals, demand sense-perception to take cognizance of those individuals.]

CHAPTER V.

INTELLECTUAL EDUCATION. (*a*) *Psychology* (continued).

(1) *The Intuitive Epoch.*

§ 85. Sense-perception, as the beginning of intellectual culture, is the free grasping of an object immediately present to the mind. Education can do nothing directly toward the performance of this act; it can only assist in making it easy: (1) it can isolate the object of consideration; (2) it can give facility in the transition to another; (3) it can promote the many-sidedness of the interest, by which means the return to a perception already obtained has always a fresh charm.

[Sense-perception (German *Anschauung*) is called *intuition* in all the earlier translations of Kant, because the Latin word *intueri* was suggested by Kant as an equivalent for *anschauen.* Hence "intuitive epoch" means *epoch of sense-perception.* Perception can be assisted by isolation of the object to be perceived. The pupil should be trained to look for certain properties and attributes, and to note their peculiarities. The categories under which one may classify these properties and attributes are furnished by reflection. Hence, when one in the so-called "object-lessons" trains the pupil to note in all objects certain constantly recurring predicates, such as color, shape, frangibility, solubility, size, number, taste, smell, etc., he is bringing thought and conception "back into perception" (see previous section) and elevating mere perception into *thinking perception.* The difference between ordinary perception and scientific perception lies just here: while the former is unsystematic and fragmentary, and does not accumulate or collect and retain data in the form of general ideas, the latter is systematic, exhaustive and cumulative. Thinking gives the system. Hence, the training of perception is the subordination of it to the will, and the introduction of complete systematic habits of activity in place of accidental perception.]

§ 86. There are many things which can not be presented to immediate perception, however desirable it may be. We must then have recourse to a mediated perception, and supply the lack of actual seeing by representations through pictures and models. But here the difficulty presents itself, that there are many objects which we are not able to represent in their true size, and we must have a reduced scale, whence results a difficulty as to the selection of the best standard. An explanation is then also necessary as a judicious supplement to the picture.

[All perceivable objects should be learned by actual perception so far as is possible. When remoteness in space and time or inaccessibility on account of size prevents this, a good substitute offers itself in the way of pictorial representation. The picture, of course, idealizes much—it magnifies some objects and reduces others, and it never presents all of the features found in nature. But it omits unessential details for the most part, and this fact makes a picture much easier to learn than the real object, although the knowledge is not so practical. The picture is commonly nearer the *type* or general form of the object than real specimens; the real specimens have much about them that is accidental, and need much comparison to discover what is the normal type. The picture gives this type at once, and hence gives assistance to the pupil—half digests his mental food for him, in fact. Hence the pictorial representation has advantages (it is easy of apprehension because it is a perception reduced to conception), and disadvantages (the pupil does not get the strength that comes from reducing the specimens of nature to their types by his own efforts).]

§ 87. Pictures are extremely valuable aids to instruction when they are correct and characteristic. Correctness must be demanded in these substitutes for natural objects, historical persons, and scenes. Without this correctness, the picture, if not an impediment, is, to say the least, useless.

It is only since the last half of the seventeenth century, i. e., since the disappearance of the genuine art of painting, that the picture-book has appeared as an educational means; first of all, coming from miniature-painting. Up to that time, public life was more picturesque with its display of arms, furniture, houses, and churches; and men, from their fondness for constant travel, had their hunger for immediate perception sated. It was only afterward, when, in the excitement of the Thirty Years' War, the arts of sculpture and painting and Christian and pagan mythology became extinct, that there arose a greater necessity for pictured representations. The *Orbis Rerum Sensualium Pictus*, which was also to be a *janua linguarum reserata*, of Amos Comenius, appeared first in 1658, and was reprinted in 1805. Many valuable illustrated books followed. Since that time innumerable illustrated Bibles and histories have appeared, but many of them look only to the pecuniary profit of the author or the publisher. [The remainder of this section, devoted to a criticism of the German illustrated books of the period, is omitted.]

[Accuracy is, above all, demanded in pictorial representations. The picture-book came into use chiefly after the decline of painting. Comenius (1658) gave a great impulse to education by his book, which attempts to convey a knowledge of the world by pictures.]

§ 88. Children have naturally a desire to collect things, and this may be so guided that they shall collect and arrange plants, butterflies, beetles, shells, skeletons, etc., and thus gain exactness and reality in their perception. Especially should they practice drawing, which leads them to form exact images of objects. But drawing, as children practice it, does not have the educational significance of cultivating in them an appreciation of art, but rather that of educating the eye, as this must be exercised in estimating distances, sizes, and colors. It is, moreover, a great gain in many ways, if, through a suitable course of lessons in drawing, the child is advanced to a knowledge of the elementary forms of nature.

That pictures should affect children as works of art is not to be required. They confine themselves at first to distinguishing the outlines and colors, and do not yet appreciate the execution. If the children have access to real works of art, we may safely trust in their power, and quietly await their moral and æsthetic effect. [Notice of a work on drawing omitted.]

[Children should be exercised in classification. They should collect and arrange cabinets for themselves. This will give them ability in recognizing the type in the specimen, the general in the particular. Drawing, too, is excellent for the training of sense-perception, if from objects direct, inasmuch as it requires the pupil to omit all that is not characteristic of the object. How far lines suffice to delineate an object, and fix it unmistakably, and what these few lines are, the art of drawing teaches. Characterization must be learned first before any attempt at æsthetic effect. But true works of art must be placed where the child will receive a silent education from them, although no positive instruction is given in them.]

§ 89. In order that looking at pictures shall not degenerate into mere diversion, explanations should accompany them. Only when the thought embodied in the illustrations is pointed out, can they be useful as a means of instruction. Simply looking at them is of as little value toward this end as is water for baptism without the Holy Spirit. Our age inclines at present to the superstition that man is able, by means of simple sense-perception, to attain a knowledge of the essence of things, and thereby dispense with the trouble of thinking. Illustrations are the order of the day, and, in the place of enjoyable descriptions, we find inferior pictures. It is in vain to try to get behind things, or to comprehend them, except by thinking.

[Pictorial representation is of little service, unless accompanied by analysis and explanation. Mere gazing upon a picture is like the thoughtless gazing upon real objects—it is not systematic, and does not separate the essential from the accidental, nor exhaust the subject.]

§ 90. The ear as well as the eye must be cultivated. Music must be considered the first educational means to this end, but it should be music inspired by ethical purity. Hearing is the most internal [i. e., it reveals to us the internal character of objects] of all the senses, and should on this account be treated with the greatest delicacy. Especially should the child be taught that he is not to look upon speech as merely a useful vehicle for communication and for gaining information; it should also give pleasure, and therefore he should be taught to speak distinctly and with a good intonation, and this can be reached only through careful attention.

Among the Greeks, extraordinary care was given to musical cultivation, especially in its ethical relation. Sufficient proof of this is found in the admirable detailed statements on this point in the "Republic" of Plato, and in the last book of the "Politics" of Aristotle. Among modern nations, also, music holds a high place, and makes its appearance as a constant element of education. Piano-playing has become general, and singing is also taught. But the ethical significance of music is too little considered. Instruction in music often aims only to train pupils for display in society, and the tendency of the melodies which are played is restricted more and more to orchestral airs of an exciting or bacchanalian character. The railroad-gallop style only makes the nerves of youth vibrate with stimulating excitement. Oral speech, the highest form of the personal manifestation of mind, was also treated with great reverence by the ancients. Among us, communication is so generally carried on by writing and reading that the art of speaking distinctly, correctly and agreeably, has become very much neglected. Practice in declamation accomplishes, on the whole, very little in this direction. But we may expect that the increase of public speaking occasioned by our political and religious assemblies may have a favorable influence in this particular.

[Training of the ear by music and by correct speaking. Tones are of all kinds—solemn, joyous, lively, sad, contemplative, discordant and suggestive of hate and bitterness, harmonious and sweet and suggestive of love and agreement, etc. There is a long scale of degrees to each one of these feelings and passions, and music can present all shades of each. Even the keys have each a special character. The German composers have used these and other properties of tones to advantage in constructing great musical dramas, in which pure music accomplishes results similar to words in poetry.]

CHAPTER VI.

INTELLECTUAL EDUCATION. (*a*) *Psychology* (continued).

(2) *The Imaginative Epoch.*

§ 91. The activity of perception results in the formation of an internal picture or image which intelligence can call up at any time at pleasure, and imagine it as occupying an ideal space, although the object is absent, in fact, and thus this image or picture becomes a sort of general schema (or pattern applicable to a class of objects), and hence an image-concept. The mental image may (1) be compared with the perception from which it sprang, or (2) it may be arbitrarily altered and combined with other images, or (3) it may be held fast in the form of abstract signs or symbols which intelligence invents for it. Thus originate the functions (1) of the verification of conceptions, (2) of creative imagination, and (3) of memory. For their full treatment, we must refer to psychology.

[(1) Verification of conceptions through comparison of the conception with the perception; (2) creative imagination, which modifies or combines images; (3) memory, which holds fast perceptions by attaching them to arbitrary or conventional symbols, such as words.]

§ 92. (1) The mental image which we form of an object may be correct; again, it may be partly or wholly defective, if we have neglected some of the predicates of the perception which presented themselves, or in so far as we have added to it other predicates which only seemingly belonged to it, and which were attached to it only by its accidental connection with other existences. Education must, therefore, foster the habit of comparing our conceptions with the perceptions from which they arose; and these perceptions, since they are liable to change by reason of their connection with other objects, must be frequently compared with our conceptions previously derived by abstraction from them.

[Method of verification and its function.]

§ 93. (2) We are thus limited in our conceptions by our perceptions, but we exercise a free control over our conceptions. We can create out of them, as simple elements, the manifold mental shapes which we do not treat as given to us by objects, but as essentially our own work. In the science of education, we must not look upon this freedom as if its exercise were only to afford gratification, but we must see in it the reaction of the absolute independence of mind against the dependence in which the empirical reception of impressions from without and their reproduction in conceptions place it. In this process, it not only fashions in itself or reproduces the phenomenal world, but it produces for itself a world which is all its own.

[Emancipation of the mind takes place through its ascent into formative power, and this is realized in two ways: (a) in reaching the general types of objects, the mind finds the one form that stands for many, and gains ability to see the one in the many, the power to hold the essential and permanent without depending on any one particular object or specimen or act of sense-perception; (b) in reproducing, by aid of the general conception or abstract definition, a number of special examples, it is able to fashion them in various ways, and yet endow them all with possible attributes and characteristics. The mind thus has free scope of realization, and can, in an ideal world of its own creation, participate in creative activity.]

§ 94. The study of art comes here to the aid of education, especially of poetry, the highest art and at the same time the most easily communicated. The imagination of the pupil can be led by means of the classical works of creative imagination to the formation of a good taste both as regards ethical merit and beauty of form. The proper classical works for youth are those which nations have produced in the childhood of their culture. These works bring children face to face with the picture of the world which the human mind has sketched for itself in one of the necessary stages of its development. This is the real reason why our children never weary of reading Homer and the stories of the Old Testament. Polytheism and the heroism (as well as hero-worship) which belongs to it are just as substantial an element of the view of the world that childhood forms as monotheism with its prophets and patriarchs. The standpoint of modern civilization is above both of these, because it is mediated by both, and embraces both in itself.

The best literature designed for the amusement of children from their seventh to their fourteenth year consists always of that which is honored by nations and the world at large. One has only to notice in how many thousand forms the story of Ulysses is reproduced by the writers of children's tales. Becker's "Ancient Stories," Gustav Schwab's most admirable "Sagas of Antiquity," Karl Grimm's "Tales of Olden Times," etc., what were they without the well-talking, wily favorite of Pallas and the divine swine-herd? And just as indestructible are the stories of the Old Testament up to the separation of Judah and Israel. These patriarchs with their wives and daughters, these judges and prophets, these kings and priests, are by no means ideals of virtue from the standpoint of our modern lifeless morality, which would smooth out of its pattern-stories for the "dear children" everything that is hard and uncouth. For the very reason that the shadow-side is not wanting here, and that we find envy, vanity, evil desire, ingratitude, craftiness, and deceit, among these fathers of the race and leaders of God's chosen people, have these stories so great an educational value. Adam, Cain, Abraham, Joseph, Samson, and David, have justly become as truly world-historical types as Achilles and Patroclus, Agamemnon and Iphigenia, Hector and Andromache, Ulysses and Penelope.

[In the epoch of the development of the imagination the study of art and literature comes in. The first classics for youth are those which have been developed by nations in their earliest stages. Not only the light sides, but the darker sides of character in these *naïve* stories, are essential to their educative effect. They furnish types of human character, and types of human situations, a knowledge of which constitutes wisdom. The conception of the characters of Cain, Joseph, Samson, David, Saul, Ulysses, Penelope, Achilles, and the like, furnishes a ready classification for special instances of character that we encounter in our experience.]

§ 95. There may be produced, also, out of the simplest and *naïvest* phases of different epochs of culture of one and the same people, stories which answer to the imagination of children, and represent to them the characteristic features of the past of their people.

The Germans possess such a collection of their stories in their popular books of the "Invulnerable Sigfried," of the "Heymon Children," of "Beautiful Magelone," "Fortunatus," "The Wandering Jew," "Faust," "The Adventurous Simplicissimus," "The Schildbürger," "The Island of Felsenburg," "Leonard and Gertrude," etc. Also, the poetical art works of the great masters which possess national significance must be mentioned here, as the "Don Quixote" of Cervantes.

[Every child should read as indispensable the stock of stories which furnish these general types of character and situation. "Robinson Crusoe," "Gulliver's Travels," "Don Quixote," the "Arabian Nights," Plutarch's "Lives," Homer's "Iliad" and "Odyssey," and the dramas of Shakespeare, should be read sooner or later. Earlier than these, the old English stories and fairy-tales, and even "Mother Goose's Melodies." A scale thus extending from the earth to the fixed stars of genius furnishes pictures of human life of all degrees of concreteness.

The meager and abstract outline is given in the nursery-tale, and the deep, comprehensive grasp of the situation with all of its motives is found in Shakespeare. The summation of the events of life in "Solomon Grundy" has been compared to the epitome furnished by Shakespeare in the "Seven Ages," and the disastrous voyage of the "Three Men of Gotham" is made a universal type of human disaster arising from rash adventure. The bald incident related in the nursery rhyme gives the child a typical fact or event which answers for a general concept and enables him to "re-enforce" (see commentary to § 84) his sense-perception, so that he acquires conscious experience far more rapidly than he could do without its aid.]

§ 96. The commonest form in which the childish imagination finds exercise is that of fairy-tales; but education must take care that it has these in their proper shape as national productions, and that they are not of the morbid kind which artificial poetry so often gives us in this species of literature, and which not seldom degenerate into sentimental caricatures and silliness.

The East Indian stories are most excellent because they have their origin with a child-like people who live wholly in the imagination. By means of the Arabian filtration, which took place in Cairo in the flourishing period of the Egyptian caliphs, all that was too characteristically Indian was excluded, and they were made in the "Tales of Sheherazade," a book for all peoples, with whose far-reaching power in child-literature the local stories of a single people, as, e. g., Grimm's admirable ones of German tradition, can not compare. Fairy-tales made to order, like those with a mediæval Catholic tendency, or very moral and dry, as we often see them, are a bane to the youthful imagination in their insipid sweetness. We must here add, however, that lately we have had some better success in our attempts since we have learned to distinguish between the *naïve* natural poetry, which is without reflection, and the poetry of art, which is more or less molded by criticism and a conscious ideal. This distinction has produced good fruits even in the picture-books of children. The pretensions of the gentlemen who printed illustrated books containing nothing more solid than the alphabet and the multiplication-table have become less prominent since such men as Speckter, Fröhlich, Gutsmuths, Hofmann (the writer of "Slovenly Peter"), and others have shown that seemingly trivial things can be handled with intellectual power, if one is blessed with it, and that nothing is more opposed to the child's imagination than the *childishness* into which so many writers for children have fallen when they attempted to descend with dignity from their assumed lofty standpoint. Men are beginning to understand that Christ promised the kingdom of heaven to little children on other grounds than because they had, as it were, the privilege of being thoughtless and foolish.

[Importance of avoiding morbid tendencies in the stories for children. They must be *naïve* and not sentimental; but mere childishness is to be avoided.]

§ 97. For youth and maidens, especially as they approach manhood and womanhood, the cultivation of the imagination must yield place and allow the earnestness which deals with the actual affairs of the world to manifest itself in its undisguised energy. This earnestness, no longer through the symbolism of play but in its objective reality, must now thoroughly penetrate the conceptions of the youth so that it shall prepare him to seize hold of the machinery of active life. Instead of the all-embracing Epos, now comes Tragedy, whose purifying process, through the feelings of fear and pity, unfolds to the youth the secret of all human destiny—sin, and its expiation. The works best adapted to lead to an interest in history and the affairs of the actual world are those of biography—of ancient times, Plutarch; of modern times, the autobiographies of Augustine, Cellini, Rousseau, Goethe, Varnhagen, Jung-Stilling, Moritz Arndt, etc. These autobiographies contain a view of the growth of individuality through its interaction with the influences of its time, and, together with the letters and memoirs of great or at least noteworthy men, tend to produce a healthy excitement in the youth, who must learn to fight his own battles through a knowledge of the battles of others. To introduce the youth to a knowledge of nature and man no means are better than books of travels which describe for us the charm of the first interview, the joy of discovery, instead of the general consciousness of the conquests of mind.

If educative literature on the one hand broadens the field of knowledge, on the other it may also promote its elaboration into ideal forms. This happens, in a strict sense, through philosophical literature. But only two species of this are to be recommended to youth: (1) well-written treatises which endeavor to solve a single problem with spirit and thoroughness; or, (2) when the intelligence has grown strong enough for it, the classical works of a true philosopher. German literature is fortunately very rich in treatises of this kind in the works of Lessing, Herder, Kant, Fichte, Schleiermacher, Wilhelm von Humboldt, and Schiller. But nothing does more harm to youth than the study of works of mediocrity, or those of a still lower rank. They stupefy and narrow the youthful mind by their empty, hollow, and constrained style. It is generally supposed that these standard works are too difficult, and that one must first seize them in a trivial and diluted form in order to understand them. This is one of the most prevalent and most dangerous errors, for these "introductions" or "explanations," "easily comprehended treatises," "summary abstracts," are, because of their want of originality and of the acuteness which belongs to it, much more difficult to understand than the standard work itself, to which they propose to conduct us. Education must train the youth to the courage which will attempt classical works in philosophy, and it must not allow any such miserable preconceived opinions to grow up in his mind as that his understanding is totally unable to comprehend works like Fichte's "Science of Knowledge," the "Metaphysics" of Aristotle, or Hegel's "Phenomenology." No science suffers so much as philosophy from this false popular opinion, which understands neither itself nor its authority. The youth must *learn how to learn to understand*, and, in order to do this, he must know that one can not immediately understand everything in its minutest subdivisions, and that on this account he must have patience, and must resolve to read over and over again and to think over what he has read.

[Earnestness must predominate over play, as the child advances into youth and youth into riper age. Aristotle said that tragedy purifies the mind, by fear and pity, from the passions depicted in the drama as having tragic results. Certainly in the dramas of Sophocles and Æschylus we see presented the great problem of a human deed and its reaction on the doer. But the Greek consciousness had not arrived at the solution of the problem of sin and responsibility which Christian nations now accept. Œdipus sins through ignorance but suffers all the same as if perfectly enlightened. According to modern ideas of justice, involuntary ignorance palliates the crime. The remarks on the study of the deepest and most original works in philosophy can not be too highly praised. The "courage" which will attempt Aristotle, Kant, or Hegel is a rare and valuable discipline, at least for the sake of what it can do in mastering other subjects than philosophy. There is no lesson the student can learn so important to him as this: The most difficult of writings can be mastered by repeated attacks that concentrate the whole energy on a small portion. Let a student read one page of Kant's "Critique of Pure Reason" when his mind is fresh, concentrating his full attention upon it. His first reading will not suffice to give him much insight. But if he repeats his reading of this one page every week for six months he will discover within himself not only new ideas but new *faculties*. While this progresses he will be delighted to find that other less difficult works, which, however, formerly had required his full strength to master, have now become quite easy. It is like substituting for the flame of an alcohol-lamp that of an oxy-hydrogen blowpipe: the difficulties melt away before his new power of analysis disciplined on the dry and abstruse philosophical work. By this exercise the youth overcomes that worst of intellectual obstacles—the belief that what he can not understand at first trial is permanently beyond his powers:—"My mind was not made for that kind of work." The motto of the school-room should be, "Each may master the deepest and wisest thoughts that the human race has transmitted to us." Repeated attacks by concentrated attention not only master the abstruse problem, but leave the mind with a permanent acquisition of power of analysis for new problems.—The biographies of Plutarch present well-executed pictures of men of colossal characters placed in difficult situations. Philosophical works, if taken up in later youth, should be classical treatises on special problems of thought. Abstracts and summaries are generally to be avoided.]

§ 98. (3) Imagination returns again within itself to perception in that it replaces, for conceptions, perceptions themselves, which are to remind it of the previous conception [as, for example, imagination calls a crafty man a "fox," and indicates a whole class of men by this symbol. The *symbol* retains under the new meaning also the old meaning]. These perceptions may resemble in some way the perception which lies at the basis of the conception, and be thus more or less symbolical; or they may be merely arbitrary creations of the creative imagination, and are in this case pure signs. [When the symbolic term loses its old meaning, and retains only its new meaning, it becomes a "pure sign," and is no longer a symbol. Thus, a studious man may be called a "book-worm," which at first would suggest the mite that destroys books, but by-and-by loses that suggestion, and suggests only the concept of a person devoted to books. Thus "book-worm" is first a symbol, and then becomes a mere conventional sign of a conception.] In common speech and writing, we call the free retaining of these perceptions created by imagination, and the recalling of the conceptions denoted by them, *memory*. It is by no means a particular faculty of the mind, which is again subdivided into memory of persons, names, numbers, etc. As to its form, memory is the stage of the dissolution of image-making representation; but, as to its content, it arises from the interest which we take in a subject-matter. From this interest results careful attention, and from this latter, facility in the reproductive imagination. If these acts have preceded, the fixing of a name, or of a number, in which the content interesting us is, as it were, summed up, is not difficult. When interest and attention animate us, it seems as if we did not need to be at all troubled to remember anything. All the so-called mnemonic helps only serve to make more difficult the act of memory. This act is in itself a double function, consisting of, first, the fixing of the sign, and second, the fixing of the conception subsumed under it. Since the mnemonic technique adds to these one more conception, through whose means the things with which we have to deal are to be fixed, it makes the function of remembering three-fold, and forgets that the connecting link and its relations to the sign and the subsumed conception—wholly arbitrary and highly artificial—must also be remembered. The true aid for memory consists in not helping it at all, but in simply taking up the object into the ideal regions of the mind by the force of the infinite self-determination which mind possesses [that is to say, the true help consists in associating the object with its kindred through ideas of species and genera or classes].

Lists of names, as e. g., of the Roman emperors, of the popes, of the caliphs, of rivers, mountains, authors, cities, etc.; also numbers, as, e. g., the multiplication-table, the melting-points of minerals, the dates of battles, of births and deaths, etc., must be learned without aid. All indirect means only serve to do harm here, and are required as self-discovered devices only in case that interest or attention has become weakened.

[Memory. The German word *Gedächtniss* is contrasted with the word *Erinnerung*; the former may be translated "memory," and the latter "recollection"—recollection, the reproduction of the perceived object in its particular existence, and memory the reproduction of it by its general type. With the general type the mind is able to master the infinite diversity of nature and reduce all to a few classes. Mnemonic artifices are to be eschewed. "Memory is the stage of the dissolution of the conception"; this means that the power of representation becomes less and less, a mere recalling of what has been perceived, and, as the mind strengthens, it passes over into a faculty which calls up universals, or general concepts in the place of particular images. Memory, in this technical sense, deals with words—each word standing for some universal concept. Language is therefore something that can be used by a whole people—its words, standing, as they do, for universals, express for each individual the contents of his observations, no matter how peculiar they may be. Memory, as thus contradistinguished from mere recollection, is therefore synthetic, inasmuch as it constructs or puts together the essential characteristics of the object in the form of a definition and subsumes objects perceived under it. While recollection recalls the exact object which it perceived before, memory recognizes in the object before it its class or species, and thus recalls and adds to the object the sum total of previous experience in regard to this object. (See commentary to § 84 for further discussion of this. The difference between the memory of the scientific man and that of the unscientific is there illustrated.) It must not be understood here that the "definition" implied in the "word" is a conscious one. Most of the words we use have never been defined consciously, that is to say, we have never reflected on the definition; but we carry with us an unconscious definition all the same, and, when we identify or recognize objects before us, we use the unconscious definition, taking notice of the features of the object one after the other, to see whether they correspond to the features which we remember as general characteristics of the class.

How what is symbolic becomes conventional is perhaps the most interesting question in the psychology of early education. The child passes from the symbolical stage to the conventional stage of culture, and enters the stage of "youth" in the technical sense of the word, as here employed. Conventional studies, like the alphabet and orthography, can not be well taken up until the child has reached this conventional epoch of growth. In the old hieroglyphic system, the letter A represented the face of an ox, and was symbolic. Since the Phœnicians transplanted the alphabet among other peoples, A has been a conventional sign for a particular sound.

Recollection may be cultivated. A magnet will increase its force if a slight increase is made daily to the weight it supports. So the memory of numbers and dates may be indefinitely increased by committing an additional one or two each day to memory, and taking care by frequent reviews that nothing once memorized shall escape. But equal care should be taken not to overburden the power of recollection by undertaking too many new items at a time. Let the student make a special effort with precisely the kind of recollection that he is most deficient in, be it names, dates, shapes, or whatever it be, and he will find that, by persistent practice for a few months, he can bring the special power to the front. The habit of attention to likeness and difference, so that the mind at once takes in the species and differentia involuntarily, is the habit that secures good memory.]

§ 99. The means to be used (and these are based on the nature of memory itself) are, on the one hand, the pronouncing and writing of the names or numbers, and, on the other, repetition; by the former means we gain distinctness and by the latter sureness of memory.

All artificial contrivances for quickening the memory dwindle in comparison with the art of writing, in so far as this is not looked upon as a means of relieving the memory. That a name or a number should be this or that, is for the intelligence a mere result of chance, an entirely meaningless accident to which we have unconditionally to submit ourselves as something not dependent on our wills. The intelligence must be accustomed to put upon itself this constraint. In the sciences, especially in philosophy, our reason helps to derive one thought from another by means of its dependence on it, and we can discover names through this fact of dependence and derivation.

[Repetition and the writing down of names and numbers are the best means for fixing them in the memory.]

CHAPTER VII.

INTELLECTUAL EDUCATION. (a) *Psychology* (continued).

(3) *The Logical Epoch.*

§ 100. In representation by means of mental images there is attained a general idea or a notion in so far as the empirical details are referred to a *schema*, as Kant called it. But the *necessity* of the connection of the particular details with the general schema is wanting to it. To develop this idea of necessity is the task of the thinking activity, which frees itself from all mental pictures, and with its clearly defined determinations transcends image-concepts. The thinking activity, therefore, is emancipated from dependence on the senses, to a higher degree than the processes of conception and perception. The notion, judgment, and syllogism, develop forms which, as such, have no power of being perceived by the senses. But it does not follow from this that he who thinks can not return out of the thinking activity and carry it with him into the sphere of image-concepts and perception. The true thinking activity deprives itself of no content. The form of abstraction affecting a logical purism which looks down upon conception and perception as forms of intelligence quite inferior to itself is a pseudo-thinking, a morbid and scholastic error. Education will be the better on its guard against this the more it has led the pupil by the legitimate road of perception and conception to thinking. Memorizing especially is an excellent preparatory school for the thinking activity, because it gives practice to the intelligence in exercising itself in abstract ideas.

[In the general images of the faculty of conception, necessity of connection is yet wanting. Thinking, technically so called, discovers necessary relations. The logical distinctions are notions, judgment, syllogism. Within the notion are the ideas of universal, particular and individual (or singular). The thinking activity "returns" to perception and conception, as illustrated in § 84, re-enforcing them. It is important for the teacher to be able to recognize the grades of simple perception from those grades re-enforced by thought as explained in that section. As an example of necessary relations, take the quantitative phases of any thing or event. In every triangle the sum of its three angles is 180°. Every circumference of a round object is equal to the diameter multiplied by 3·14159 +.]

§ 101. The fostering of the sense of truth, from the earliest years up, is the surest way of leading the pupil to gain the power of thinking. The unprejudiced, disinterested yielding to truth, as well as the effort to shun all deception and false seeming, is of the greatest value in strengthening the power of reflection, as this considers nothing of value but the actually existing objective interaction of things and events.

The indulging of an illusion as a pleasing recreation of the intelligence should be allowed, while lying must not be tolerated. Children have a natural inclination for mystifications, for masquerades, for raillery, and for theatrical performances, etc. This inclination to illusion is perfectly normal with them, and should be permitted. The graceful kingdom of art is developed from it, as also the poetry of conversation with its jest and wit. Although this sometimes becomes stereotyped into very prosaic conventional forms of speech, it is more tolerable than the awkward honesty which takes everything in its simple literal sense. And it is easy to discover whether children in such play, in the activity of free joyousness, incline to the side of mischief by their showing a desire of satisfying their selfish interest. Then they must be checked, for in that case the sprightliness of harmless joking gives way to gloomy calculation and dissimulation.

[A sense of truth should be fostered from childhood up. Prejudice and self-interest must be habitually set aside for the truth—for the perception of things as they actually are. Great care, therefore, must be exercised to prevent an undue tendency to illusions (the activity of the productive imagination, however essential it may be) from weakening the sense of truth.]

§ 102. An acquaintance with logical forms is to be recommended as a special educational help in the culture of intelligence. The study of mathematics does not suffice, because it, itself, already presupposes logic. Mathematics is related to logic in the same way as grammar, the physical sciences, etc. The logical forms must be known explicitly in their pure independence and not merely in their implicit state as immanent in objective shapes.

[An acquaintance with logical forms is important for the thorough education of the intellect. Logical forms give the archetypes or simplest shapes of all problems that occur elsewhere. Neither mathematics nor any other application of logic in the sciences can supply the place of a logical training.]

CHAPTER VIII.

INTELLECTUAL EDUCATION (*continued*).

(*b.*) *The Logical Presupposition, or the Method.*

§ 103. THE logical presupposition of instruction is the order in which the subject-matter develops for the consciousness. The subject, the consciousness of the pupil, and the activity of the instructor, interpenetrate each other in instruction, and constitute in actuality one whole.

[Instruction presupposes a certain logical order of development in its theme. In arithmetic, for example, fractions must not be studied before simple addition. Political geography should be studied after mathematical and physical geography; grammar, after reading and writing; general history after the history of one's own country.

The three elements which instruction combines are: (1) the subject to be taught; (2) the consciousness of the pupil; (3) the insight and labor of the teacher.]

§ 104. (1) First of all, the subject which is to be learned has a specific determinateness which demands in its exposition a certain fixed order of sequence. However arbitrary we may be, the subject has a certain determination of its own which no mistreatment can wholly crush out, and this inherent immortal rationality is the general foundation of instruction.

To illustrate: however one may handle a language in teaching it, he can not change the words in it, or the inflections of the declensions and conjugations. And the same restriction is laid upon our inclinations in the different divisions of natural history in the theorems of arithmetic, geometry, etc. The theorem of Pascal remains still the same theorem wherever it is set forth.

[The subject has a nature of its own which requires it to be studied in a certain definite order. Whatever modifications are made in the subject to adapt it to the immature mind of the pupil, this essential nature of the subject must not be changed.

As regards the "logical presupposition" above spoken of, it is clear enough that all subjects to be taught possess logical relations of dependence of one part on another and of the parts on the whole. There must be therefore a certain order of exposition of the subject: the dependent parts must be shown in their dependence, otherwise the subject will not be taught properly. We can not teach the zones or parallels and meridians unless we have previously taught the spherical form of the earth.

Much change and adaptation will be made by the teacher in order to make the subject entertaining to his pupil and easy of access, but the logical order of dependence of one topic on another within arithmetic, geometry, natural history, grammar, etc., can not be changed; he must take it as it is, for that is its intelligible order and must be followed. The words of the classic author must be translated as they stand, and not from the end backward, if we would find sense in them.]

§ 105. (2) But the subject must be adapted to the consciousness of the pupil, and here the order of procedure and the exposition depend upon the stage which he has reached intellectually, for the special manner of the instruction must be conditioned by this. If he is in the stage of sense-perception, we must use the illustrative method; if in the stage of image-conception, that of combination; and if in the stage of thinking, that of demonstration. The first exhibits the object directly, or some representation of it; the second considers it according to the different possibilities which exist in it, and turns it around on all sides (and examines its relations to other things); the third demonstrates the necessity of the relations in which it stands either with itself or with others. This is the natural order from the standpoint of the developing intelligence: first, the object is presented to the perception; then combination with other things shows its relations and presents its different phases; and, finally, the thinking activity circumscribes the restlessly moving reflection by the idea of necessity. Experiment in the method of combination is an excellent means for a discovery of relations, for a sharpening of the attention, for the arousing of a many-sided interest; but it is no true dialectic, though it be often denoted by that name.

Illustration is especially necessary in the natural sciences and also in æsthetics, because both of these departments appeal to sense-perception. [Omission here of reference to editions of atlases and wall-maps.]

[With regard to the second point mentioned above—the consciousness of the pupil or his grade of advancement, this too must be considered, as well as the logical order of the development of the subject. Inasmuch as instruction is a leading of the ignorant into knowledge by translating the unknown into the known, there are two factors involved: (a) the unknown subject; (b) the stock of knowledge already possessed by the pupil. The knowledge already possessed is the means by which the unknown can be grasped and retained. All learning is a translating of an unknown into a known, just as the learning of a foreign language proceeds by translating the unfamiliar words into familiar words and thereby changing the strange into the familiar. This being so, unless constant reference is had by the teacher to the stock of familiar ideas belonging to the pupil, there is imminent danger to instruction; it may pass off into the process of exchanging unknown words for unknown words—a movement entirely within the realm of the unfamiliar. Such a process is not instruction, whatever else it may be. Thus the method of instruction must be largely determined by the consciousness (what he knows) or stage of advancement of the pupil. If the pupil is young and has few ideas of abstract depth, but mostly ideas of objects perceived by the senses, then the method must be one of *illustration*. It must translate the subject into particular objects of sense-perception so far as this is possible. If such a process is not possible with a given branch of instruction, then that branch must not be taken up now; its logical presupposition requires it to be preceded by other studies.

If the pupil has reached the stage of thinking by means of mental images or pictures of the mind (Vorstellungen), then the method may be less illustrative and may combine objects and symbolize to some extent (as in fairy-stories, or as in any stories when the objects used are types of whole classes of objects); or, in the stage of reflection there may be demonstration or the showing up of logical necessity, or the relations of cause and effect, or of power and manifestation, or of fact and logical presupposition, or any logical relation the object may have to other objects or to the whole environment in which it is found.

These three stages make up the range of the "consciousness" of the pupil—he may be in the (a) first stage, and mere perception or beholding of external objects be his chief mental activity, or (b) he may be active in representing objects, that is to say, active in his fancy, imagination, or recollections; or (c) active in discovering relations between objects, and hence active in the application of such abstract conceptions as identity and difference, likeness and unlikeness, force and manifestation, whole and parts, cause and effect, thing and properties, etc.

"Combination," spoken of in the text, means the consideration of the various phases and properties of the subject under different relations. It is necessary to multiply the examples and see the object under new combinations in order to discover all of the possibilities in it. The individual oak-tree before us is only one of infinite possible examples of the oak, and, as each actual oak differs from every other in some respect, we learn some new possibility with each new specimen. Thus we add or combine by experience the possibilities which together make up the nature or entire being of an object. Water is easily discovered to have three states—liquid, solid (as ice), and aëriform (as steam). It is only one of these states at a time, and all only in succession. Hence the necessity of "combination" or of discovery of different relations or of the behavior of the object under different "combinations" or environments, in order to learn its totality of possible being. The idea of necessity arrives when one has reached a totality of "combination." This may be reached only relatively in the realm of experience; we may treat the total of states actually discovered thus far as the absolute totality—this we do as a fact in practical experience, e. g., we do not hesitate to treat water as though it had only three possible states, liquid, solid, and gaseous. But the true absolute necessity comes only from the logical side of presupposition. Every fact has a presupposition which is the logical condition of its existence. This oak-tree presupposes space and time, and could not exist without them. All the properties that follow from the nature of space and time may be named as logical conditions absolutely necessary to the existence of the oak-tree.

"Experiment in the method of combination is an excellent

means for the discovery of relations," but "it is no true dialectic," or, in other words, it does not discover the inward necessity which appertains only to the logical presupposition, because the dialectical method does not make combinations or experiments at hap-hazard, but by careful analysis and observation of the object discovers in what manner its essential properties demand or presuppose other objects. Given one object, it unfolds the system to which it belongs. The dialectic proceeds from the part to the whole, following the thread of dependence which may be discovered in any object.

In æsthetics, or the science of art (architecture, sculpture, painting, and music), illustration is necessary, because *presentation to the senses* is essential to the nature of art.

§ 106. The demonstrative method, in order to bring about its proof of necessity, has a choice of many different ways. But we must not imagine, either that there are an unlimited number, and that it is only a chance which one we shall take; or that they have no connection among themselves, and run, as it were, side by side. It is not, however, the business of pedagogics to develop different methods of proof; this belongs to logic. We have only to remember that, logically taken, proof must be analytic, synthetic, or dialectic. Analysis begins with the single individual, and leads out from it by induction to the general principle from which its existence results. Synthesis, on the contrary, begins with a general which is presupposed as true, and leads from this through deduction to the special determinations which were implicit in it. The regressive search of analysis for a determining principle is *invention;* the forward progress of synthesis from the simple elements seeking for the multiplicity of single individuals is *construction.* The former method has been called the heuristic [from the Greek word for to discover, εὑρεῖν]; the latter, the *architectonic*. Each, in its result, passes over into the other; but their truth is found in the dialectic method, which in each phase allows unity (of principle) to separate into diversity (of particulars), and diversity to return into unity. While in the analytic as well as in the synthetic method the mediation of the individual with the general, or of the general with the individual, brings in the phase of particularity as only subjectively connected with it, in the dialectic method we have the going over of the general through the particular to the individual, or to the self-determination of the idea, and it therefore rightly claims the title of the "genetic" method. We can also say that while the inventive method gives us the idea (notion) and the constructive the judgment, the genetic gives us the syllogism which leads the determinations of reflection back again into substantial identity.

[The demonstrative method deals with necessary relations, and uses the forms of demonstration furnished it by logic, namely, analytic, synthetic, or dialectic. Analytic demonstration, according to Rosenkranz, begins with some object, as a whole, and proceeds to find its derivation or dependence on something else, and thus gradually leads out to the idea of that larger whole in which the object exists as a part (invention). Synthetic demonstration, on the other hand, proceeds from a principle to the particular results that follow from it (construction). "Each of these passes over into the other in its result," i. e., the result of analysis is synthesis, because in our analysis of the object we discovered dependence and derivation, and hence discovered that it was not a true whole or totality, but involved something else —hence we found that the compass of its being was greater than we had at first supposed—we have *added* to it, and our analysis proves to have been synthesis rather.

So, too, synthesis or construction is really an analysis of the constituent elements of the principle. By deducing (analyzing) what is given us in the principle, we discover the results or special characteristics that the principle produces; hence we rise to the idea of the total, which includes both the principle and its results, and the demonstration involves both analysis and synthesis.

The one-sided methods of analysis and synthesis are therefore always united in fact, although they seem to be separate when we consider them abstractly; we find them to be dialectic methods, therefore, if we look upon both of the phases of their activity. In the former (analytic), diversity returns to unity—the subordinate unities are traced back to their higher unity, or in the latter (synthesis) unity separates into diversity; the higher unity gives rise to lower unities. In the analytic method there is a "mediation of the individual" object with the general object, i. e., a tracing of the relations of the individual to other individuals with which it forms a totality or higher unity. In the synthetic method there is a "mediation of the general or total with the particular object," because we see how a force, power, energy, or principle develops particular forms. In both of these, when considered superficially or inadequately and one-sidedly, there is only a subjective connection stated between the particulars and the general—"subjective connection" meaning a connection only in our minds, and not an *essential* connection which would be one existing in the object as a real dependence upon other objects. In the dialectic method, or in the method which sees both synthesis and analysis in each step, we see in every phase the principle of self-activity, because we see that the subordinate objects arise through the energy of the totality, and the energy of the totality produces the subordinate phases and unities. All totalities must be self-determined or self-active, because they can not be at the same time totalities and depend on anything beyond them for their movement or form. This self-active totality is called by the Hegelian philosophy (from which Rosenkranz borrows it) "the self-determination of the notion (*Begriff*) or idea," because in that philosophy the technical term for self-activity is *Begriff* (idea or notion). Inasmuch as it shows self-activity as the principle that connects the general with the particular, and hence explains all things through evolution, it "rightly claims the title of *genetic* (or development) method."

"The inventive or analytic method gives us the idea or notion" (*Begriff*), because it proceeds beyond the particular object to its genesis in a higher unity whose energy or self-activity has produced it; it has therefore explained the object through self-activity (*Begriff*).

"The constructive method (synthetic) gives the judgment (*Urtheil*)." In Hegelian technique, the distinction arising through self-activity (distinction into active and passive or actor and acted upon) in the notion (*Begriff*) is called judgment (*Urtheil*).

The analytic method leads us back to self-activity (*Begriff*, notion). The synthetic method leads us to distinction of universal and individual (*Urtheil*, judgment). The genetic method leads us to syllogism (*Schluss*). In the same system of philosophy, *Schluss*, or syllogism, is the technical term for the unity of all the phases of self-activity, and includes the universal or self-active, and the particular (or distinguished phases of active and passive that form an antithesis), and it is the unity of these two, or that which is self-identical and self-distinct in one act (just as mind or consciousness is subject and object of itself).]

§ 107. (3) The living mediation of the pupil with the content which is to be impressed upon his consciousness is the work of the teacher, whose personality creates an individual or peculiar method; for, however clearly the subject may be defined, however exactly the psychological stage of the pupil may be regulated, the teacher can not do away with his own individuality even in the most objective relations. This individuality must penetrate the whole with its own exposition, and that peculiarity which we call his *manner*, and which can not be determined *a priori*, must appear. The teacher must place himself on the standpoint of the pupil, i. e., he must adapt himself; he must see that the abstract is made clear to him in the concrete, i. e., he must illustrate; he must fill up the gaps which will certainly appear, and which may mar the thorough seizing of the subject, i. e., he must supply. In all these relations the pedagogical tact of the teacher may prove itself truly ingenious in varying the method according to the changefulness of the ever-varying needs, in contracting or expanding the extent, in omitting or accumulating examples, in stating, or only indicating, what is to be supplied. The true teacher is free from any superstitious belief in any one procedure as a sure specific which he follows always in a monotonous bondage. This freedom can only be enjoyed by him who is capable of the highest method. The teacher has arrived at the highest point of ability in teaching when he can make use of all means, from the loftiness of solemn seriousness, through smooth statement, to the play of jest—yes, even to the incentive of irony, and to humor.

Education can be in nothing more ostentatious than in its method, and it is here that charlatanism can most readily intrude itself. Every little change, every pitiful modification, is proclaimed aloud as a new or an improved method; and even the most foolish and superficial changes find at once their imitators, who themselves conceal their effrontery behind some trifling differences, and, with ridiculous conceit, hail themselves as inventors.

["The living mediation of the pupil," etc. "Mediation" here refers to the *adjustment* and *adaptation* of the subjects taught to the pupil, so as to suit his intellectual and moral capacity and meet his special difficulties. The teacher adopts his own method within limits. He finds that his capacity and peculiarities make it most convenient to lead the pupil to his task in this way rather than in that way. But all teachers must (a) keep in view the standpoint of the pupil, (b) use illustration, (c) supply necessary steps to make the connection clear to the pupil. The live teacher is careful to avoid being hampered by the limits of any one method, although he finds use for all on occasions.]

CHAPTER IX.

INTELLECTUAL EDUCATION (*continued*).

(c) *Instruction.*

§ 108. All instruction starts from the inequality between those who possess knowledge and ability and those who have not yet obtained them. The former are qualified to teach, the latter to learn. Instruction is the act which gradually cancels the original inequality of teacher and pupil, in that it converts what was at first the property of the former into the property of the latter by means of his own activity.

[Instruction presupposes two parties, one possessing knowledge and ability, and the other lacking them.]

(1) *The Subjects of Instruction.*

§ 109. The pupil is the apprentice, the teacher the master, whether in the practice of any craft or art, or in the exposition of any systematic knowledge. The pupil passes from the state of the apprentice to that of the master through that of the journeyman. The apprentice has to appropriate to himself the elements; journeymanship begins, by means of their possession, to become independent; the master combines with his technical skill the freedom of production. His authority over his pupil consists only in his knowledge and ability. If he has not these, no external support, no trick of false appearances which he may put on, will serve to create it for him.

[Distinction of three stages: (*a*) apprenticeship, (*b*) journeymanship, (*c*) mastership—after the old distinction of degrees of perfection in the trades.]

§ 110. These stages—(1) apprenticeship, (2) journeymanship, (3) mastership—are fixed limitations in the didactic process; but they are relative in the concrete. The standard of special excellence varies with the different grades of culture, and must be varied that it may have validity for each period of time. The master is complete only in relation to the journeyman and apprentice; to them he is superior. But, on the other hand, in relation to the infinity of the problems of his art or science, he is by no means complete; to himself he must appear as one who begins ever anew, one who is ever striving, one to whom a new problem ever rises from every achieved result. He can not discharge himself from work, he must never desire to rest on his laurels. He is the truest master whose finished performances only force him on to never-resting progress.

[The standard of mastership varies with the demands of the age or nation. In judging a particular example, we must always take the standard into consideration. The true master always regards himself an apprentice before the new problems that step forth out of the solution of the old ones.]

§ 111. The possibility of culture is found in general, it is true, in every human being; nevertheless, as a practical matter, there are distinguished: (1) incapacity, as the want of all gifts; (2) mediocrity; (3) talent and genius. It is the part of psychology to give an account of all these. Mediocrity characterizes the great mass of intelligences that are merely mechanical, and that wait for external impulse as to what direction their endeavors shall take. Not without truth, perhaps, may we hypothetically presuppose a special talent in each individual, but this special talent in many men never makes its appearance, because under the circumstances in which it finds itself placed it fails to find the exciting occasion which shall give them the knowledge of its existence. The majority of mankind are contented with the mechanical impulse which makes them into something, and impresses upon them certain characteristics. Talent shows itself by means of the confidence in its own especial productive possibility, which manifests itself as an inclination, or as a strong impulse, to occupy itself with the special object which constitutes the object of its ability. Education has no difficulty in dealing with mechanical natures, because their passivity is only too ready to follow prescribed patterns. It is more difficult to manage talent, because it lies between mediocrity and genius, and is therefore uncertain, and not only unequal to itself, but also is tossed now too low, now too high, is by turns despondent and over-excited. The general maxim for dealing with it is to spare it no difficulty that lies in the subject to which its efforts are directed. Genius must be treated much in the same way as talent. The difference consists only in this, that genius, with a premonition of its creative power, usually manifests its decision with less doubt for a special province of activity, and, with a more intense thirst for culture, subjects itself more willingly to the demands of instruction. Genius is in its nature the purest self-determination, in that it feels, in its own inner existence, the necessity which exists in the object to which it devotes itself; it lives, as it were, in its object. But it can create no valid place for the new idea, which is in it already immediately and subjectively, if it has not united itself to the already existing culture as its objective presupposition; on this ground it thankfully receives instruction.

[Abstractly speaking, each human being has the possibility in him of every talent that has appeared or will appear in the human race. But, practically, there is immense difference in the facility with which individuals can realize this possibility. Hence we have the scale: (1) incapacity (pure dunce); (2) mediocrity (mechanical intelligence, who can do the average task as others do); (3) the talent and genius who have great self-activity. The talent has an inclination to his vocation, but is not perfectly clear as to all of the means that lead to it; does not value industry as much as he ought, or despises the methods discovered before him. The genius is clear as to methods—sees all that has been as tools and materials out of which to build his ideals—and therefore works with a passion.]

§ 112. But talent and genius offer a special difficulty to education in the precocity which often accompanies them. But by precocity we do not mean that they early render themselves perceptible, since the early manifestation of gifts by talent and genius, through their intensity of decision and self-confidence, is to be looked at as perfectly legitimate. But precocity is rather the hastening forward of the human being in feeling and moral sense, so that, where in the ordinary course of nature we should have a child, we have a youth, and a man in the place of a youth. We may therefore find precocity among those who belong to the class of mediocrity, but it is developed most readily among those possessed of talent and genius, because with them the early appearance of superior gifts may very easily bring in its train a derangement of the feelings and the moral nature. Education must deal with it in so far as it is inharmonious, and reminds us of the *pourri avant d'être mûri,* and see to it strictly that the demands made on it from without shall not minister to vanity; and must take care, in order to accomplish this, that social naturalness and lack of affectation be preserved in the pupil.

Our age has to combat this precocity much more than others. We find, e. g., authors, who, at the age of thirty years, in which they publish their collected works or write their biography, are chilly with the feelings of old age. . . . Music has been the sphere in which the earliest development of talent has shown itself, and here we find the absurdity that the cupidity of parents has so forced early talents that children of four or five years of age have been made to appear in public.

[Precocity defined: not intense self-confidence, but the omission of some natural stage of development. Education must take care that its vanity is not encouraged, and do all in its power to prevent affectation and self-consciousness, which destroy the proper relation of the pupil to his fellows.]

§ 113. Every sphere of culture contains a certain quantity of knowledge and ready skill which may be looked at, as it were, as the created result of the culture. It is desirable that every one who turns his attention to a certain line of culture should take up into himself the traditional learning which controls it. In so far as he does this, he is professionally educated. The consciousness that one has in the usual way gone through a school of art or science, and has been made familiar with the general inheritance of the acquisitions of a special department, creates externally a salutary composure which is very favorable to internal progress. We must distinguish from the professionally educated the dilettant and the self-taught man. The dilettant or amateur busies himself with an art, a science, or a trade, from free inclination, without having gone through any strict training in it. As a rule, he dispenses with elementary thoroughness, and hastens toward the enjoyment which production gives. The conscious amateur confesses this himself, makes no pretension to mastership, and calls himself—in distinction from the professional, who subjects himself to rules—a tyro. But the self-deluded dilettant, on the contrary, conceals his weakness, cherishes in himself the self-conceit that he is equal to the heroes of his art or science, constitutes himself the first admirer of his own performances, explains their want of success by accidental circumstances, never by their own want of excellence; and, if he has money, or edits a paper, is intoxicated with being the patron of talent which produces such works as he would willingly produce or pretends to produce. The self-taught man has often true talent, or even genius, to whose development nevertheless the inherited culture has been denied, and who by good fortune has through his own strength worked his way into a field of effort. The self-taught man is distinguished from the amateur by the thoroughness and the industry with which he acts: he is not only equally unfortunate with him in the absence of school-training, but is much less assisted by advice of the competent. Even if the self-taught man has for years studied and practiced much, he is still haunted by a feeling of uncertainty as to whether he has yet reached the standpoint at which a science, an art, or a trade, will receive him publicly. It is of very great consequence that man should be comprehended and recognized by man. The self-taught man, therefore, remains embarrassed, and does not free himself from the apprehension that he may expose some weak point to a professional, or he falls into the other extreme—he becomes presumptuous, steps forth as a reformer, and, if he accomplishes nothing, or earns only ridicule, he sets himself down as a martyr unrecognized by an unappreciative and unjust world.

It is possible that the dilettant may get beyond the stage of superficiality and subject himself to a thorough training; then he ceases to be a dilettant. It is also possible that the self-taught man may be on the right track, and may accomplish as much as, or even more than, one trained in the usual way. In general, however, it is very desirable that every one should go through the regular course of the inherited means of education, partly that he may be thorough in the elements, partly to free him from the anxiety which he may feel lest he in his solitary efforts spend labor on some superfluous work—superfluous because done long before, and of which he, through the accident of his want of culture, had not heard. We must all *learn* by ourselves, but we can not *teach* ourselves. Only genius can do this, for it must be its own leader in the new paths which it opens. Genius alone passes beyond where inherited culture ceases. It bears this in itself as of the past, and uses it as material for its new creation; but the self-taught man, who may possibly be a genius, wastes his time in doing things already accomplished, or sinks into eccentricity, into secret arts and sciences, etc.

[The professionally educated, the dilettant or amateur, and the self-taught. (a) The professionally educated masters thoroughly what the experience of the race has transmitted to his own specialty, and hence increases his own stature by standing on the shoulders of the human race. (b) The dilettant wishes to eat of the kernel without breaking the shell, and is a sort of futile individual who amuses himself by producing what is good for nothing when produced. (c) The self-taught man works with great industry and thoroughness, but has not access to the best means, i. e., the traditional culture of the race as taught in the schools. He works under embarrassment, haunted with the feeling that the professionally educated see defects in his training, or, throwing off his embarrassment, he plays the *rôle* of "reformer," and becomes imbittered against the world.]

§ 114. These ideas of the general steps of culture, of special gifts, and of the ways of culture appropriate to each, which we have set forth above, have a manifold connection with each other which can not be established *a priori*. We can, however, remark that apprenticeship, the mechanical intelligence and the professional education; secondly, journeymanship, talent, and dilettanteism; and, finally, mastership, genius, and self-education, have a relationship to each other.

[Correspondence (a) between apprenticeship, mechanical intelligence, and professional education; also (b) between journeymanship, talent, and dilettanteism; (c) between mastership, genius, and self-education.]

CHAPTER X.

INTELLECTUAL EDUCATION. (*c*) *Instruction* (continued).

(2) *The Act of Learning.*

§ 115. In the process of instruction the interaction between pupil and teacher must be so managed that the exposition by the teacher shall excite in the pupil the impulse to reproduction. The teacher must not treat his exposition as if it were a work of art which is its own end and aim, but he must always bear in mind the need of the pupil. The artistic exposition, as such, will, by its completeness, produce admiration; but the didactic, on the contrary, will, through its perfect adaptation, call out the imitative instinct, the power of new creation.

From this consideration we may justify the frequent statement that is made, that teachers who have an elegant diction do not really accomplish so much as others who resemble in their statements less a canal flowing smoothly between straight banks than a river which works its foaming way over rocks and between ever-shifting banks. The pupil perceives that the first is considering himself when he speaks so finely, perhaps not without some coquettish self-complacency; and that the second, in the repetitions and the sentences which are never finished, is concerning himself solely with *him.* The pupil feels that not want of facility or awkwardness, but the holy zeal of the *teacher*, is the principal thing, and that this latter uses rhetoric only as a means.

[The teacher should expound the subject in such a way as to arouse in the pupil an impulse to reproduce it. It differs in this respect from a work of art, which seeks only complete presentation and the *appearance of self-existence.* The pupil sees in the elegant diction of one teacher a studied attempt to win admiration for himself, while in the inelegant repetitions and unfinished sentences of another teacher he feels the genuine and exclusive interest manifested in his own progress.]

§ 116. In the act of learning there appears (*a*) a mechanical element, (*b*) a dynamic element, and (*c*) one in which the dynamic again mechanically strengthens itself.

[The process of learning involves (*a*) a mechanical element; (*b*) a dynamic element; (*c*) a dynamic element re-enforced by the mechanical element (i. e., dynamic *attention* re-enforced by mechanic *regularity, punctuality, and system*, so as to constitute *industry*).]

§ 117. (*a*) The mechanical element consists in this, that the right time be chosen for each lesson, an exact arrangement observed, and the suitable apparatus, which is necessary, procured. It is in the arrangement that especially consists the educational power of the lesson. The spirit of scrupulousness, of accuracy, of neatness, is developed by the external technique, which, however, should be subordinated to the interests of the subject studied. The teacher must, therefore, insist upon it that work shall cease at the exact time, that the work be well done, etc., for on these little things many greater things, in an ethical sense, depend.

To choose one's time for any work is often difficult because of the pressure of a multitude of demands, but in general it should be determined that the work requiring the strongest and keenest energy of the thinking activity and of memory should have appropriated to it the first half of the day.

[The mechanical element consists in (1) right time (punctuality); (2) exact arrangement (regularity); (3) neatness and accuracy (system). These constitute the mechanical morals of the school-room, and furnish a sort of training in self-control and obedience to rule that forms the basis of all more spiritual morality. Attention to these punctilios often seems a waste of energy; but it tells on the moral character as nothing else does, and makes his future life far more successful. The importance of choosing the morning hours for studies requiring hardest thinking or greatest strain on the memory.]

§ 118. (*b*) The dynamical element (i. e., the self-activity of the pupil) consists of the previously developed power of attention, without which all the exposition made by the teacher to the pupil remains entirely foreign to him. All apparatus is dead, all arrangement of no avail, all teaching fruitless, if the pupil does not by his free self-activity receive into his inner self what one teaches him, and thus make it his own property.

[The dynamical element is the activity of the pupil's will directed on the intellect; its general form being attention (see §§ 82, 83). It is the door that opens the mind of the pupil—the mechanical element relates to externals, the dynamical to the internal, the self-activity of the pupil.]

§ 119. This appropriation must not limit itself, however, to the first acquisition of any knowledge or skill, but it must give perfect command over whatever the pupil has learned; it must make it perfectly familiar and natural, so that it shall appear to be a part of himself. This must be brought about by means of repetition. This will mechanically secure that which the attention first grasped.

[Besides attention, there must be *repetition*—frequent reviews —in order to transmute the new knowledge and skill into permanent possession ("into *faculty*," as Herbert Spencer says). *Repetition* corresponds to *habit* in will-training, and is itself mechanical—hence with it the dynamical is re-enforced by the mechanical, and the best name for the union of the two is *industry*.]

§ 120. (*c*) The careful, persistent, living activity of the pupil in these acts we call industry. Its negative opposite is laziness, which is deserving of punishment inasmuch as it proceeds from a want of self-determination. Man is by nature lazy. But mind, which is only what it does, must resolve upon activity. This connection of industry with human freedom, with the very essence of mind, makes laziness appear blameworthy. The really civilized man, therefore, no longer knows that absolute inaction which is the greatest enjoyment to the barbarian, and he fills up his leisure with a variety of easier and lighter work. The positive opposite of industry is the unreasonable activity which rushes in breathless chase from one action to another, from this to that, over-tasking the person with the immense quantity of his work. Such an activity, seldom directed with proper deliberation, is unworthy of a man. It destroys the serenity and repose which in all industry should penetrate and inspire the deed. Nothing is more repulsive than the beggarly pride of such stupid laboriousness. One should not permit for a moment the pupil, seeking for distinction, to begin to pride himself on an extra industry. Education must accustom him to use a regular diligence. The frame of mind suitable for work often does not exist at the time when work should begin, but more frequently it makes its appearance after we have begun. The subject takes its own time to awaken us. Industry, inspired by a love and regard for work, has in its quiet uniformity a great force, without which no one can accomplish anything essential. The world, therefore, holds industry worthy of honor; and to the Romans, a nation of the most enduring perseverance, we owe the inspiring words, "*Incepto tantum opus est, cœtera res expediet*"; and, "*Labor improbus omnia vincit.*" Unflinching labor conquers everything.

"Every one may glory in his industry!" This is a true word from the lips of a truly industrious man, who was also one of the most modest. But Lessing did not, however, mean by them to charter Pharisaical pedantry. The necessity sometimes of giving one's self to an excess of work injurious to the health generally arises from the fact that he has not at other times made use of the requisite attention and the necessary industry, and then attempts suddenly and as by a forced march to storm his way to his goal. The result of such over-exertion is naturally entire prostration. The pupil is, therefore, to be accustomed to a generally uniform industry, which may increase from time to time without his thereby overstraining himself. What is really gained by a youth who has hitherto neglected time and opportunity, and who, when examination presses, overworks himself, perhaps standing the test with honor, and then must rest for months afterward from the over-effort? On all such occasions attention is not objective and dispassionate, but rather becomes, through anxiety to pass the examination, restless and corrupted by egotism; and the usual evil result of such compulsory industry is the ephemeral character of the knowledge thus gained. "Lightly come, lightly go," says the proverb.

A special worth is always attached to study far into the night. The student's "midnight oil" always claims for itself a certain veneration. But this is a sad vanity. In the first place, it is injurious to contradict Nature by working through the night, which she has ordained for sleep; secondly, the question is not as to the number of hours spent in work and their position in the twenty-four, but as to the quality of the work. With regard to the value of my work, it is of no moment whatsoever whether I have done it in the morning or in the evening, or how long I have labored, and it is of no consequence to any one except to my own very unimportant self. Finally, the question presents itself whether these gentlemen who boast so much of their midnight work do not sleep in the daytime!

[Industry defined as the vital, circumspect, persistent activity of the pupil. Its opposite is laziness, which deserves *corrective* punishment. Man by nature is lazy. Since mind develops into existence only through self-activity, industry is a fundamental virtue because through it alone can spiritual growth take place. Spiritual growth produces freedom, i. e., emancipation from the limitations of time and space, giving man possession of the past and present within himself and in his environment, however distant. The savage loves intervals of absolute inaction; the civilized man hates torpidity, but rests himself by change of work. He supplements his vocation by avocations. Industry has besides its negative opposite a positive opposite which is over-haste and over-exertion.]

§ 121. But industry has also two other opposites—seeming-laziness and seeming-industry. Seeming-laziness is the neglecting of the usual activity in one department by the individual because he is so much more active in another. The mind possessed with the liveliest interest in one subject buries itself in it, and, because of this, can not give itself up to another which before had engrossed the attention. Thus it appears more idle than it is, or rather it appears to be idle just because it is more industrious. This is especially the case in passing from one subject of instruction to another. The pupil should acquire such a flexibility in his intellectual powers that the rapid relinquishment of one subject and the taking up of another should not be too difficult. Nothing is more natural than that when he has become thoroughly aroused on one subject he should, on going back to the subject that has just been presented to him, feel himself still attracted to the former, and remain indifferent to the following lesson, which may relate to an entirely different topic. The young soul is brooding over what has been said, and is really exercising an intense activity, though it appears to be idle. But in seeming-industry all the external motions of activity, all the mechanism of work, manifest themselves noisily, while there is no true energy of attention and productivity. One busies himself with all the apparatus of work; he heaps up instruments and books around him; he sketches plans; he spends many hours staring into vacancy, biting his pen, gazing at words, drawings, numbers, etc. Boys, under the protection of so great a scaffolding for work erected around them, often carry on their own amusements. Men, who arrive at no real concentration of their force, no clear defining of their vocation, no firm decision as to their action, dissipate their power in what is too often a great activity with absolutely no result. They are busy, very busy; they have hardly time to do this thing because they really wish or ought to do that; but, with all their driving, their energy is all dissipated, and nothing comes from their countless labors.

[Industry is opposed to (*1*) seeming-laziness, which neglects some things to attend to others which are considered more important; all specialization is of this character. (*2*) It is opposed likewise to seeming-industry, which goes through all the motions of industry in a noisy and ostentatious manner, but is internally idle. Importance of disciplining the mind to turn completely from one subject to another.]

CHAPTER XI.

INTELLECTUAL EDUCATION. (*c*) *Instruction* (continued).

(3) *The Modality of the Process of Teaching.*

§ 122. Now that we have learned something of the relation of the teacher to the taught, and of the process of learning itself, we must examine the mode and manner of instruction. This may have (*1*) the character of contingency: the way in which our immediate existence in the world, our life, teaches us; or it may be given (*2*) by the printed page; or (*3*) it may take the shape of formal oral instruction.

[The modality—that is to say, the mode and manner in which the instruction is given, hence its form or *method.* Instruction (*1*) the lessons of experience; (*2*) by the written or printed page; (*3*) oral.]

§ 123. (*1*) For the most, the best, and the mightiest things that we know we are indebted to life itself. The sum of perceptions which a human being makes for himself up to the fourth or fifth year of his life is incalculable; and after this time we continue involuntarily to gain by immediate contact with the world countless ideas. But we understand, by the phrase "the school of life," especially the ethical knowledge which we gain by what happens in our own lives.

If one may say, *Vitæ non scholæ discendum est,* one can also say, *Vita docet.* Without the power exercised by the immediate world our intelligence would remain abstract and lifeless.

[Instruction by experience begins with infancy and continues through life. Especially in the first four or five years the sum of perceptions from this source is enormous. What the child learns of the ways of life, manners, and customs, and moral principles; proper habits of eating and drinking, care of the person and clothing, forms to be observed toward the various ranks in the family and society; glimpses of the action of the law of the state, its resistless might, its punishment of crime; numerous observations on the division of labor and its sustentation by trade and commerce; the daily and weekly spectacle of the rites and ceremonies of religion: here is the education of life through the four institutions of civilization—family, civil community, state, and church. The education that one gets by adopting a trade or form of industry and earning his living, or by acting as a citizen, obeying the laws and assisting at the ballot-box to make them, or in the army risking one's life to defend them—each of these is a peculiar form of the education that life offers, and its results can not be obtained through any other form—certainly not by the school—however much the school may re-enforce them.]

§ 124. (*2*) What we learn through books forms a contrast to that which we learn through living. Life *forces* upon us its wisdom; the book, on the contrary, is entirely passive. It is locked up in itself; it can not be altered; but it waits by us till we wish to use it. We can read it rapidly or slowly; we can simply turn over its leaves—what in modern times one calls reading—we can read it from beginning to end or from end to beginning; we can stop, begin again, skip over passages, or cut them short, as we like. To this extent the book is the most convenient means for instruction. If we are indebted to life for our perceptions, we must chiefly thank books for our understanding of our perceptions. We call book-instruction "dead" when it lacks, for the exposition which it gives, a foundation in illustration addressed to sense-perception, or when we do not add to the printed description the perceptions which it implies; and these two are quite different.

[Instruction through books is in some respects the opposite of instruction through living, because life forces its wisdom on us, while the book is entirely passive. The book is the most convenient form of instruction. We must have gained by experience from real life a sort of alphabet or key, with which we may spell out or unlock the meaning of the wisdom stored up in books. Unless we can translate what the book says into elements of our own experience, it is dead to us.]

§ 125. Books, as well as life, teach us many things which we did not previously expect to learn directly from them. From the romances of Walter Scott, for example, we learn, first of all, while we read them for entertainment, the English language, and English and Scotch history and geography. . . . We must distinguish from such books as those which bring to us, as it were accidentally, a knowledge for which we were not seeking, the books which are expressly intended to instruct. These "text-books" must (*a*) in their consideration of the subject give us the principal results of any department of knowledge, and denote the points from which the next advance must be made, because every science comes to results which are themselves again new problems; (*b*) in the consideration of the particulars they must be exhaustive, i. e., no essential elements of a science must be omitted. But this exhaustiveness of execution has different meanings according to the standpoints of those for whom it is made. How far we shall pass from the universality of the principal determinations into the multiplicity of the particular, into the fullness of detail, can not be definitely determined, and must vary, according to the aim of the book, whether for the apprentice, the journeyman, or the master; (*c*) the expression must be precise, i. e., the maximum of clearness must be combined with the maximum of brevity.

The writing of a text-book is on this account one of the most difficult tasks, and it can be successfully accomplished only by those who are masters in a science or art, and who combine with great culture and talent great experience as teachers. Unfortunately, many masters of science hold in low esteem the writing of text-books because they think that they are called upon to devote themselves entirely to the spread of science, and because the writing of compendiums has come to be in bad repute through the fact that authors and publishers have made out of text-books a profitable business and good incomes. In all sciences and arts there exists a quantity of material which is common property, which is disposed of now in one way, now in another. Hence the majority of compendiums can be distinguished from each other only by the kind of paper, printing, the name of the publisher or bookseller, or by arbitrary changes in the arrangement and execution. The want of principle with which this work is sometimes carried on is incredible. Many governments have on this account fixed prices for text-books, and commissioners to select them. This in itself is right and proper, but the use of any such book should be left optional, so as to avoid the one-sidedness of a science patronized by government and as it were licensed or introduced by law. A state may through its censorship oppose poor text-books, and recommend good ones for introduction; but it may not . . . establish as it were a national system of science or of art, in which only the ideas, laws, and forms sanctioned by it shall be allowed. The Germans are fortunate, in consequence of their philosophical criticism, in the production of better and better text-books. . . . So much the more unaccountable is it that, with such excellent books, the evil of such characterless books, some of them defectively, some of them atrociously written, should still exist when there is no necessity for it. The good old fashion of paragraph-writing has become obnoxious, under the name of compendium-style, as the most stiff and affected style of writing.

[The recorded wisdom of the entire human race is preserved in books, and hence the chief province of the school is to endow the pupil with the power to use books profitably through life so that he may perpetually draw from that reservoir of wisdom, and re-enforce and interpret his own life. A "text-book" (a) gives us the summed-up results in a department of knowledge, and indicates the new problems that occupy present attention; (b) it must include all phases, so as to give a rounded view of the entire subject without going exhaustively into details; (c) it must use clear and precise language, and be brief. Government prescription of text-books.]

§ 126. A text-book must be differently written according as it is intended as a book for private study or to be accompanied by oral explanation. If the former, it must go more into details, and must develop more clearly the internal relations; if the second, it should be shorter, and proceed from axiomatic and clear postulates to hints and suggestions that must have an epigrammatic keenness which should leave something to be guessed. Because for these a commentary is expected which it is the teacher's duty to supply, such a sketch is usually accompanied by the fuller text-book which was arranged for private study. [Illustrations here omitted.]

[Text-books (a) for private study; (b) for use in school.]

§ 127. (*3*) The text-book which presupposes oral explanation forms the transition to oral instruction itself. Since speech is the natural and original form in which mind manifests itself, no book can rival it. The living word is the most powerful agent of instruction. However common and cheap the art of printing may have rendered books as the most convenient means of education—however the multiplication of facilities for intercourse and the increasing rapidity of transportation may have facilitated the immediate viewing of human life as the most impressive educational means—nevertheless the living word still asserts its value. In two cases especially it is indispensable: one is when some knowledge is to be communicated which is in process of discovery and as yet is found in no compendium; and the other when a living language is to be taught, for in this case the printed page is entirely inadequate. One can learn from books to understand Spanish, French, English, Danish, etc., but not to speak them; to do this he must hear them, partly that his ear may become accustomed to the sounds, partly that his vocal organs may learn correctly to imitate them.

[Oral instruction. The living word is the most powerful agent of instruction, and hence can produce effects where other means are inadequate. The latest discoveries, the commentary on the book, as well as the pronunciation of foreign languages —for these things oral instruction is indispensable.]

§ 128. Life surprises and overpowers us with the knowledge which it offers; the book, impassive, waits our convenience; the teacher, superior to us, perfectly prepared in comparison with us, consults our necessity, and with his living speech uses a gentle force to which we can yield without losing our freedom. Listening is easier than reading.

Princes seldom read themselves, but have servants who read to them.

[Although oral instruction is the most powerful means of arousing and interesting the pupil, yet its object should be to emancipate the pupil from the need of it, and (*a*) make him interested in knowledge for itself, so that he will eagerly follow it through the (*1*) text-book, (*2*) reference-book, and (*3*) library; (*b*) seek to master the material poured in upon him by experience of life.]

§ 129. Oral instruction may (*1*) give the subject, which is to be learned, in a connected statement, or (*2*) it may develop it by means of question and answer. The first method is called the acroamatic, the second the erotematic. The first (the acroamatic or lecture-system) presupposes the theoretical inequality of the teacher and the taught. Because one can speak while many listen, this is especially adapted to the instruction of large numbers. The second method (the erotematic) is either that of the catechism or the dialogue. The catechetical is connected with the first kind of oral instruction above designated because it makes demand upon the memory only for what is already learned, and is very often and very absurdly called the Socratic method. In the dialogue, we try, by means of an interchange of thought, to investigate in company with others some problem, proceeding according to the necessary forms of reason. But in this we can make a distinction. One speaker may be superior to the rest, may hold in his own hand the thread of the conversation, and may guide * it himself; or, those who mingle in it may be perfectly equal in intellect and culture, and may each take part in the development with equal independence. In this latter case, the true reciprocity gives us the proper dramatic dialogue, which contains in itself all forms of exposition, and may pass from narration, description, and analysis, through satire and irony, to genuine humor. When it does this, the dialogue is the highest product of the intellect, and the means of its purest enjoyment.

The system of alternate teaching, in which the pupil takes the teacher's place and instructs others, can be used only where the subject taught admits of a mechanical treatment. The Hindoos made use of it in very ancient times. Bell and Lancaster † have transplanted it for the teaching of poor children in Europe and America. For the teaching of the elementary accomplishments—reading, writing, and arithmetic—as well as for the learning by heart of names,

* ὁδαγός or ὁδηγητής, a guide.

† Monitorial system.

sentences, etc., it suffices, but not for any scientific culture. Where we have large numbers to instruct, the giving of the fully developed statement (the acroamatic method) is necessary, since the dialogue, though it may be elsewhere suitable, allows only a few to take part in it. And, if we take the interrogative (erotematic), we must, if we have a large number of pupils, make use of the catechetical method only. What is known as the conversational method has been sometimes suggested for our university instruction. Diesterweg, in Berlin, insists upon it. Here and there the attempt has been made, but without any result. In the university, the lecture of the teacher as a self-developing whole stands in contrast with the scientific discussion of the students by themselves, in which they as equals work over with perfect freedom what they have heard. Diesterweg was wrong in considering the lecture-system as the principal cause of the lack of scientific interest which he thought he perceived in our universities. Kant, Fichte, Schelling, Schleiermacher, Wolf, Niebuhr, etc., taught by lectures and awakened the liveliest enthusiasm. But Diesterweg is quite right in saying that the students should not be degraded into writing-machines. This is generally conceded, and a pedantic amount of copying more and more begins to be considered as out of date at our universities. Nevertheless, a new pedantry, that of the mere lecture, should not be introduced; but a brief summary of the lecture may be dictated and answer all purposes, or the lecture may be afterward written out by the pupil from memory. The great efficacy of the oral exposition does not so much consist in the fact that it is perfectly free, as that it presents to immediate view a person who has made himself the bearer of a science or an art, and has found what constitutes its essence. Its power springs, above all, from the solidity of the lecture, the originality of its content, and the elegance of its form; whether it is read or declaimed is a matter of little moment. Niebuhr, e. g., read, word for word, from his manuscript, and what a teacher was he! The catechetical way of teaching is not demanded at the university except in special examinations; it belongs to the private work of the students, who must learn to be industrious of their own free impulse. The private tutor can best conduct reviews. The institution which presupposing the lecture-system combines in itself original production with criticism, and the connected exposition with the conversation, is the professional school. It pursues a well-defined path, and confines itself to small classes of scholars whose grades of culture are very nearly the same. Here, therefore, the dialogue can be developed with best effect because it has a fixed foundation, and each one can take part in the conversation; whereas, from the variety of opinions in a large class, it is easily perverted into an aimless talk, and the majority, having no chance to speak, become weary.

[Oral instruction of two kinds: (1) the lecture, acroamatic, and (2) erotematic, or the form of catechism and dialogue. (Acroamatic, from ἀκροάομαι, the Greek verb for *to hear lectures*, was applied to Aristotle's oral lectures, which were given to a few pupils, and related to his most profound and abstruse doctrines; hence, also called *esoteric*, i. e., *inner*, doctrines as opposed to the *exoteric*, or outer, doctrines. Erotematic, from ἐρωτάω, the Greek verb *to ask*, means the interrogative method.)]

§ 130. As to the way in which the lecture is carried out, it may be arranged for those who have undertaken the entire course of instruction in its thorough, systematic form, or for those who have in view only a general, inexact education, without intending to go through the complete course. The ancients called the first method the esoteric and the second the exoteric, as we give to such lectures now, respectively, the names *scholastic* and *popular*. The first makes use of terms which have become technical in science or art, and proceeds to combine the isolated ideas in a strict, logical manner; the second endeavors to substitute for technicalities generally understood designations, and conceals the exactness of the formal conclusion by means of a style of narration. It is possible to conceive of a perfectly methodical treatment of a science which at the same time shall be generally comprehensible if it strives to attain the transparency of real beauty. A scientific work of art may be correctly said to be popular, as, e. g., has happened to Herder's "Ideas toward a Philosophy of the History of Mankind."

Beauty is the element which is comprehended by all, and as we declare our enmity to caricatures in picture-books and books of amusement, and to the mischievous character of "compendiums," so we must also oppose the popular publications which style themselves "Science made easy," etc., in order to attract more purchasers by this alluring title. . . . Kant says: "In the effort to produce in our knowledge the completeness of scholarly thoroughness, and at the same time a popular character, without in the effort falling into the errors of an affected thoroughness or an affected popularity, we must, first of all, look out for the scholarly completeness of our scientific knowledge, the methodical form of thoroughness, and first ask how we can make really popular the knowledge methodically acquired at school, i. e., how we can make it easy and generally communicable, and yet at the same time not supplant thoroughness by popularity. For scholarly completeness must not be sacrificed to popularity to please the people, unless science is to become a plaything or a trifling." It is perfectly plain that all that has been said above (§§ 81–107) on the psychological and the logical methods must be taken into account in the style of the exposition in the two kinds of oral method.

[Technical and popular lectures.]

§ 131. It has been already remarked (§ 21), in speaking of the nature of education, that the office of the instructor must necessarily vary with the growing culture. But attention must here again be called to the fact that education, in whatever stage of culture, must conform to the law which, as the internal logic of being, determines all objective developments of Nature and of history. The family gives the child his first instruction; between this and the school comes the teaching of the tutor; the school stands by itself over against the family, and presents three essentially different forms according as (1) it imparts a general preparatory instruction, or (2) special teaching for different callings, or (3) a universal scientific cultivation. Universality and particularity are united in individuality, which therefore contains both the general and the particular freely in itself. All citizens of a state should have (1) a general education which (*a*) makes them familiar with reading, writing, and arithmetic, these being the means of all theoretical culture; then (*b*) hands over to them a picture of the world in its principal phases, so that they as citizens of the world can direct their course on our planet; and, finally, it must (*c*) instruct each in the history of his own state, so that he may see that the circumstances in which he lives are the result of special circumstances in the past in their connection with the history of the rest of the world, and so may learn rightly to estimate the interests of his own country in view of their necessary relation to the future. This work the elementary schools have to perform. From this through the *Realschule* [our scientific course in the high-school] they pass into the school where some particular branch of art is taught, or through the *Gymnasium* [classical course of a high-school or college] to the university. Upon the general basis of university training develop (2) the educational institutions that aim at some special education which leads to the exercise of some art. These we call technological schools, where one may learn farming, mining, a craft, a trade, navigation, war, etc. This kind of education may be specialized indefinitely with the growth of culture, because any one branch is capable in its negative aspect of such division into special schools, as, e. g., foundling hospitals and orphan asylums, blind, and deaf and dumb, institutions. The abstract universality of the elementary (common) school and the one-sided particularity of the technological school, however, unite in a sort of concrete universality as a ground that includes both, which, without aiming directly at utility, treat science and art on all sides as their own end and aim (and constitutes what is called the scientific spirit). "*Scientia est potentia*," said Lord Bacon. Practical utility results indirectly through the progress which scientific cognition makes in this free attitude toward the world, because it collects itself and avoids dissipation through manifold details by seizing the idea of the whole and getting insight into the details by that means. This organic whole of instruction is properly called a university. By it the educational system is perfected.

It is important to note that no more than these three types of schools can exist, and that they must all exist in a perfectly organized civilization. Their titles and their plans and arrangements may be very different among different nations at different epochs, but this need not prevent the recognition in them of the three essential logical phases—universal, particular, singular—on which they are founded. Still less should the imperfect ways in which they manifest themselves induce us to condemn them. It is the modern tendency to undervalue the university as an institution which we had inherited from the middle ages, and with which we could at present dispense. This is an error. The university presents just as necessary a form of instruction as the elementary school or the technological school. Not the abolition of the university, but a reform which shall adapt it to the spirit of the age, is the advance which we have to make.* That there are to be found, outside of the university, men of the most thorough and elegant culture, who can give the most excellent instruction in a science or an art, is most certain. But it is a characteristic of the university in its teaching to do away with the dependence on hap-hazard and mere luck which is unavoidable in case of private voluntary efforts. The university offers to the student an organic, self-conscious, encyclopedic representation of all the sciences, and thus it creates to a greater or less degree an intellectual atmosphere which no other place can give. Through this, all sciences and their aims are seen in their just claims for con-

* Rosenkranz wrote this in 1847, on the eve of revolutionary scenes.

sideration, and a personal stress is laid upon the connection of one science with another. The imperfections of a university, which arise through the rivalry of external ambition, through the necessity of financial success, through scholarships, etc., are finite affairs which it has in common with all human institutions, and on whose account they are not all to be thrown away. Art-academies are for art what universities are for science. They are inferior to them in so far as they appear more under the form of special schools, as schools of architecture, of painting, and conservatories of music; because it must be granted that architecture, sculpture, painting, music, the orchestra, and the drama, are, like the sciences, bound together in a *universitas artium*, and that by means of their internal reciprocal action new results would follow. Academies of art, as isolated schools for masters, which have no teaching properly so called, are not indispensable, and serve only as a *prytaneum* for meritorious scholars, and to reward industry through the prizes which they offer. In their idea they belong with the university, this appearing externally in the fact that most of their members are university professors. But as institutions for ostentation by which the ambition of the learned was flattered, and princes surrounded with a halo of science—as scientific corporations attached to courts, they have lost all significance. They flourished with the Ptolemies and the Egyptian caliphs, and with absolute monarchical governments. In modern times we have passed beyond the abstract jealousy between the so-called "humanities" and the natural sciences, because we comprehend that each part of the totality can be realized in a proper sense only by its development as relatively independent. Thus the *Gymnasium* has its place as that elementary school which, besides giving a general culture, by means of the knowledge of the language and history of the Greeks and Romans, prepares for the university; while, on the other hand, the *Realschule*, by special attention to natural science and the living languages, furnishes the required preparation to the technological schools. Nevertheless, because the university embraces the science of Nature, of technology, of trade, of finance, and of statistics, the pupils who have graduated from the so-called high-schools (*höhern Bürgerschulen*) and from the *Realschulen* will also be brought together at the university with the graduates of the *Gymnasia*.

[The order of educational institutions; the course of study; the kinds of schools. (1) Family; (2) private tutor or governess; (3) district school; (4) high-school, general or classical course; (5) university. District-school course of study, (*a*) the rudiments, reading, writing, arithmetic, the means of all theoretical culture; (*b*) a picture of the world in geography, and selections of poetry and prose given in the school readers; (*c*) history of one's own state, and its relation to the history of the world. The necessity of three institutions to complete the whole course of study—district or elementary school, high or secondary school, the university. Art academies. The jealousy between the "humanities" (classical studies) and the natural sciences.]

§ 132. The organization of the school will be determined in its details by its peculiar aim. But in general every school, no matter what it teaches, ought to have some system of rules and regulations by which the relation of the pupils to the institution, to each other, to the teacher, and that of one teacher to another, as well as to the supervisory authority, the programme of lessons, the apparatus, the changes of work and recreation, shall be clearly set forth. The course of study must be arranged so as to avoid two extremes: on the one hand, it has to keep in view the special aim of the school, and according to this it tends to contract itself. But, on the other hand, it must consider the relative dependence of one specialty upon other specialties and upon general culture. It must leave the transition free, and in this it tends to expand itself. Experience alone is competent so to assign the limits that the special task of the school shall neither be sacrificed nor deprived of the means of performance which it (since it is also always only a part of the whole culture) receives by means of its reciprocal action with other departments. The programme must assign the exact amount of time which can be appropriated to each study. It must prescribe the order in which they shall follow each other; it must, as far as possible, unite kindred subjects, so as to avoid the useless repetition which dulls the charm of study; it must, in determining the order, bear in mind at the same time the necessity imposed by the subject itself and the psychological progression of intelligence from perception, through conception, to the thinking activity which grasps all. It must be periodically submitted to revision, so that all matter which has, through the changed state of general culture, become out of date, may be rejected, and that which has proved itself indispensable may be appropriated, so that it may be kept up to the requirements of the times. And, finally, the school must, by examinations and reports, aid the pupil in the acquirement of a knowledge of his real standing. The examination lets him know what he has really learned, and what he is able to do: the report shows him a history of his culture, exhibits to him in what he has made improvement and in what he has fallen behind, what defects he has shown, what talents he has displayed, what errors committed, and in what relation stands his theoretical development to his ethical status.

The struggle between the *Gymnasia* and the industrial interests of the community is a very interesting phase of educational history. They were asked to widen their course so as to embrace mathematics, physics, natural history, geography, and the modern languages. At first they stoutly resisted; then they made some concessions; finally, the further they went the more they found themselves in contradiction with their true work, and so they produced, as an independent correlate, the *Realschule*. After this was founded, the *Gymnasium* returned to its old plan, and is now again able to place in the foreground the pursuit of classical literature and history. It was thus set free from demands made upon it which were entirely foreign to its nature.—The examination is, on its pedagogic side, so adapted to the pupil as to make him conscious of his own condition. As to its external side, it determines whether the pupil shall pass from one class to another or from one school to another, or it decides whether the school as a whole shall display its results to the public—an exhibition which ought to have no trace of ostentation, but which, as a matter of fact, is often tinctured with pedagogical charlatanism.

[The rules and regulations of the school. The course of study, limited by the aim of the school, but, on account of the dependence of one specialty upon all the rest, must include some general outline of the whole that will indicate the position and scope of the specialty. The programme defines the amount of time given to each study, and the order of their sequence. It must conform to the laws of logical arrangement of topic, and of psychological development of the pupil. Examinations and reports aid the pupil by showing him where his work is successful and where defective.]

§ 133. The direction of the school on the side of science must be held by the school itself, for the process of the intellect in acquiring science, the progress of the method, the peculiarities of the subject-matter and the order of its development, have their own laws, to which instruction must submit itself if it would attain its end. The school is, however, only one part of the whole of culture. In itself it divides into numerous departments, together constituting a great organism which in manifold ways comes into contact with the other organisms of the state. So long as teaching is of a private character, so long as it is the reciprocal relation of one individual to another, or so long as it is shut up within the circle of the family and belongs to it alone, so long it has no objective character. It receives this first when it grows to a school. Historically speaking, the school first appears as an auxiliary of the church; but this first form, in time, disappears. Religion is the absolute relation of man to God which subsumes all other relations. In so far as religion exists in the form of a church, those who are members of the same church may have common instruction given them on the nature of religion. Instruction on the subject is proper, and it is even enjoined upon them as a law—as a duty. But beyond the limits of their own society they may not extend their sway. The church may exert itself to make a religious spirit felt in the school and to make it penetrate all the teaching; but it may not presume, because it has for its subject the absolute interest of men, the interest which is superior to all others, to determine also the other objects of education or the method of treating them. The technical acquisitions of reading, writing, and arithmetic, drawing and music, the natural sciences, mathematics, logic, anthropology and psychology, the practical sciences of finance and the municipal regulations, have no direct relation to religion. If we attempt to establish one, there inevitably appears in them a morbid state which destroys them; not only so, but piety itself disappears, for these accomplishments and branches of knowledge are not included in its province.

Such treatment of art and science may be well-meant, but it is always an error. It may even make a ludicrous impression, which is a very dangerous thing for the authority of religion. If a church has founded a system of schools, it must see to it that all which is there taught except the religious instruction, i. e., all of science and art, shall have no direct connection with it as a religious institution.

[The management of the school, as regards its course of study, the methods used, and the interpretation given to knowledge, must be vested in the faculty of the school. But, as the school is only a part of the entire system of education, it receives direction from all other institutions of society. The school had its origin in the church.]

§ 134. The church, as the external manifestation of religion, is concerned with the absolute relation of man to God, which, however, is special in itself as opposed to man's other relations; the state, on the contrary, seizes the life of a nation according to its *explicit totality*. The state should conduct the education of all its citizens. To it, then, the church must appear only as a school, for the church instructs its own people concerning the nature of religion, partly by teaching proper (that of the catechism), partly in an edifying way, by preaching. From this point of view, the state can look upon the church only as standing side by side in the same rank with those schools which prepare for a special vocation. The church appears to the state as that school which assumes the task of educating the religious faculty. Just as little as the church should the state attempt to exercise any influence over the essential matters of science and art. In this they are exactly alike, and must acknowledge the necessity which both science and art contain within themselves and by which they develop their contents. The laws of logic, mathematics, astronomy, morals, æsthetics, physiology, etc., are entirely independent of the state. It can decree neither discoveries nor inventions. The state occupies the same ground as science, both presupposing the freedom of self-consciousness. It is true that the church teaches man, but it demands from him at the same time belief in the truth of its dogmas. It rests, as the actual church, on presupposed authority, and sinks finally all contradictions which arise in experience in the absolute mystery of the existence of God. The state, on the contrary, elaborates its idea into the form of laws, i. e., into general determinations, of whose necessity it convinces itself. It seeks to give to these laws the clearest possible form, so that every one may understand them. It concedes validity only to that which can be proved, and sentences the individual according to the external side of the *deed* ("overt act"), not, as the church does, on its internal side—that of *disposition* (the state of the heart). Finally, it demands in him consciousness of his deed, because it makes each one responsible for his own deed. It has, therefore, the same principle as science, for the proof of necessity and the unity of consciousness with its object constitute the essence of science. Since the state includes the school as one of its educational instrumentalities, it is from its very nature called upon to guide its regulation in accordance with the principles that govern the unfolding of consciousness.

The church calls this "profanation." One might say that the church, in the absolute mystery which is the object of its faith, always represents the absolute problem for science, while the state, as to its form, coincides with science. Whenever the state abandons strictness of proof—when it begins to measure the individual citizen by his disposition and not by his deed, and, in place of the clear insight of the rational self-consciousness, sets up the psychological compulsion of a hollow mechanical authority, it destroys itself.

["The state seizes the life of a people in its explicit totality," i. e., all human relations, and hence must conduct the education of its citizens. To the state the church is not *the* institution, but one of several co-ordinate institutions. The state should not dictate in matters of science and art, nor in matters of conscience. The state and science are alike in presupposing the freedom of self-consciousness; the state in making the individual responsible for his deed requires consciousness and freedom as conditions of conviction in case of crime; science presupposes freedom of thought, freedom from authority, and clear insight into the necessity of the demonstration, i. e., clear consciousness. The church, however, does not relinquish the demand for authority.]

§ 135. Neither the church nor the state should attempt to control the school in its internal management. Still less can the school constitute itself into a state within the state; for, while it is only one of the temporary means which are necessary for developing citizens, the state and the church lay claim to the whole man his whole life long. The independence of the school can then only consist in this, that a directory is created within the state which takes the schools under its control, and which as a school board endeavors to provide for the needs of the school, while externally it adjusts them to the church and state with the other ethical powers. The emancipation of the school can never reasonably mean its abstract isolation, or the absorption of the ecclesiastical and political life into the school; it can signify only the free reciprocal action of the school with state and church. It must never be forgotten that what makes the school a school is not the total process of education, for this falls also within the family, the state, and the church; but that the proper work of the school is the process of instruction, by which the pupils shall gain knowledge, and the acquirement of accomplishments by practice.

The confusion of the idea of instruction with that of education in general is a common defect in superficial treatises on these themes. The radicals, among those who are in favor of so-called "emancipation," often erroneously appeal to "free Greece," which generally for this fond ignorance is made to stand as authority for a thousand things of which it never dreamed. In this fictitious Hellas of "free beautiful humanity," they say the limits against which we strive to-day did not exist. The biographies of Anaxagoras, Protagoras, Diagoras, Socrates, Aristotle, Theophrastus, and of others, who were condemned on account of their "impiety" (ἀσέβεια), tell quite another story.

[Limitations of church and state in their control over the school—school independent in the control of its internal management. "Emancipation of the school," in 1848, a great political watchword. Education (*Erziehung*) distinguished from instruction (*Unterricht*).]

§ 136. The inspection of the school may be carried out in different ways, but it must be required that its special institutions shall be included and cared for as an organized and interrelated whole, framed in accordance with the idea of the state, and that one division of the ministry shall occupy itself exclusively with it. The division of labor will specially affect the schools for teaching particular vocations. The prescription of the subjects to be studied in each school as appropriate to it, of the course of study, and of the object thereof, properly falls to this department of government (the school board), is its immediate work, and its theory must be changed according to the progress and needs of the time. . . . Sketches of plans for school systems, however correct they may be, depend upon the actual sum of culture of a people and a time, and must therefore continually modify their fundamental ideal. The same is true of the methods of instruction in the special arts and sciences. Niemeyer, Schwarz, Herbart, in their sketches of pedagogics, Beneke in his "Theory of Education," and others, have set forth in detail the method of teaching reading, writing, and arithmetic, languages, natural science, geography, history, etc. Such directions are, however, ephemeral in value, and only relatively useful, and must, in order to be truly practical, be often revised in accordance with universal educational principles, and with the progress of science and art. [Notes on questions of school supervision in Prussia, in 1848, here omitted.]

[School inspection. Inspection ought to extend over the whole, so that it may treat each part in its organic relation to the rest. Programmes of studies, methods of teaching special branches, are of ephemeral value and need frequent revision.]

CHAPTER XII.

PRAGMATICS (EDUCATION OF THE WILL).

§ 137. BOTH physical and intellectual education are in the highest degree practical. The first reduces the merely natural (i. e., the body) to a tool which mind shall use for its own ends; the second guides the intelligence, by ways conformable to its nature, to the necessary method of the art of teaching and learning, which finally branches out in the nation into a system of mutually dependent school organizations. But in a narrower sense we mean by practical education the methodical development of the will. This phrase more clearly expresses the topic to be considered in this division than another sometimes used in the science of education (*Bestrebungsvermögen*, conative power). The will is already the subject of a science of its own, i. e., of ethics; and if the science of education would proceed in anywise scientifically, it must recognize and presuppose the idea and the existence of this science. It should not restate in full the doctrines of freedom, of duty, of virtue, and of conscience, although we have often seen this done in works on education. Education has to deal with the ideas of freedom and morality only so far as to fix the technique of their process, and at the same time to confess itself weakest just here, where nothing is of any worth without pure self-determination.

[The special elements of education are: A. Physical Education; B. Intellectual Education; C. Pragmatics, or Education of the Will. "Practical" refers to the will-power. The complete science of the will is called Ethics. Education borrows the conclusions of that science and restates them only in outline.]

§ 138. The pupil must (1) become civilized; i. e., he must learn to govern, as a thing external to him, his natural egotism, and to make the forms which civilized society has adopted his own. (2) He must become imbued with morality; i. e., he must learn to determine his actions, not only with reference to what is agreeable and useful, but according to the principle of the good; he must become internally free, form a character, and must habitually look upon the necessity of freedom as the absolute measure of his actions. (3) He must become religious; i. e., he must discern that the world, with all its changes, himself included, is only phenomenal; the affirmative side of this insight into the emptiness of the finite and transitory (which man would so willingly make everlasting) is the consciousness of the *Absolute* existing in and for itself. The Absolute, without change and entirely unaffected by the process of manifestation, constitutes no factor of its changes, but, while it actually makes them its object, permeates them all, and freely distinguishes itself from them. In so far as man relates himself to God, he cancels all finitude and transitoriness, and by this feeling frees himself from the externality of phenomena. Virtue on the side of civilization is politeness; on that of morality, conscientiousness; and on that of religion, humility.

[The youth must (1) become civilized; (2) acquire a moral will; (3) become religious. Civilized man subordinates his animal selfishness and wears the forms of society as though they were his nature. Morality subjects all motives to one supreme motive, the principle of the good. Religion sees the world and all its phenomena, including the "deeds done in the body," to be mere transient appearances, while, on the other hand, in God it contemplates absolute existence above the realm of change and decay.

Three stages of virtue: (a) politeness the virtue of civilization; (b) conscientiousness the virtue of morality; (c) humility the virtue of religion. Humility is the virtue named in the Beatitudes as possessed by "the poor in spirit," the "poverty" wedded by St. Francis (Dante's *Paradiso*, canto xi, 58).]

CHAPTER XIII.

EDUCATION OF THE WILL (*continued*).

(*a*) *Social Culture.*

§ 139. The social development of man constitutes the beginning of practical education. It is not necessary to suppose a special social instinct. The inclination of man to the society of men does not arise from the identity of their nature alone, but is also in each special instance affected by particular relations. The natural starting-point of social culture is the family. But this in turn educates the child for society, and by means of society the individual enters into relation with the world at large. Thus natural sympathy changes to polite behavior, and the latter again to the thrifty and circumspect deportment, whose proper ideal nevertheless is before all the ethical purity which combines with the wisdom of the serpent the harmlessness of the dove.

[The beginning of all education of the will is to be found in social manners and customs. This is given in the family, where the child learns the manifold forms of behavior toward others, his equals, inferiors, and superiors.]

§ 140. (1) The family is the natural social circle to which man primarily belongs. In it all the immediate differences which exist are compensated by the equally immediate unity of the relationship. The subordination of the wife to the husband, of the children to their parents, of the younger children to their elder brothers and sisters, ceases to be subordination, through the intimacy of love. The child learns obedience to authority, while it satisfies its parents and finds its own gratification in their approval. All the relations in which he finds himself within the family are penetrated by the warmth of implicit confidence, which can be replaced for the child by nothing else. In this sacred circle the tenderest emotions of the heart are developed by the personal interest of all its members in what happens to any one of their number, and thus the foundation is laid of a susceptibility to all genuine or hearty social intercourse.

Nothing more unreasonable or inhuman could exist than those modern theories (of French socialists) which would destroy the family and would leave the children, the offspring of the unbridled natural instinct, to grow up in public nurseries. This appears to be very humane to them; indeed, these socialists talk of nothing but the interests of "humanity"—they are never weary of uttering their insipid jests on the institution of the family, as if it were the principle of all narrow-mindedness. Have these fanatics, who are seeking after an abstraction of humanity, ever examined our foundling-hospitals, orphan asylums, barracks, and prisons, to discover in some degree to what an atomic barren intelligence a human being develops who has never formed a part of a family? The family is, of course, only one phase in the grand order of the ethical organization; but it is the substantial phase from which man passively proceeds, but into which, as he founds a family of his own, he actively returns. The child lives in the family, shares the common joy and grief, and feels sympathy with all. In the emotion with which he sees his parents approach death while he is hastening toward the full enjoyment of existence, he experiences the finer feelings which are so powerful in creating in him a deeper and more tender understanding of everything human. . . .

[The family is the natural social circle—its association does not depend on free choice, but on the natural accident of birth. All the differences of rank, all subordination and inferiority, are at once compensated by the natural intimacy of kinship and family love. Each one feels his unity of substance with the other members of the family, and hence suffers in their sorrow and rejoices in their happiness. Hence, obedience to the authority of the parents is rendered by the child with an intense feeling of gratification at winning their approval. This development of living for others and through others in the family lays the foundation of social intercourse.]

§ 141. (2) The family, however, educates the children not for itself but for civil society. In the latter a system of manners and customs is formed which furnishes a social formula or fixed code of etiquette to determine the behavior of the individual in society. This social code endeavors to subdue the natural roughness of man, at least as far as it manifests itself externally. Because he is a spiritual being, man is not to yield himself to his immediate impulses; he is to exhibit to man his naturalness as under the control of spirit. The etiquette of propriety on the one hand facilitates the manifestation of individuality by means of which one person becomes interesting to others, inasmuch as it encourages free expression of individual differences, and, on the other hand, since its forms are alike for all, it makes them recognize the equality of each individual with all others, and so makes their intercourse easier.

The conventional form is no mere constraint; but essentially a protection not only for the freedom of the individual, but much more the protection of the individual against the rude impetuosity of his own naturalness. Savages and peasants for this reason are, in their relations to each other, by no means as unconstrained as one often represents them, but hold closely to a ceremonious behavior. There is in one of Immerman's stories, "The Village Justice," a very excellent picture of the conventional forms with which the peasant loves to surround himself. The scene in which the townsman, who thinks that he can dispense with forms among the peasants, is very entertainingly taught better, is exceedingly valuable in an educational point of view. The feeling of shame which man has in regard to his mere naturalness is often extended to relations where it has no direct significance, when this sense of shame is appealed to in children in reference to things which are really perfectly indifferent externalities.

[The object of the social code is to subdue the natural rudeness that belongs to man as a mere animal, and thus clothe the brutal with a garb of unselfish forms. The essence of politeness consists in treating others as if they were perfectly ideal people. The polite person utterly ignores all rudeness shown him, and treats others as if they intended the same politeness toward him. He prefers others before himself, and adopts as a second nature the form of divine charity or "altruism," which devotes itself to the good of others. Politeness is only the *form* of this altruism; morality and religion are the *substance* of it. Since the form of politeness is the same for all—the same for the king as for the beggar—it follows that politeness is the ceremonial form by which we celebrate the equality of all men in the substance of their humanity. "All are equal before God"; and also before the ideal of politeness. This, as Rosenkranz says, makes social intercourse easier.]

§ 142. Education with regard to social culture has two extremes to avoid: the youth may, in his effort to prove his individuality, become vain and conceited, and fall into a sort of mania for attracting the attention of others; or he may become slavishly dependent on conventional forms, a kind of social pedant. This state of nullity which contents itself with the mechanical polish of social formalism is ethically more dangerous than the tendency to a marked individuality, for it betrays emptiness; while the effort toward a peculiar differentiation from others, and the desire to become interesting to others, indicate power.

[Two extremes of social culture to be avoided: (1) accentuation of individuality by deviations from the code of politeness to such a degree as to become a mania for attracting attention; (2) slavish dependence on the conventional forms to such an extent as to appear constrained and pedantic. The latter indicates weakness of individuality, the former strength.]

§ 143. When we have a harmony of the manifestation of the individual with the expression of the recognition of the equality of others, we have what is called proper deportment or politeness, which combines dignity and grace, self-respect and modesty. We call it, when fully complete, urbanity. It treats the conventional forms with irony, since, at the same time that it yields to them, it allows the productivity of spirit to shine through them in small deviations from them, as if it were fully able to make others in their place.

True politeness shows that it remains master of forms. It is very necessary to accustom children to courtesy and to bring them up in the etiquette of the prevailing social custom; but they must be prevented from falling into silly formality which makes the highest perfection of polite behavior to consist in a blind following of the dictates of the last fashion-journal, and in the exact copying of the phraseology and directions of some book on manners. One can best teach and practice politeness when he does not merely copy the social technique, but comprehends its original idea. . . .

[Urbanity the name for perfect politeness.—(Notice that *urbanity* is from *urbs*, the Latin for *city*, while *politeness* is from *polis*, the Greek for *city*—as if social culture were born in cities, where the constant intercourse of people renders necessary a code of manners.) Urbanity "treats the conventional forms of politeness with irony," i. e., it lets it be apparent that it does not practice the strict forms of etiquette mechanically, but merely *submits* to them outwardly, while within it feels a much more tender and hearty respect for others than is or can be expressed by those stiff, conventional forms. It therefore "makes small deviation from them" in the direction of greater familiarity and friendliness, showing that it possesses the substance of politeness in its devotion to the good of others, and that it can therefore invent new forms of etiquette. Within the family there reigns the unconstrained expression of devotion to others —in polite society, the conventional forms of considerateness for others' welfare—in its perfect form of urbanity, a sort of shining through of the family love.]

§ 144. (3) But to fully initiate the youth into the institutions of civilization one must not only call out the feelings of his heart in the bosom of the family, not only give to him the formal refinement necessary to his intercourse with society; it must also perform the painful duty of making him acquainted with the mysteries of the ways of the world. This duty is painful, because the child naturally feels an unlimited confidence in all men. This confidence must be modified and restricted but not destroyed. The mystery of the way of the world is the practice of deception which originates in selfishness. We must provide against it by a proper degree of distrust. We must teach the youth that he may be imposed upon by cunning, dissimulation, and hypocrisy, and that therefore he must not give his confidence lightly and credulously. He himself must learn how he can, without using deceit, gain his own ends in the midst of the throng of opposing interests.

Kant in his pedagogics calls that worldly-wise behavior, by which the individual is to demean himself in opposition to others, impenetrability. By its means man learns how to "manage men." Egotism is like the blast of a simoom in its withering effects on the moral character when it is practiced as Lord Chesterfield recommends it in his letters to his son. . . . The sum of his teachings amounts to this, that we are to consider every man to be an egotist, and to convert his very egotism into a means of finding out his weak side, i. e., to flatter him by exciting his vanity, and by means of such flattery to ascertain his limits. In common life, the expression "to know the world" means about the same thing as having been deceived and betrayed.

[Social culture has also a negative duty—that of forewarning youth against the selfishness of the world and its forms of deceit and violence. Cunning, dissimulation, and hypocrisy, may impose on the youth. He must be on his guard.]

CHAPTER XIV.

EDUCATION OF THE WILL (*continued*).

(*b*) *Moral Culture.*

§ 145. The essential element of social culture is found in moral character. Without this latter, every graceful device of behavior remains worthless, and can never attain that purity of humility and dignity which are possible to it in its unity with morality. For the detailed treatment of this idea the science of education must refer to ethics itself, and can here give the part of its content which relates to education only in the form of educational maxims. The principal categories of ethics in the domain of morality are the ideas of duty, virtue, and conscience. Education must lay stress on the truth that nothing in the world has any absolute value except will guided by the right.

[Morality is a department of Ethics in the system here followed. Ethics includes manners and customs, forms of etiquette, statute laws, forms of government, the organized forms of human industry and the like as well as morality, which is only the subjective aspect of Ethics. Ethics relates, therefore, to the whole of the formal part of life that fits man to live in the institutions of civilization. Morality refers to the individual conviction of duty—hence, to the internal ideal, the form of the perfect man. The principal categories of Morality are (1) Duty; (2) Virtue; (3) Conscience. "Nothing in the world has an absolute value except will guided by the right," Rosenkranz says, "except the pure will." In his philosophy "pure will" means the will as self-related. When I guide my action by moral law I guide my will by my will instead of letting external circumstances or internal impulses guide it. The will acting upon the will is pure will, and this is the essence of morality. Again, morality is the form of will or that general form of volition which will not contradict itself and reduce to zero. Immoral acts injure one's self and society, and, if persisted in, would ultimately cripple or destroy the self and society, and thus cancel the will itself. Hence, the pure will is the form in which the will of the individual re-enforces the will of society, and is in turn re-enforced by it.]

§ 146. Thence follows (1) the maxim relating to the idea of duty, that we must accustom the pupil to unconditional obedience to it, so that he shall perform it for no other reason than that it is duty. The performance of a duty may bring with it externally a result agreeable or disagreeable, useful or harmful; but the consideration of such consequences ought never to determine us. This moral demand, though it may appear to be excessive severity, is the absolute foundation of all genuine ethical practice. All "highest happiness" theories, however finely spun they may be, when taken as a guide for life, lead at last to sophistry, and to contradictions ruinous to life.

[The pupil must be accustomed to unconditional obedience to duty. Eudemonism, or the doctrine that we should seek the highest happiness, is not a sufficient theory, because it implies that the individual shall weigh the consequences of his deed. But no individual can weigh the consequences of his puniest act.]

§ 147. (2) Virtue must make actual what duty commands, or, rather, the actualizing of duty is virtue. And here we may mention, by way of caption, that the principal things to be considered under virtue are (*a*) the dialectic of particular virtues, (*b*) moral discipline, and (*c*) character.

[Virtue, which is the practice of actualizing duty, involves three things: (*a*) the dialectic of the different forms of virtue; (*b*) moral discipline; (*c*) character as the result.]

§ 148. (*a*) From the dialectic [i. e., the consideration of the interdependence of the virtues and their mutual support, as well as their reciprocal limitation] of particular virtues there follows the educational maxim that we must practice all with equal faithfulness, for all together constitute an ethical system complete in itself, in which no one virtue is indifferent to another.

Morality should recognize no distinction of superiority among the different virtues. They reciprocally determine each other. There is no such thing as one virtue which shines out above the others, nor is there any special gift for virtue. The pupil must be taught that there are no great and no small among the virtues, for that one which may at first sight seem small is inseparably connected with that which is seemingly the greatest. Many virtues are attractive by reason of their external consequences, as, e. g., industry because of success in business, worthy conduct because of the respect paid to it, charity because of the pleasure attending it; but man should not practice these virtues because he enjoys them: he must devote the same amount of self-sacrifice and of assiduity to those virtues which (as Christ said) are to be performed in secret.

It is especially valuable, in an educational respect, to gain an insight into the transition, of which each virtue is empirically capable, into a negative as well as into a positive extreme. The differences between the extremes and the golden mean are differences in quality, although they arrive at this difference in quality by means of difference in quantity. Kant has, as is well known, attacked the Aristotelian doctrine of the ethical μεσότης, since he was considering the qualitative difference of the disposition or intention as the deciding principle. This is the correct procedure when treating of the moral subject that acts, but in the objective development of the actions themselves, we arrive, on the other hand, at the determination of a quantitative limit, e. g., a man, with the most earnest intention of doing right, may be in doubt whether he has not, in any task, done more or less than was fitting for him.

As no virtue can cease its demands upon us, no one can permit any exceptions or any provisional circumstances to come in the way of his duties. Our moral culture will always certainly manifest itself in very unequal phases if we, out of narrowness and weakness, neglect entirely one virtue while we diligently cultivate another. If we are forced into such unequal action, we are not responsible for the result; but it is dangerous and deserves punishment if we voluntarily encourage it. The pupil must be warned against a certain moral negligence which consists in yielding to certain weaknesses, faults, or crimes, a little longer and a little longer, because he has fixed a certain time after which he intends to do better. Up to that time he allows himself to be a loiterer in ethics. Perhaps he will assert that his companions, his surroundings, his position, etc., must be changed before he can alter his internal conduct. Wherever education or temperament favors sentimentality, we shall find birth-days, new-year's-day, confirmation-day, etc., selected as these turning-points. It is not to be denied that man proceeds in his internal life from epoch to epoch, and renews himself in his most internal nature, nor can we deny that moments like those mentioned are especially favorable in man to an effort toward self-transformation because they invite self-examination; but it is not to be permitted that the youth, while looking forward to such a moment, should consciously persist in his evil-doing. If he does, we shall have as consequences that when the appointed time which he has set at last arrives, at the stirring of the first emotion he perceives with terror that he has changed nothing in himself; that the same temptations are present to him, the same weakness takes possession of him. In our business, in our theoretical endeavors, it may certainly happen that, on account of want of time, or means, or humor, we may put off some work to another time; but morality stands on a higher plane than these, because it, as the concrete absoluteness of the will [see commentary to § 145: morality demands only such actions as do not contradict the will of the social whole; immoral acts are therefore such as would destroy society if persisted in], makes unceasing demand on the whole and undivided man. In morality there are no vacations, no interims. As we in ascending a flight of stairs take good care not to make a single misstep, and give our conscious attention to every step, so we must not allow any exceptions in moral affairs, must not appoint given times for better conduct, but must await these last as natural crises, and must seek to live in time as in eternity.

[The dialectic is the interaction of the several species of virtues, where they conflict, or where they mutually limit, or, finally, where they re-enforce each other.

Virtues are to be practiced not because they are pleasurable, but because of the duties they involve.

Some virtues, however, have negative and positive extremes—wherein they conflict, and find quantitative limits. Aristotle mentions the following virtues as consisting in a mean (μεσότης) between two extremes—courage (between rashness and cowardice), temperance, liberality, magnificence, magnanimity, proper mean between ambition and the want of it, meekness, plain speaking of the truth, pleasantry, sociability, modesty, righteous indignation.

No virtue may be neglected for another. The worst results follow from the habit of procrastinating the performance of a duty or the indulgence of a weakness until a fixed day. The person who "turns over a new leaf" on an important epoch is apt to turn it back again soon after. The will must not be trifled with. Duty must be obeyed now. To permit a temporary lapse from virtue occasionally is as inadmissible as allowing one's self now and then a misstep in ascending a flight of stairs. Such missteps undo the whole work.]

§ 149. (*b*) From moral culture springs the injunction of self-government. The action of education on the will with a view to form habits in it, is discipline or training in a narrower sense. Moral training teaches us to know the relation in which we in fact, as historical persons, stand to the idea of the good. From our personal knowledge of ourselves as individuals we derive the idea of our limits; from the absolute knowledge of ourselves as human, on the other hand, which reveals to us freedom as the innermost ideal of our spiritual nature, we derive the conception of the resistless power of the genuine will for the good. But to actualize this conception we must have practice. This practice constitutes the proper moral culture. Every man must devise for himself some special set of rules, which shall be determined by his peculiarities and his resulting temptations. These rules must have as their innermost essence the subduing of self, the vanquishing of his negative arbitrariness by means of the universality and necessity of the will.

In order to make this easy, the youth may be practiced in renouncing for himself even the arbitrariness which is permitted to him. One often speaks of moral discipline as if it belonged especially to the middle ages and to Catholicism; but this is an error. Ascetic discipline in its one-sided form as relying on works of piety, and for the purpose of mortification, belongs to them; but discipline in general is a necessary instrumentality of morals. The keeping of a journal is said to assist in the practice of virtue, but its value depends on how it is kept. To one it may be a curse, to another a blessing. Fichte, Goethe, Byron, and others, have kept journals and have been assisted thereby; while others, as Lavater, have been hindered by them. Vain people will every evening record with pen and ink their admiration of the correct course of life which they have led during the day.

[From the exercise of virtue (German *Askese*, not quite "asceticism," from the Greek Ἄσκησις) arises the maxim enjoining self-control. The will for the good is (see § 145, commentary) the will for the form of all will that does not contradict itself—the form in which all may act, never contradict, but always re-enforce each other, and hence the good is the form of resistless human might.]

§ 150. (*c*) The result of the practice in virtue, or, to express it philosophically, of the individual actualization of freedom, is the methodical development of the individual will as character. This conception of character is a merely formal one, for it considers only the unchangeable habit formed by the will, and according to which it directs its course in dealing with external affairs. As there are good, strong, and beautiful characters, so there are also bad, weak, and detestable ones. When in the science of education, therefore, we speak so much of the building up of a character, we mean *good* character, or the making permanent of a direction of the individual will toward the actualization of the good. Freedom ought to be the character of character. Education must, therefore, observe closely the interaction of the factors which go to form character, viz., (*α*) the temperament, as the *natural* character of the man; (*β*) external events, the historical element; (*γ*) the energy of the will, by which, within its limits of nature and history, it realizes the idea of the good in and for itself as the proper ethical character. Temperament determines the mode and manner of our external manifestation of ourselves; the events in which we live assign to us the ethical problems, but the will in its sovereignty stamps its seal on the structure built up from these materials. Education aims at accustoming the youth to freedom, so that he shall always measure his deed by the idea of the good. It does not desire a formal independence, which may also be called character, but a real independence resting upon the conception of freedom as that which is absolutely necessary. The pedagogical maxim is, then: Be independent, but be so through doing good.

According to preconceived opinion, stubbornness and obstinacy indicate a firm basis of character. But these may spring from weakness and indecision, on which account one needs to be well on his guard. A gentle disposition, through enthusiasm for the good, may attain to quite as great a firmness of will. Coarseness and meanness are on no account to be tolerated.

[The methodical development of the individual will, by the practice of virtue or vice, produces character, in the formal sense of the word as indicating either good or bad character. We mean *good* character when we use the word absolutely, and speak of a "person of character." Education takes account of the factors that form character. (1) The temperament and natural proclivities; (2) the external historic environment; (3) the energy of the will.]

§ 151. (3) The consideration of the culture of character leads to the subject of conscience. This is the comparison which the moral agent makes between himself as he is and his ideal self. He compares himself, in his past or future, with his nature, and judges himself accordingly as good or bad. This independence which belongs to the ethical judgment is the true soul of all morality, the negation of all self-illusion and of all deception through another. The educational maxim is: Be conscientious. Depend in your final decision entirely on your conception of what is right.

The self-examination prompted by conscience prevails throughout all the situations of life, and is the ground of all our rational progress. Fichte's stern words remain, therefore, eternally true: "He who has a bad character, must absolutely create for himself a better one."

[Conscience the criticism which the ideal self makes on the realized self. This is the highest authority within man.]

CHAPTER XV.

EDUCATION OF THE WILL (*continued*).

(c) *Religious Culture.*

§ 152. Social culture contains the formal phase, moral culture the real phase, of the practical mind. Conscience forms the transition to religious culture. In its universal and necessary nature, it reveals the absolute authority of spirit. The individual discerns in the depths of his own consciousness commands possessing universality and necessity to which he has to subject himself. They appear to him as the voice of God. Religion makes its appearance as soon as the individual distinguishes the Absolute from himself, as a personal Subject existing for and by Himself, and therefore for him. The atheist remains at the stage of insight into the absoluteness of the logical and physical, æsthetic and practical categories. He may, therefore, be perfectly moral. But he lacks religion, though he loves to characterize his uprightness by this name, and to transfer the dogmatic definitions of positive religion into the ethical sphere. It belongs to the province of religion that I demean myself toward the Absolute not merely as my own substance, I alone being the conscious subject, but that for me the substance in itself is also a conscious personal subject. If I look upon myself as the only absolute, I make myself devoid of spiritual essence. If I am the only absolute self-consciousness, there remains only the impulse to a persistent conflict with every self-consciousness not identical with me. Such a self-consciousness would be only theoretical irony [i. e., it would deny itself in another, while it pretended to recognize itself in that other]. In religion I know the Absolute as essence, when I am known by Him. Everything else, myself included, is finite and transitory, however significant it may be, however relatively and for the moment the Infinite may exist in it. In all finite existence the Infinite manifests itself only temporarily. But the Absolute, realizing itself, distinguishing itself from itself even in its unity with itself, is always self-identical, and takes up all the unrest of the phenomenal world back again into its simple essence.

[Politeness is the form, morality the substance or reality of the will or practical side of man. Conscience is the bridge that leads from morality over to religion. Religion begins when the individual recognizes personality in the highest principle in the universe. A "moral order of the world," a "persistent force," a "supreme idea," and "an absolute harmony" are, respectively, practical, physical, logical, and æsthetic categories, but neither of them is a religious category. The highest principle must be a Person, and I must recognize him as such, and his recognition of me is the highest object of my destiny.]

§ 153. This process of the individual spirit, in which it rises out of the multiplicity of all relations into union with the absolute as the substantial subject, and in whom nature and history are united, we may call, in a restricted sense, a change of heart. . . . The highest emotions of the heart culminate in religion, whose warmth is inspired by practical activity and conscientiousness.

[" Change of heart "—Rosenkranz says *Gemüth*, which means the inner life of the soul and also a cheerful disposition. Hegel says that only the Teutonic branches of the human race possess *Gemüth*, "that undeveloped, indefinite totality of spiritual being realized in the will rather than in the intellect." The Romanic nations he distinguishes as having "character," but not *Gemüth*. Character surrenders itself to a principle, but heart surrenders itself to a principle only with a reserve, for "heart" feels its own personality, and will not surrender to an abstraction, but only to a person.]

§ 154. Education has to prepare man for religion in the following respects: (1) It gives him the conception of it; (2) it endeavors to have this conception realized in his life; (3) it subordinates the theoretical and practical process in adapting him to a special standpoint of religious culture.

In the *working out* or detailed treatment of the science of education, the position which the conception of religion occupies is very uncertain. Many writers on education place it at the beginning, while others reserve it for the end. Others naïvely bring it forward abruptly in the midst of heterogeneous surroundings, but know very little to say concerning it, and urge teachers to kindle the fire of religious feeling in their pupils by teaching them to fear God. Through all their writing, we hear the cry that in education nothing is so important as religion. Rightly understood, this saying is quite true. The religious spirit, the consciousness of the Absolute, and the reverence for Him, should permeate all. Not unfrequently, however, we find that what is meant by religion is theology, or the church ceremonial, and these are only one-sided phases of the total religious process. [Allusion to religion in English colleges and universities omitted.] Religion must form the culminating point of education. It takes up into itself the didactical and practical elements, and gives to their matter a universal form.

[The respects in which education has to prepare the youth for religion are threefold: (*1*) It must teach him its theory; (*2*) it must train him into the habit of religious observances and a religious life; (*3*) it must make these theoretical and practical phases of religion conform to the tenets of some particular denomination or "to some special standpoint of religious culture."]

CHAPTER XVI.

EDUCATION OF THE WILL. (*c*) *Religious Culture* (continued).

(*1*) *The Theoretical Process of Religious Culture.*

§ 155. RELIGION, in common with every spiritual activity, must pass through three stages—feeling, conception, and comprehension. Whatever the special character of any religion may be, it can not avoid this psychological necessity, either in its general history or in the history of the individual. The teacher must understand this process, partly in order that he may make it easier to the pupil, partly that he may guard against the perversion of the religious feeling which may arise through the fact of the youth's remaining in one stage after he is ready for another and needs it. The science of education must therefore here refer to the philosophy of religion for a complete discussion of this idea.

[Religion has three stages: (*a*) feeling; (*b*) conception or representation; (*c*) comprehension or insight. These, it will be noted, correspond to the three psychological stages of the intellect (§ 84), the perceptive (or intuitive), imaginative, and logical epochs.]

§ 156. (1) Religion exists first as religious feeling. The individual is through feeling still immediately under the control of the divine, does not yet distinguish himself from the absoluteness of his own essence, and is in so far swayed by it. In so far as he feels the divine, he is a mystery to himself. This beginning is indispensable. Religion can not be produced in men by an education in external matters; its genesis belongs rather to the primitive depths in which God himself and the individual soul are essentially one.

The educator must not allow himself to suppose that he is able to make a religion. Religion dwells originally in every individual soul, for every one is born of God. Education can only aid the development of the religious feeling. As far as regards the psychological form, it was quite correct for Schleiermacher and his followers to characterize the essential element of the religious feeling as the feeling of dependence, for feeling takes its character from that which it feels; it depends upon its object. But in so far as God constitutes the object of the feeling, there enters it absolute emancipation, or the opposite of all dependence. I have maintained this in opposition to Schleiermacher. Religion lifts man above the finite, temporal, and transitory, and frees him from the pressure of external circumstances. Even the lowest form of religion does this; and when it is said that Schleiermacher has been unjustly criticised for this expression of dependence, this distinction is overlooked.

[Feeling or emotion is the indispensable first basis of religion. But if it goes no further than mere feeling, the devotee does not find himself able to recognize God as personal. To him God is therefore a fetich, an immediate manifestation in matter, and hostile to man's freedom and intelligence. Schleiermacher held that religion arose in the feeling of dependence, and that this remained its essential element. But Rosenkranz points out that religion lifts man above the trammels of the finite and transitory, and therefore gives him independence of the world.]

§ 157. But religious feeling as such rises into something higher when the spirit distinguishes the content of this religious feeling from any other content which it also feels, forms for itself a mental image of it, and thus objectifies it, and thereby is enabled to assume a free attitude toward it.

We must not understand that the religious feeling is destroyed in this process; in rising from vague feeling to a mental image of the object of feeling, it persists as a necessary form of the intelligence.

[A higher stage of religion rises out of this vague and nebulous condition of mere feeling, and begins to define the divine as an object of the imagination.]

§ 158. If the mind is held back and prevented from passing out of the simplicity of feeling into the act of distinguishing its object by perception, or recalling it and representing it as a mental image, if its efforts toward the forming of this representation are continually redissolved into feeling, then feeling, which was as the first step perfectly healthy and correct, will become morbid and degenerate into a wretched mysticism. Education must, therefore, remember that this feeling is not destroyed by the progress of its content into perception and conception on the side of psychological form, but rather that it attains truth thereby.

[Mysticism is produced by the arrested development of religious feeling. The devotee holds back from mental images and forms of the imagination, fearing to anthropomorphize the conception of the Divine Being. He does not, however, for this reason, attain a purer idea of Him, but tends rather to destroy all the attributes of personality in his conception of the Absolute, and leave it an empty abstraction like the Brahm of the Hindoos, or the Supreme Being (*l'Être Suprême*) of the French deists.

Education, therefore, makes a mistake if it attempts to elevate the pupil at once from the stage of feeling to that of comprehension and insight without passing through the stage of imagination.]

§ 159. (2) Representation retains perception, transformed into conception. It develops the different phases of the religious content, and follows each of these to its consequence. Imagination controls the individual conceptions, but by no means with that absoluteness which is often supposed; for each picture has in itself its logical consequence to which imagination must yield; e. g., if a religion represents God as an animal, or as half animal and half man, or as man, the conception chosen has in its development its consequences for the imagination.

[Religious imagination is not mere idle fancy, but its images have a logical sequence, and adumbrate a series of profound ideas.]

§ 160. We rise out of the stage of representation when the mind tries to define the universality of its content according to its necessity, i. e., when it begins to think. But for the imagination the necessity of its pictures is a hidden assumption. The thinking activity, however, recognizes not only the contradiction which exists between the sensuous, limited form of the individual representation, and the essential nature of its content, but also the contradiction in which the conceptions find themselves with respect to each other.

[It is in attempting to discover the contents of these religious images that the mind rises to the true concrete insight. Thought needs at first these mental pictures, and without them can not begin at all. Hence so-called deism, which rejects the imaginative stage of religious culture altogether, is not able to rise to a concrete doctrine of God as a divine human Person such as Christianity reveals, but makes Him to be a being with the negation of all attributes, because such a deity transcends everything finite, and everything thinkable is regarded as finite.]

§ 161. If the mind is prevented from passing out of the motley pictures of conception to the supersensuous clearness and simplicity possessed by the object of the thinking activity—if the content which it already begins to seize as idea is again dissolved into the disconnected images of the picture-world—then the religion of imagination, which was a perfectly proper form as the second step, becomes perverted into some form of idolatry, either coarse or refined. Education must therefore not oppose the thinking activity if the latter undertakes to criticise the images and pictures in which religious conceptions are embodied; on the contrary, it must seek to guide this thinking activity so that the discovery of the contradictions which unavoidably adhere to sensuous form shall not mislead the youth into the folly of throwing away, with the husk that has become useless, also the religious kernel itself.

It is an error for educators to desire to hold back the imagination from religious feeling, but it is also an error to detain the mind, which is on its formal side essentially the activity of knowing, in the stage of imagination, and confine it to the office of picturing the conventional religious allegories. The more, in opposition to this, the mind is carried away with the charm of thinking, the more is it in danger of condemning the essence of religion itself as a mere fictitious conception. As a transition-stage the religion of imagination is perfectly normal, and it does not in the least impair freedom if, for example, one has personified evil as a living devil in bodily shape. The error does not lie in this, but in the making independent existences out of these sensuous forms of religion. The reaction of the thinking activity against such sensuous embodiment then undertakes in its negative freedom and independence as realized in critical thought to despise the content also, as if it were a mere conception.

[Again, if religion is arrested at the standpoint of imagination, it becomes fixed in the form of idolatry. Hence, education has before it the difficult task (especially in our Sunday-schools) of guiding rather than repressing the critical tendency of pupils who are beginning to inquire for themselves into the contradictions and absurdities of the images and allegories in which the imagination has embodied religious truth. Spiritually understood, these very contradictions are the most wonderful and admirable product of the history of religion, and altogether the most valuable and profound part of its revelation.]

§ 162. (3) In the thinking activity the mind attains that form of the religious content which is identical with that of its simple self-consciousness, and above which there is no further progress for the intelligence as theoretical. But we distinguish three varieties in this thinking activity: the abstract, the reflective, and the speculative. The abstract gives us the religious content of consciousness in the form of abstractions or dogmas, i. e., propositions which set up some doctrine as a universal, and add to it a reason for its necessity. The reflective stage busies itself with the mutual relation of dogmas, and with an examination of the grounds alleged for their necessity: it is essentially critical, and hence skeptical. The discussion of the dogmas, which is carried on in this process of reasoning and skeptical investigation, gives place to speculative thinking, which recognizes the free unity of the content and its form as its own proper self-determination of the content, creating its own differences. Education must know these three stages of the intelligence, partly that it may in advance preserve an equipoise, and prevent going to extremes in the midst of the changes which the progressive development produces in the consciousness; partly that it may be able to direct the process of change itself, in accordance with the proper order of development of these phases of mind. We should, for example, not try to prevent the criticism of the abstract understanding by the reflective stage nor that of the imagination by the thinking activity. But the stage of reflection is not to be regarded as the last and highest possibility of the thinking activity, although, in the vain conceit of its skepticism, it often takes itself for such, and, with the emptiness of mere negation to which it holds, often brings itself forward into undesirable prominence. It becomes evident, in this view, how very necessary for man, with respect to religion, is a genuine philosophical culture, so that he may not lose a sure conviction of the existence of the Absolute in a life of culture divided between adherence to unyielding dogmas on the one hand, and shifting, unstable opinions on the other hand.

[Three varieties of religious thought on the plane of insight: (*a*) abstract, (*b*) reflective, (*c*) speculative. The abstract sets forth the doctrines as abstract dogmas. The reflective busies itself over the mutual relation of the dogmas and the proofs of their necessity. This leads to skepticism. The speculative thinking sees the logical necessity of self-activity in the Absolute, and hence the consequent logical necessity for concrete attributes such as belong to a Creator. It recognizes the personality of the Absolute, and now comprehends the contradictions and apparent absurdities in the allegorical forms submitted to it.]

§ 163. Education must then not fear the overthrow of dogmatic abstraction, since its downfall is an indispensable means for theoretical culture in its totality, and the consciousness can not dispense with it in its history. But education has, in dealing with concrete cases, carefully to discern in which of these stages of culture its pupil is. For if mankind as a race can not get along without philosophy, it by no means follows that this necessity exists for each individual. To children, to women, and to all simple and limited lives, the form of the religion of the imagination is well suited, and the form of religion for the speculative intellect has only a small degree of significance to them. Education must not, then, desire powerfully and prematurely to develop the thinking activity before the intelligence has grown through the earlier stages of development.

The forced efforts at thinking which many teachers demand in the sphere of religion is no less impractical than the want of all guidance into rightly ordered meditations on religious subjects. It is natural that to the lower form of intelligence a higher form should appear to be frivolous in its behavior toward it, because it has as yet felt no need of change of form as the higher has; and on this account it looks upon the discrediting of a sacred symbol or emblem or the overthrow of a dogma as the destruction of religion itself. In our time the idea is very prevalent that the substance itself must change with the changing of the psychological form, and that therefore a religion on the stage of feeling can no longer be the same in its essence with a religion on the stage of representation in mental images, or on the stage of clear thought. These suppositions, which are so popular, and are considered to be high philosophy, spring from the superficiality of psychological inquiry.

[Religious education, therefore, must not fear these changes from feeling to imagination and from imagination to reflection, for they are indispensable to the full religious consciousness, and Christianity is essentially a religion of all these stages, and especially of the highest thought. Just as in psychology we said that thinking goes back and re-enforces sense-perception and conception (§ 100), so the stage of insight goes back and re-enforces religious feeling and religious imagination. And it is for feeling and imagination only as thus re-enforced by thinking insight that Christianity is the true religion. But for all this it is by no means proper to attempt to prematurely develop the stage of religious insight, for such attempt can only end in producing that critical skeptical stage above described. It is interesting to notice the view that Rosenkranz holds concerning the capacity of women to understand philosophy. It was the common view held throughout the civilized world forty years ago, when this book was written. Since that time the education of girls has ascended step by step until college education has proved the mind of woman specially adapted to high studies.]

§ 164. The theoretical education of the religious feeling endeavors, therefore, to unite the presupposition of reason in the religious content with the freedom of philosophical criticism, and to elevate it to self-assured insight by means of the proof of the necessity of its determinations. This is the only reasonable pedagogical way, not only to prevent the degeneration of the religious consciousness into a miserable mysticism or into empty formality, but also to remove these if they are already existent.

External seclusion avails nothing. The crises of the world-historical changes in the religious consciousness penetrate the thickest cloister-walls. . . .

[Theoretical religious education endeavors to re-enforce the stages of religious emotion and religious imagination by the stage of insight into the necessary nature of the divine.]

CHAPTER XVII.

EDUCATION OF THE WILL. (*c*) *Religious Culture* (continued).

(2) *The Practical Process of Religious Culture.*

§ 165. THEORETICAL education has already a practical implication, for it gives man definite conceptions and thoughts of the Divine, and defines his relation to God. But in a narrower sense that education is practical which relates to the Will as such. Education has in this respect to distinguish (1) *consecration*, (2) the *initiation* of the youth into the forms of worship as found in some particular religion, and (3) his *reconciliation* with his lot.

[The will side of religious education is treated under three heads: (*a*) consecration of self; (*b*) ceremonial initiation, and uniting with the church; (*c*) religious reconciliation with one's lot in life.]

§ 166. (1) Religious feeling presupposes morality as an indispensable condition without which it can not attain its ideal. But while man from a merely moral standpoint places himself in relation to the idea of duty, the religious standpoint of the Church differs from it in this, that it holds the necessity of the good to be the self-determination of the Divine Will, and thus gives all human conduct a personal relation to God, changing the good to the holy and evil to sin. Education must, therefore, first accustom the youth to the idea that, in doing the good, he unites himself with God as with the absolute Person, but that in doing evil he separates himself from him. The consciousness that through his deed he comes into relation with God himself, affirmatively or negatively, deepens the moral standpoint with its formal obedience to the commands of virtue, to the standpoint of the heart that finds its all-sufficient principle in love.

[Distinction between the moral and the religious standpoint. While the moral makes duty the highest, the religious looks upon the good as the action of the Divine Will, and thus places the individual in a direct personal relation to God. The good thus becomes the holy, and evil becomes sin. The distinction between *sin*, *crime*, and *evil* is a very interesting one: sin is violence done by the individual to his relation to God's will; evil is a general negation of the form of self-activity, and hence negative to the interests of humanity—moral evil being the self-contradiction of the will, or the will of the individual set against the will of mankind in general; crime is the negation of the law of the state; crime must be an overt act—a deed actually done and not merely deliberated upon; but it must be a deed intended to be done. Sin is internal, and may or may not be accompanied by external deeds. In contrast to crime it lies in the disposition of the heart. Moral evil may be conscious or unconscious—strictly moral evil must be conscious and a violation of conscience. But ethically all attacks upon institutions, family, society, state, church, are moral evils, whether the intention is good or bad. The plea of conscience is not valid to justify a murder, an assault on the state or the church, or on the sacredness of the family.]

§ 167. (2) The ceremonial recognition of the sense which grows in the child that he has an uninterrupted personal relation to the Absolute as a person, constitutes the beginning of the practical education in religion. The second step is the initiation of the child into the objective forms of worship established in some particular religion. Through religious training the child learns to renounce his egotism; through attendance on religious services he learns to give expression to his religious feeling in prayer, in the use of symbols, and in church festivals. Education must, however, endeavor to retain freedom with regard to these forms, so that they shall not be confounded with religion itself. Religion presents itself in these ceremonies, but they as mere forms are of value only in so far as there dwells in them the spirit which produces them as its external manifestation.

If the mechanism of ceremonial forms is taken as religion itself, the service of God degenerates into the false service of religion, as

Kant has designated it in "Religion within the Limits of Pure Reason." Nothing is more destructive of the sensibility to all real religious culture than the want of earnestness with which prayers, readings from the Bible, attendance on church, the communion, etc., are often practiced by teachers. But one must not conclude, from this defect on the part of teachers, that an ignorance of all sacred forms in general would be more desirable for the child.

[The religious discipline of consecration educates to renunciation of selfish egotism, while the union with the church teaches the expression of the religious feeling in prayer, the use of symbols, and the observance of the solemnities of the church. Education has to guard, however, against the danger of confounding forms with religion itself.]

§ 168. (3) It is possible that a man on the standpoint of ecclesiastical religious observances may be fully contented; he may be entirely taken up with the ceremonies of worship, and pass his life in these occupations in perfect religious peace. But by far the greater number of men will see themselves forced to experience the truth of religion in the hard vicissitudes of their lot, since they engage in secular activities, and create for themselves a past whose consequences condition their future. They limit themselves through their deeds, which they perform as partly voluntary and partly involuntary authors: involuntary, in so far as they are impelled to their deeds by the totality of events; voluntary, in so far as they originate them and react on the world around them. Nay, man is responsible for deeds of omission as well as of commission. The history of the individual man appears, therefore, on the one hand, if we consider its material, as the work of circumstances; but, on the other hand, if we reflect on the form, as the act of a self-determining agent. Want of freedom (the being determined through the given situation) and freedom (the origination of the act) are united in actual life as a finality which is exactly so, and can not become anything else. The essence of the spiritual being stands always over against this unavoidable limitation as that which is in itself infinite and eternal, as beyond all history, because the absolute spirit, in and for itself, has no history. That which man calls his history is only the manifesting of himself and his continual withdrawal out of this manifestation into himself, an act which coincides with the transcending of all manifestation on the part of the absolute spirit. From this infinite essential nature which belongs to him there arises for the individual spirit the impulse toward a beatific life, i. e., a life freed from external contingencies even in the midst of their process. He gratifies this impulse negatively through the contemplation of what has happened as past and gone, as that which lives now only ideally in the memory; or he contemplates it in a new actual existence more perfect than the old one which he has planned in order to realize the idea of freedom which constitutes his ideal nature. This constant new-birth out of the grave of the past to the life of a more beautiful future is the true solution of the problem of life. The false solution may assume different forms. It may abstain from all action because man through action limits himself and becomes accountable to others; but this is to despair of freedom, for it condemns the spiritual being to the loss of its selfhood; for its nature demands activity. The abstract quietism of the Indian *yogis*, of the Buddhists, of the fanatical ascetics, of the Protestant recluses, etc., is an error of this kind. Or, secondly, man may become indifferent to the ethical consequences of his deeds. In this case he acts, it is true; but, because he has no faith in the necessary connection of his deeds with their consequences as results of his choice, a connection which he would ascribe to mere chance, he loses his spiritual essence. This is the error of indifference and its trifling, which denies the open mystery of human life as built up by freedom out of materials furnished by Fate. Education must, therefore, imbue man with respect for the circumstances and events of his environment, and at the same time inspire with faith in the inexhaustible resources of the human spirit, since only by continually producing better things can he elevate himself above his past. This practical acknowledgment of the necessity of freedom as the determining principle of life gives the highest satisfaction to which practical religious feeling may arrive, for the state of beatitude develops itself in it—that blessedness which refuses to admit that it is circumscribed by finitude and transitoriness, and which possesses the undying courage to strive always anew for perfection, with cheerful resignation when defeated; and by this means happiness and misery, pleasure and pain, are conquered by the power of disinterested self-sacrifice and sincere humility.

The escape from action in an artificial exclusion of all relation to external events, which often sinks to a veritable brutifying of man, is the distinguishing feature of all monkish education. In our time [1848] there is especial need of a reconciliation between man and destiny, for all the world is discontented. The worst form of discontent is when one is, as the French say, *blasé;* though the word is not, as many fancy, originally French, but from the Greek βλάζειν, to wither. It is true that all culture passes through phases, each of which becomes temporarily and relatively wearisome, and that in so far one may be *blasé* in any age. But in modern times this state of feeling has increased to that of thorough disgust at existence—disgust which nevertheless at the same time hungers for enjoyment. The one who is *blasé* has enjoyed everything, experienced everything, mocked at everything. He has passed from the enjoyment of pleasure to sentimentality, i. e., to rioting in feeling; from sentimentality to that irony which despises the shallowness of mere feeling, and from this to the tormenting consciousness of his entire weakness and emptiness when he has discarded feeling. He ridicules this also, as if it were a consolation to fling away the universe like a squeezed lemon, and to assert that in empty nothing lies the truth of all things. And yet, nevertheless, this irony furnishes the point on which education can fasten, in order to kindle anew in him the religious feeling, and to lead him back to a loving recognition of the world, and to a proper interest in the circumstances and events of his time. The greatest difficulty which education has to encounter here is the coquetting with this *blasé* mood, the miserable affectation of superiority, and the self-complacency which have undermined the man and made him incapable of all simple and natural enjoyment. It is not too much to assert that many pupils of our *Gymnasia* are affected with this malady. Our literature is full of its products. We inveigh against its dissipation, and nevertheless at the same time can not resist a certain kind of pleasure in it. Diabolical sentimentality!

[Religious peace does not often come to the individual solely through personal consecration and the strict performance of ceremonial observances. It is the encountering of the hard vicissitudes of life that brings home to the individual the lessons of religion and elevates him to that higher religious state of mind called reconciliation with one's lot, or religious peace and consolation which are a sure indication that this individual has renounced the world and has joined his life to the eternal order, and is therefore secure from the arrows of fortune, no matter how much his energies may be given to the accomplishment of temporal enterprises. Quietism, which renounces all action, is the false religious peace, for spirit is essential activity, and the will must forever realize the good anew by changing nature into a more pliant instrument of the spirit. The antithesis of this consolation of religion is the state of mind described as *blasé* and *Weltschmerz.*]

CHAPTER XVIII.

EDUCATION OF THE WILL. (*c*) *Religious Culture* (continued).

(*3*) *The Absolute Process of Religious Culture.*

§ 169. In comparing the stages of the theoretical and practical culture of the religious feeling their internal correspondence appears. Feeling, as immediate knowledge of God, and the consecration of the objects of sense to holy purposes by means of piety; imagination with all its images, and the church services with their symbolism and ceremonial observances; finally, the comprehending of religion in its highest spiritual meaning, and the reconciliation of man with his lot as the internal emancipation from the dominion of external events—all these correspond to each other. If we grasp this parallelism as a whole, we have the course which religion must take in its historical process, in which it (1) begins as natural, (2) goes on to historical differences of form, and (3) unites these finally in a rational faith. These stages await every man in so far as he lives through a complete religious culture, but this may be for the individual a question of chance.

[The absolute process of religious culture would take one through three stages: (*a*) beginning with the natural, (*b*) it would next develop differences of form, and (*c*) unite these, through insight, in a rational faith.]

§ 170. (1) A child has as yet no definite religious feeling. He is still only a possibility capable of growth in all directions. But, since he is a spiritual being, the essence of religion is active in him, though as yet in an unconscious form. The substance of spirit attests its presence in every individual, through his mysterious impulse toward the infinite and eternal, and toward intercourse with God. This is the elementary stage of natural religion, which must not be confounded with the religion which makes Nature the object of worship (fetichism, etc.).

[In the child brought up in modern civilization natural religion manifests itself as an impulse toward the infinite and eternal, and toward communion with God.]

§ 171. (2) But the child comes in contact with definite forms of religion, and will naturally, through the mediation of the family, be introduced to some one of them. His religious feeling takes now a particular direction, and he accepts religion in one of its historical forms. This special realization of religion meets the precise want of the child, because it brings into his consciousness, by means of teaching and forms of worship, the principal elements which are found in the nature of religion.

[The family introduces the child to its own chosen form of worship, and he accepts it and finds in it satisfaction.]

§ 172 (3) In contradistinction to the natural basis of religious feeling, all historical religions rest on the authoritative basis of revelation from God to man. They address themselves to the imagination, and offer a system of objective forms of worship and ceremonies. But spirit, as eternal, as self-identical, can not forbear as thinking activity to subject the traditional religion to criticism and to compare it as a phenomenal existence with its perfect ideal. From this criticism arises a religion which satisfies the demands of the reason, and which, by means of insight into the necessity of the historical process, leads to the exercise of a genuine toleration toward its many-sided forms. This religion reconciles the unity of the thinking consciousness with the religious dogmas and ceremonies, which, in the history of religious feeling, appear theoretically as dogma, and practically as the command of an absolute and incomprehensible authority. The religion of reason is just as simple as the unsophisticated natural religious feeling, but its simplicity is at the same time master of itself. It is just as specific in its determinations as any historical form of religion, but its determinateness is at the same time universal, since it is worked out by the thinking reason.

[If the individual reflects on the nature of religion in itself and the ground for its appearance in this or that denominational form, he may arrive at a justification of all forms and ceremonies, finding the occasion of each in its historic genesis. In this he reaches a genuine toleration, but not the negative state of indifference that is wont to accompany toleration; for he sees, through these forms, their revelation of the divine.]

§ 173. Education must superintend the development of the religious consciousness toward an insight into the necessary sequence of its different stages. Nothing is more absurd than for the educator to desire to avoid the introduction of a particular form of religion, or a definite creed, as a middle stage between the natural beginning of religious feeling and its end in philosophical culture. Only when a man has lived through the entire range of a one-sided phase—through the crudeness of such a concrete individualizing of religion, and has come to recognize the universal nature of religion in a special form of it which excludes other forms—only when the spirit of a church has taken him into its number, is he ripe to criticise religion in a conciliatory spirit, because he has then gained a religious character through that historical experience. The self-comprehending universality must have such a solid basis as this in the career of the man; it can never form the beginning of one's culture, but it may constitute the end which turns back again to the beginning. Most men remain at the historical standpoint. The religion of reason, as that of the minority, constitutes in the different religions the invisible church, which seeks by progressive reform to purify these religions from superstition and unbelief. It is the duty of the state, by making all churches equal in the sight of the law, to guard religion from the temptation of impure motives, and, through the granting of such freedom to religious individuality, to help forward the unity of a rational insight into religion which is distinct from the religious feeling only in its form, not in its content. Not a philosopher, but Jesus of Nazareth, freed the world from all selfishness and all bondage.

[These three phases in the absolute religious process are essential to complete religious experience. Certainly the first and second forms are indispensable—the stage of religious emotion and the stage of membership in a denominational body. The third stage, that of membership in the invisible church, has no meaning to those who have not entered the visible church in some one of its communions.]

§ 174. With this highest theoretical and practical emancipation, the general work of education ends. It remains now to be shown how the general idea of education shapes its special elements into their appropriate forms. From the nature of education, which concerns itself with man in his entirety, this exposition belongs partly to the history of culture in general, partly to the history of religion, partly to the philosophy of history. The pedagogical element in it always lies in the ideal which the spirit of a nation or of an age creates for itself, and which it seeks to realize in its youth.

[With religious education, which unites theoretical and practical education by offering to the intellect the view of the first principle of the universe, and by offering to the will a revelation of the divine purpose in creation as the ultimate guide for all practical action, education ends. The science of education, having expounded these departments, has now left for it only the survey of the historical systems that have prevailed in the world.]

THIRD PART.

PARTICULAR SYSTEMS OF EDUCATION.

THIRD PART.

PARTICULAR SYSTEMS OF EDUCATION.

INTRODUCTION.

HISTORICAL SYSTEMS OF EDUCATION.

§ 175. The general idea of education is individualized, in its realization in human history, according to its elements, into specific ideas which we call pedagogical principles. The number of these principles is not unlimited, but the idea of education admits only a certain definite number. If we deduce them, therefore, we deduce at the same time the history of pedagogics, which can from its very nature do nothing else than realize the possibilities involved in the idea of education. Such a deduction may be called an *a priori* construction of history, but it differs from what is generally denoted by this term in not pretending to deduce single events and characters. All empirical details are confirmation or illustration for it, but it does not attempt to seek this empirical element *a priori.*

The history of pedagogics is still in the stage of infancy. Sometimes it is taken up into the sphere of politics; sometimes into that of the history of culture. The productions of some of the most distinguished writers on the subject are now antiquated. [Omission here of references to the works of Niemeyer, Schwarz, Cramer, Stralsund, Alexander Kapp, of Brzoska's and Mager's "Pedagogical Reviews."] But with regard to modern pedagogics we have relatively very little. Karl von Raumer,* in 1843, began to publish a "History of Pedagogics since the Time of the Revival of Classical Studies," and has accomplished much of value on the biographical side. But the idea of the general connection and dependence of the several phases has not received much attention, and since the time of Pestalozzi books have assumed the character of biographical confessions. Strümpell, in 1843, collected and systematized the educational material found in the writings of the philosophers Kant, Fichte, and Herbart.

[The exposition of the historical systems that have prevailed in the world is derived partly from the history of culture, partly from the history of religion, and partly from the philosophy of history. The educational element in a nation must always be interpreted through the ideal which the spirit of a nation or an age creates for itself and seeks to realize in its youth.

Each historical system has a definite idea or principle lying at its basis. It may seem at first as though there might be an indefinite number of these principles, but such is not the fact. Human nature is a definite thing as a reality, and its ideal is also something definite, namely, rational culture. Reason is logical and systematic. Hence, the development of the human race into reason can give only such phases as the two extremes and their combination permit. Man starts as a natural being and becomes a spiritual being. He begins in thralldom to time and space, and develops self-determination and freedom in his intellect and will. Man's first phase of growth into civilization is characterized by absolute authority correlated with absolute subjection. The institutions which help him to free himself from nature (family, civil society, state, church) assume an attitude of absolute authority toward the individual. That is to say, the first stage of the development of civilization sets up its institutions of civilization in the form of nature. As civiliza-

---

* The larger portion of this excellent work of Karl von Raumer has been translated into English, and published under separate articles in the volumes of Dr. Henry Barnard's "American Journal of Education." The thirty volumes of Dr. Barnard's work constitute an encyclopædia of education.—Ed.

tion is the process of mediation between nature and spirit, three general phases only are possible in the history of civilization: (a) The phase in which institutions take on the form of nature, and crush out all individual freedom; (b) the phase in which pure spirit or the personal God governs his people directly as a chosen people, and sets them free from all forms of Nature-worship; (c) the phase in which man himself enters into the positive individual freedom of spirit. In § 177, Rosenkranz names three phases: (a) National Education; (b) Theocratic Education; (c) Human Education. There is in this classification an *a priori* element which necessitates three and only three general forms (the subdivisions of these three forms are, of course, indefinitely manifold). Experience alone discovers for us the nations and people who may be classified under these three classes.]

§ 176. Man is educated by man for humanity. This is the fundamental idea of all education. But, in the shaping of this science, we can not begin with the idea of humanity as such, but only with the natural form in which it primarily manifests itself—that of the people or nation. But the naturalness of this principle disappears in the course of its development, since nations act and react upon each other, and begin gradually to perceive the unity of their common humanity. But the freedom of spiritual being from nature makes its appearance explicitly in the transcendent form of abstract theistic religion, in which God is recognized as the ruler over Nature, which on the other hand is conceived as merely dependent; and his chosen people plant the root of their nationality no longer in the earth, but in this belief. The unity of the abstractly natural and abstractly spiritual determinateness is the concrete unity of the spirit with nature, in which it recognizes nature as its necessary organ, and itself as in its nature divine. Spirit in this stage, as the internal presupposition of the two previously named, takes up into itself on one hand the phase of nationality, since this is the form of the immediate individualization (of modern civilization); but it no longer distinguishes between nations as if they were abstractly severed the one from the other, as the Greeks shut out all other nations under the name of barbarians. It also takes up into itself the phase of spirituality, since it knows itself as spirit, and knows itself to be free from nature, and yet it does not estrange itself from the world as the Jews did in their representation of pure spirit, to whom nature seemed to be only the work of divine caprice. Humanity knows nature as its own, because it knows the divine spirit and its creative energy manifesting itself in nature and history, as also the essence of its own spirit. Education can be complete only with Christianity as the religion of humanity.

[Man is educated by man for humanity, i. e., for the realization of all the possibilities of humanity as a whole in each individual; education of the youth shall give him the results of all human experience. But humanity in its complete unfolding is not to be found at the beginning of history. The totality of a people or nation is the highest realization of humanity that can be found at first (countless ages pass away before science, art, philosophy, and theology come to exist). "The naturalness of this principle," i. e., the bond that unites a people, is a natural and not an artificial bond; it does not depend on leagues and treaties, but on community of descent and consequent identical race-peculiarities, common language, manners and customs, and traditions. Each individual of a people finds himself living in this identity with his people just as he finds himself living in identity with a family. The family identity (called "identity" because it is a common life, the same for each, consisting of mutual relations and common possessions in which each owns an undivided share) is a "natural" one in the fact that it, too, arises from the laws of nature and not from free choice. The individual, e. g., can not choose his ancestry. This natural unity of people gradually gives place to the recognition of common humanity and an observance of humane duties toward all men.

The spiritual nature of man (his will, intellect, and heart) is opposed to his animal nature. Matter is exclusive; animal gratifications are exclusive and selfish; spiritual life is participation; the intellect and the moral will develop through sharing all acquisitions with others. Wisdom is a product of the race, and not of one individual exclusively; the greater the number who participate in wisdom, the better for all. The second phase of the history of culture is the one in which God is revealed as a pure spiritual being, not identical with the sun or moon or any part of nature, or indeed with the whole of nature. In the contemplation of this pure ideal man begins to see that his own destiny is something transcending nature. "The chosen people plant the root of their nationality" not in any particular territory or feature of nature, but in their faith in Jehovah. The Jewish nationality is a sort of pivot on which the history of the world turns from the thralldom of nature to the freedom of spirit. Nevertheless, spirit is not free when it simply renounces nature and regards it as a work of divine caprice. It must conquer nature and use it for spiritual purposes or rational ends before it is free in the highest sense. Concrete freedom is therefore said to be a unity of spirit and nature, but it is a unity in which nature is subordinated to an instrument, and spirit is exalted to the end and aim of creation. In this it "takes up into itself the phase of nationality," or, in other words, modern civilization retains the form of the nation or of separate peoples, but at the same time it repudiates more and more the jealousy and hatred that was wont to be directed to outside nations. It also "takes up into itself the phase of spirituality," i. e., besides retaining nationality, modern civilization also worships God as a person, and places on the summit the ideal of the divine-human. By this it "knows itself to be free from nature," i. e., to be immortal and able to survive death and live without this world. "Humanity knows nature as its own" because it recognizes its right to use it for its own advantage; it sees nature as created by Absolute Reason for the behoof of reasonable creatures made in his image. Hence education becomes "complete with Christianity as the religion of humanity."]

§ 177. We have thus three different systems of education: (1) the National; (2) the Theocratic; and (3) the Humanitarian. The first works after the manner of nature, since it educates the individual as a type of his race. The original nationality endeavors sharply to distinguish itself from others, and to impress on each person the stamp of its uniform type. One individual is like every other, or at least should be so. The second system in its manner of manifestation is identical with the first. It even marks the national difference more emphatically; but the ground of the uniformity of the individuals is with it not merely the natural element in common, but the common interest is the result of the spiritual unity, which neglects nature, and concentrates its whole attention upon the events of its own history; satisfied with no present, it remains in continual self-alienation, looking back to its past, or forward to its future. The theocratic system educates the individual as the servant of God. He is the true Jew only in so far as he is this; the genealogical identity with father Abraham is a condition but not the principle of the nationality. The third system emancipates the individual, and elevates him to the enjoyment of freedom as his essence; educates him within national limits which no longer separate but unite; and, in the consciousness that each, without any kind of mediation, has a direct relation to God, makes of him a man who knows himself to be a member of the spiritual world of humanity. We can have no fourth system beyond this. From the side of the state-pedagogics we might characterize these systems as that of the nation-state, the God-state, and the humanity-state. From the time of the establishment of the last, no one nation can attain to any sovereignty over the others. By means of the world-religion of Christianity, the education of nations has come to the point of taking, for its ideal, man as determining himself according to the demands of reason.

[Three different systems of education founded on the stages of civilization: (a) National; (b) Theocratic; (c) Humanitarian—"humanitarian" not used here in a sentimental sense; it expresses rather the missionary sense—love for the souls of men of whatever race or land; the care of the civilization for its unfortunate, the care of the highest for the lowest. It is a civilization that interests itself in all nature as a revelation of the divine, and hence specializes its work in the several sciences, investigating the humblest orders of nature with as much painstaking care as the mightiest.

The National system works "after the manner of nature, since it educates the individual as a type of his race"; education among the people of Asia does not attempt to develop individualism, but only to repress individuality and produce perfect conformity to the established type of behavior, just as Nature compels new acorns to be like the old ones. Species is tyrannical in nature, allowing only the slightest of variations from the type. But in the highest civilization individuality is cherished to such a degree that social caste, intellectual modes of thought, habits of behavior, and vocation may be completely varied in the second generation.

In the second system (the Theocratic) the uniformity of individuals is based on its spiritual unity, a continual straining of the mind after what is not present—a past to which it looks back with longing as the days of patriarchal ancestors who lived in close personal favor with Jehovah, or a future in which it expects peace and plenty, and the renewal of divine favor. The Jewish child must be educated as a servant of God. The race principle, based as it is on nature, yields in the case of the Hebrews to the purely spiritual principle of service of Jehovah. If one serves Jehovah, it is not necessary that he be descended from Abraham.

The third system has for its ideal the brotherhood of all men, and continually impels the nations toward commerce in articles of use and beauty, necessity and luxury, as well as the interchange of ideas and the mutual toleration of differences.

There can be no fourth system beyond this, because this completely mediates the particular with the universal, holding as its end and aim the perfect collection of all that the individual produces into the market of the world, material and spiritual, and the perfect distribution of all thence again to the individual, so that each helps all and all help each. Each person gives his mite to the world; each person receives from the world infinitely more than he gave, not in quantity but in quality, enriched by variety and all manner of precious attributes. For each locality has a limited number of precious material productions, and likewise a few spiritual gifts; by world-commerce each locality is made to abound in the desirable productions of all climes, and the spiritual gifts of all places and all times are brought to every human being. This is achieved progressively by the inspiration of Christianity as it gradually regenerates society.]

CHAPTER I.

THE SYSTEM OF NATIONAL EDUCATION.

§ 178. The National is the primitive system of education, since the family is the organic starting-point of all education, and it grows into the basis of nationality.

Education has always in view the preparation of youth for life in institutions. Even inorganic peoples, those in a state of nature—the so-called savage races—are possessed of something more than a mere physical education; for, though they set much value upon gymnastic and warlike practices, and give much time to them, they inculcate also respect for parents, for the aged, and for the decrees of the community. Education with them is essentially family training, and its object is to cultivate in children a natural love and reverence for the elders and those in authority. That the finer forms to which we are accustomed are wanting must not be forgotten. Besides, education among all these people of nature is very simple and much the same, though great differences in its administration may exist, arising from differences of geographical situation or race characteristics.

[The National is the primitive system of education because it is the education of the family, which is the germ out of which grows civilization. The education of the family lays chief stress on what Rosenkranz calls "*natürliche Pietät*," i. e., love and reverence for parents and blood-relatives, and obedience to elders—what the Romans called *pietas*, the affection and respect due to parents and departed ancestors; it expressed the piety of ancestor-worship, which is the oldest form of religion. (See Des Coulanges' *La Cité Antique.*) Rosenkranz says: "Education has always in view the production of spirit (*Geist*)—*Geist* being the technical term in Hegel's Philosophy for the social life of man in the institutions of civilization; *Geist* might here be translated 'civilization,' although its literal ordinary meaning is *spirit.*"]

§ 179. National education is divided into three special systems: (1) passive, (2) active, (3) individual. It begins with the humble attitude of an utter subjection to nature, and ends with the arrogance of an equally entire rejection of nature.

[Three systems of National education: (1) passive (China, India, Thibet); (2) active (Persia); (3) individual (Greece and Rome).]

§ 180. Man subjects himself at first to the natural authority of the family; he obeys unconditionally its behests. Then he substitutes for the family, as he goes on in his culture, the artificial family of his caste, to whose rules he again unconditionally yields. To relieve himself from this artificiality and this tyranny, at last he breaks away from the family and from the training that prepares him for family and caste. He flees from both, and, becoming a monk, he again subjects himself to the tyranny of his order. A monk presents to us only a specimen of his species—all are alike.

[(1) The passive. (a) Man begins in the humble attitude of subjection to Nature as it is found in the family: he obeys the authorities of the family implicitly. The Chinese state is founded on patriarchal rule. (b) The Indian civilization substitutes *caste* for family, and obeys its rules. (c) Then he revolts against the tyranny of caste, and subjects himself to a new tyranny, the rules of the cloister—the Buddhist civilization in its purest form. These phases of civilization will be treated in detail further on.]

§ 181. This absolute abstraction from nature and from education that fits one for life in family and caste, this quietism of spiritual isolation, is the ultimate result of the passive system. In opposition to this, the active system seeks the positive vanquishing of natural restraints. Its people are courageous. They attack other nations in order to rule over them as conquerors. They live for the continuation of their life after death, and for this purpose build for themselves tombs of granite. They brave the dangers of the sea. The unvaried prose of the patriarchal state, the fantastic dreamy reveries of the caste-state, the ascetic self-renunciation of the cloister-state, yield gradually to the recognition of the world of reality, and the fundamental principle of Persian education consisted in the inculcation of veracity.

[The passive system (1) results in quietism or the renunciation of activity and the adoption of a life of seclusion and meditation. We shall see (§ 184) the ground for this result: its view of the world and its relation to the Absolute Being explains the peculiarity of its civilization. (2) The active system directs itself against restraints thrust upon it by Nature. (a) The Persian strives to overcome limits and boundaries, and to extend his dominion over space. (See the peculiar ground for this in his religion, § 195). (b) The Egyptian civilization is directed toward a preparation for the life after death (see § 199). (c) The Phœnician braves the dangers of the sea. Note in § 197 the remarkable thought of Hegel on the contrast between the Persians and the Hindoos in respect to the education in telling the truth—"inculcation of veracity."]

§ 182. But the nationality which is occupied with simple, natural elements—other nations, death, the mystery of the ocean—may revert to the abstractions of the previous stage, which in education often takes on cruel forms—nay, often truly horrible. First, when spiritual being begins not only to suspect its nature, but rather to recognize itself as the true essence; and when the God of Light places as the motto on his temple the command to self-knowledge, the natural individuality becomes free. Neither the passive nor the active system permits the free self-distinction of the individual from his fellows. In them, to be an individuality is a betrayal of the very idea of their existence, and even the suspicion of such a thing is sufficient to destroy utterly and mercilessly the one to whom it refers. Even the solitary individuality of the despot is not the oneness of free individuality; but he is also only a specimen of his kind, although the only specimen. Nationality rises to individuality through the free dialectic of its component peoples, whereby it dissolves its presupposition, or the peculiarities that arise from limitations by alien nationalities.

[The defects and limits of the "active" systems—liable to revert to the abstractions of the passive systems, and take on cruel forms (Phœnician Moloch-fires, Egyptian slavery, Persian luxury, etc.). (3) The individual system is far in advance of the passive and active systems in the fact that it is based on a recognition of individuality in the divine, and hence permits itself to develop individuality in men. Apollo, the god of light, places the motto "Know thyself" over his temple at Delphi, and, under the inspiration of this command, the Greek people gradually free themselves from blind obedience to custom, and seek to find a necessity in reason for all things in nature and history. The later civilization borrows this from the Greeks, and also borrows the Greek idea of the beautiful. "The free dialectic of its component peoples," as in the Persian wars, gradually wears off, or dissolves the national peculiarities of the peoples around the Eastern Mediterranean, and develops them all toward the principle of individuality, which they enter at the time of the Alexandrian conquest.]

§ 183. Nevertheless, individuality must always proceed from natural conditions. Æsthetically it seeks nature, but nature in the form of living body, in order, by penetrating it with mind, to make of it a work of art; practically it seeks it, partly to disdain it in gloomy resignation, partly to enjoy it in revels of excessive sensuality, and to heighten the extravagance of its own internal morbid self-consciousness by cruel or shameless public spectacles.

The Germans were not savage in the common signification of this term. They were men each one of whom constituted himself willingly a center for others, or, if this was not the case, renounced them in proud self-sufficiency. All the glory and all the disgrace of our history lie in the power of individualizing which is divinely infused into our veins. As a natural element, if this be not controlled, it degenerates easily into intractableness, into violence. The Germans need, therefore, in order to be educated, severe discipline, the imposition of difficult tasks; and for this reason they attack such subjects as Roman law, Greek philology, Gallic usages, etc., in order to work off their superfluous strength. The natural love of independent individuality which characterized the German found its needed complement in Christianity. The history of the German race shows that it would have been destroyed by this extreme tendency toward individuality which led to minute political divisions and to weak political ties. The German people, full of faith in their own personal resources, ventured forth upon the sea, and managed their ships as skillful horsemen their chargers.

[Individuality, however, must always have a natural basis, for its differences will not be found in the common rational endowment of intellect and will. Hence it happens that we find the first nation that sets up individuality as its principle seeking it in the form of the beautiful as it shines through physical nature, especially in the human body. The second nation, the Roman, seeks individuality practically for epicurean enjoyment and sensuality, or for Stoic renunciation, setting up its natural individual self as a target for the universe. (These peculiarities will be explained in detail in §§ 203–225.) The German "abstract individualism" (treated in § 226), which is that of the love of isolated personal freedom, needs severe discipline (such as feudal vassalage) to educate it into the necessary feeling of dependence on society.]

CHAPTER II.

FIRST GROUP—THE SYSTEM OF PASSIVE EDUCATION.

§ 184. All education desires to free man from his finitude, to make him ethical, to unite him with God. It begins, therefore, with a negative relation to natural conditions, limits, and restraints, but at once falls into a contradiction of its aim, by converting this opposition to nature into a natural necessity. Spirit (that is to say, man acting in institutions) subjects the individual (1) to the rule of the family as the institution that is the closest approximation of nature; (2) to the rule of the caste as to a principle in itself spiritual, mediated through the division of labor, which it nevertheless, through the principle of hereditary descent, joins again to the family; (3) to the abstract self-determination of the monkish quietism, which turns itself away as well from the family as from work, and makes this flight from nature and human society, this absolute passivity, his educational ideal.

We shall not here enter into the details of these systems, but simply endeavor to make clear their distinctions and remove the vagueness which is generally found in the descriptions of them abounding in educational works, which employ the terms "hierarchical and theocratical education" without historical accuracy.

[The rational ground for the system of "passive education." It sets out to free man from thralldom to Nature, and hence assumes a "negative relation" toward "natural conditions," i. e., it refuses to permit the individual to give free rein to his animal impulses, but constrains him to obey the rules and regulations ordained for the establishment and preservation of institutions. *First*, the institution of the *family* is set up as the supreme object of life in China. *Secondly*, the division of labor (the vocations of life) is made the basis of caste, which is the chief concern of the Hindoo. Then the renunciation of all concrete life for the sake of monastic institutions is the requirement of the *third* species of "passive education," as found in Central Asia, and more or less in Ceylon and Farther India.]

I. *Family Education.*

§ 185. The family is the organic starting-point of all education. The nation looks upon itself as a family. Among all uncivilized people education is family education, though they are not conscious of its necessity. Identical in principle with these people, but distinguished from them through the fact that it is conscious of it, the Chinese nation, in its laws, regulations, and customs, has established the family as the absolute basis of its life, and the only principle of its education.

[The "organic starting-point of all education" is the family, that is to say, the family is the institution that most resembles a product of Nature; it arises through the natural relations of sex and parentage on the one hand, and through the necessary ethical laws that perfect and secure these natural relations on the other hand. The first form of the nation is a direct outgrowth of the family. The tribe is patriarchal in its organization. The first collection of tribes into a nation retains the same form. The Chinese nation (437,000,000 of people!) is a vast family of families. Mere tribes can not be civilized because they have to devote their entire attention to protecting their narrow borders from neighboring tribes. When these tribes are united into a great nation the border-land recedes, and all classes of people may devote themselves to productive industry.]

§ 186. The natural element of the family is found in marriage and kinship; the spiritual element, in love. We may call the nature of family feeling, which is the immediate unity of both elements, by the Latin name of *pietas*. In so far as this appears not merely as a substantial feeling, but at the same time as conscious rule of action, there arises from it the subordination involved in the implicit obedience of the wife to the husband, of children to the parents, of the younger children to the elder. In this obedience man first renounces his willfulness and his natural selfishness; he learns to master his passions, and to conduct himself with deferential gentleness.

When the principle that governs the family is transferred to political relations, there arises the tyranny of the Chinese state, which can not be fully treated here. We find everywhere in it an analogical relation to that of parents and children. In China the ruler is the father and mother of the people; the civil officers are representatives of a paternal authority, etc. It follows that in school the children will be ranked according to their age. The authority of parents over children is absolute, but its exercise is in point of fact very mild. The abandonment of daughters by the poorest classes in the great cities is no instance to the contrary, for the government rears the children in foundling asylums, where they are cared for by nurses appointed by the state.

[The family has a natural element and a spiritual element, (a) kinship by marriage and parentage; (b) love; (c) *pietas*, or affectionate loyalty to one's relatives is the unity of love and kinship. Obedience and providential care are the mutual duties arising out of the relation of subordination within the family.]

§ 187. These relations which are conditioned by nature take on the external shape of a definite ceremonial, the learning of which is a chief element of education. In conformity with the naturalness of the pervading principle all crimes against it are punished by whipping with the rod, which, however, does not entail dishonor. In order to lead man to self-control and to obedience to those who are naturally set over him, education develops an endless number of fragmentary maxims to keep his attention ever watchful over himself, and his behavior always fenced in by a code of prescriptions.

We find in such moral sentences the substance of what is called, in China, philosophy.

[The family preserves itself by a code of observances constituting a ceremonial or system of etiquette which forms the chief part of education. How to behave, is the important question. For details regarding the rules of etiquette in China, see Hegel's "Philosophy of History." Five mutual duties named in the Shu-King as fundamental, (1) between the emperor and his people; (2) between parents and children; (3) between elder and younger brothers; (4) between husband and wife; (5) between friend and friend. "The son may not accost the father when he comes into the room; he must seem to contract himself to nothing at the side of the door, and may not leave the room without his father's permission." The same obedience must be shown to the elder brother. The son does not receive honor for his meritorious deeds; they are attributed to his father. The school flourishes there because it is the road to all preferment in the state. The Chinese alphabet has a separate sign for each word, and has to be mastered by an enormous effort of the memory—ten thousand of these characters being necessary for graduating as a scribe. The primary reading-books are filled with maxims relating to etiquette and behavior, and have to be memorized, words, characters, and all. Strict examinations are held to sift out the incompetent and admit the competent to a higher course of study. The third grade of examination is held by the chancellor of the province twice in three years, and successful candidates receive the degree of Blooming Talent (*B. T.*, instead of *B. A.!*), and are qualified for primary teachers, lawyers, notaries public, or physicians. The fourth examination is held at the capital of the province and under the direction of two imperial examiners sent from Pekin. In some instances as many as twenty thousand "blooming talents" attend this examination, but only one in a hundred of the candidates is successful in obtaining the degree of "Licentiate." The licentiates may enter the fifth and highest examination held in the Imperial Palace at Pekin, and if they pass are entitled at once to membership in the Imperial Academy and a salary for life. This academy furnishes committees of counsel to whom the emperor refers all difficult matters for consideration and report. These five sifting examinations have at last obtained as net result the men best fitted of all for carrying on the Chinese government in the prescribed path, for they have had not only to learn by heart the five classics of Confucius, filled with maxims of family piety and patriarchal etiquette, but they have had to prove in the final examination that they understand and are able to defend the doctrines on which the government is founded. In the first and second examinations only verbal memory is tested and no insight required. The minute details of Chinese education are of importance to us as proving clearly the function of the exclusive education of the memory. Conservative people without aspiration and firmly bound to the established order of things can be produced without fail by schools that lay great stress on verbal memory (e. g., "learning by heart" the capricious orthography of the English spelling-book, historical dates, geographical names, arithmetical tables, etc., etc.).]

§ 188. The theoretical education includes reading, writing—i. e., painting the letters with a brush—arithmetic, and the making of verses. But these accomplishments are not looked at as means of culture, but as qualifications for official position. The Chinese possess formally all the means for literary culture—printing, libraries, schools, and academies; but the extent to which these appliances are used is not great. Their value has been often overrated because of their external resemblance to those found among us.

[The effort requisite to learn the Chinese alphabet is sufficient to commit to memory all the Chinese classics. Hence, the library is not so important in that country as in Europe and America, where one may learn to read with so little trouble. Hence, too, the obstacle in the way of original literary production.]

II. *Caste Education.*

§ 189. The members of the family, as a matter of course, differ from each other in sex and age, but this difference is entirely immaterial as far as the nature of their employment goes. In China, therefore, every position is open to each man; he who is of humblest birth in the great state-family can climb to the highest honor. But the next step in the development of the state, as an institution, is that on which the division of labor is made the principle, and a new distinction added to that of the family: each one shall perfect himself only in that labor which was allotted to him as his own through his birth into a particular family. This fatalism (the distinction of caste) breaks up the life, but increases the social tension, by the necessary mutual dependence that flows from the division of labor; for human civilization moves on the one hand toward the deepening of its distinctions; on the other, toward leading them back into the unity which continually works against the natural tendency to fix human activity in ruts.

[Distinction of caste imposes a new yoke on the individual. The highest preferment is not open to each as in the family state; in India, the station of life is absolutely determined by birth. If born a Brahman, he may be a religious teacher, and the object of unbounded reverence on the part of the other castes. There are warriors and merchants and common laborers, besides many mixed castes founded on intermarriages. The members of the lowest castes are far more degraded and brutally treated than the negro slaves of the West India Islands.]

§ 190. The chief work of education thus consists in teaching each one the rights and duties of his caste so that he shall observe their precise limits, and not pollute himself by passing beyond them. As the family-state concerns itself with fortifying the distinctions founded on nature by a far-reaching and vigorous ceremonial, so the caste-state must do the same with the distinctions of caste. A painful etiquette becomes more and more exacting in its requisitions, the higher the caste, in order to make the isolation more sharply defined and more perceptible.

This feature penetrates all exclusively caste-education. All aristocracy exiles itself on this account from its native country, speaks a foreign language and loves its literature, adopts foreign customs, lives in foreign countries—in Italy, Paris, etc. In this way man becomes "distinguished." But that he should strive thus to "distinguish" himself has its ultimate ground in the accident of his birth, and this is assuredly always the principle of the caste-state in which it is to be found in its most perfect form. The castes require genealogical records, which are of the greatest importance in determining the destiny of the individual. The Brahman may strike dead one of a lower caste who has defiled him by contact, without becoming thereby liable to punishment; he would be regarded as criminal, in fact, if he neglected to kill him. Thus it was formerly with the officer who did not immediately kill the citizen or common soldier who struck him a blow.

[Education consists chiefly in teaching the etiquette and ceremonies proper to one's caste. To omit one of these observances is to become defiled, and requires a complicated ceremony of purification. The Chinese etiquette is very simple compared with that of India: "The Brahman must rest on a particular foot when rising; read the Vedas, each word separately, or doubling them alternately, or forward and backward; must not look at the sun when rising or setting, nor at its reflection in the water; must not step over a rope at which a calf is fastened, nor go out when it rains; must not look at his wife when she eats, or when she sneezes; must not step on ashes, cotton-seeds, or broken crockery," etc., etc. One of the lowest caste may be struck dead if he comes in the way of a Brahman; if he hears the Vedas read, he must have melted lead poured into his ears, etc.]

§ 191. The East Indian education is far deeper and richer than the Chinese. Its theoretical instruction also includes reading, writing, and arithmetic; but these are subordinate, as mere means for the higher activities of poetry, speculation, science, and art. The practical education limits itself strictly by the lines of caste, and since the caste system constitutes a whole in itself, and each for its permanence needs the others, it can not forbear giving utterance suggestively to what is universally human in the soul, in a multitude of fables (Hitopadesa) and apothegms (sentences of Bartrihari), especially intended for the education of princes, and furnishing a sort of mirror of the world.

Xenophon's Cyropedia is not Greek but Indian in its plan.

[The Brahman caste may be said to be devoted to religious literature and worship. Through them have arisen epic and dramatic poems, systems of philosophy, science, and art. The Hitopadesa is the Indian Æsop, and contains a multitude of fables for the instruction of the sons of a king. They are ingeniously interwoven. The animals of one fable relate other fables. The pigeon relates to the crow the fable of the tiger and the traveler; the king of the mice relates the fable of the deer, the jackal, and the crow; the crow relates the fable of the blind vulture, the cat, and the birds, etc.]

III. *Monkish Education.*

§ 192. Family education demands unconditional obedience toward parents and toward all who stand in an analogous position. Caste-education demands unconditional obedience to the duties of the caste. The family punishes with the rod; the caste, by excommunication, by loss of honor. The negative tendency against nature appears in both systems in the form of a strict ceremonial, distinguishing between the differences arising from nature. The family as well as the caste has within it a fountain of manifold activity, but it has also just as manifold a limitation of the individual. The impulse toward higher civilization is forced, therefore, to turn against nature in general. It must become indifferent to the family. But it must also oppose the social order, and the fixed distinctions of division of labor as necessitated by nature. It must become indifferent to labor and the fruits derived from it. That it may not be conditioned either by nature or by human civilization, it denies both, and makes its action to consist in producing an abstinence from all action.

[Monkish education "turns against nature" altogether, and does not, like the family and the caste, lay emphasis on differences arising from nature (such as sex, age, birth, hereditary descent, etc.). Labor, and even the fruits of labor, are a matter of indifference to it. The activity of Buddhism is directed toward abstention from activity. Here the passive education culminates.]

§ 193. Such an indifference toward nature and the social order produces the education which we have called monkish. Those who perpetuate the race, care for food, clothing, and shelter, and for these material contributions, as the laity, receive in return from those who live this contemplative life the spiritual reward of participation in the blessings which wait upon ascetic contemplation. The family institution as well as the institution of human labor is subordinated to the abstract isolation of the cloister, in which the individual lives only for the purification of his soul. All things are justified by this end. Castes are found no more; only those are bound to the observance of a special ceremonial who as nuns or monks subject themselves to unconditional obedience to the rules of the cloister, these rules solemnly enjoining on the negative side celibacy and cessation from business, and on the positive side prayer and performance of ceremonial rites.

[Such a system requires a distinction of the people into laity and monks. For with Buddhist monks alone the race would soon perish. The laity supply the material wants of the monks, and keep up the race. The dreadful oppression of ceremonial which prevails in Chinese etiquette and Hindoo observance of caste is avoided in Buddhism. All is simplified. There are three hundred million Buddhists scattered over China, Farther India, Ceylon, and among the Mongolians of Siberia. In China Buddhism takes on an essentially modified form; it does not replace the family principle as in Thibet.]

§ 194. In the school of the Chinese Tao-tse, and in the command to the Brahman after he has established a family to become a hermit, we find the transition as it actually exists to the Buddhistic quietism which has covered the rocky heights of Thibet with countless cloisters, and reared the people who are dependent upon it into a child-like amiability, into a contented repose. Art and science have here no value in themselves, and are regarded only as ministering to religion. To be able to read, in order to mutter the prayers, is desirable.

With the conscious purpose of the monk to reduce self to nothing, as the highest good, the system of passive education attains its highest point. But civilization can not content itself with this abstract and dreamy absence of all action, though it demands a high stage of culture; it has recourse therefore to action, partly on the positive side to conquer nature, partly to double its own existence by building up human institutions. Inspired with affirmative courage, it descends triumphantly from the mountain-heights, and fears secularization no more.

[In Thibet every father who has four sons must dedicate one of them to monastic life. The supreme object of life among the Buddhists where Lamaism prevails—for Lamaism is a political form, not at all coextensive with Buddhism as a religion—is to attain the elevated spiritual condition of the monastic order. Failing in this highest object, the people strive to share in the divine favors dispensed or obtained by the priests. The Buddhistic view of the world is in sharp contrast with the Christian view, although its monasticism as well as its ceremonial has a close external resemblance to the forms of the Catholic Church; and, in fact, Lamaism may have borrowed its ceremonial from Eastern Christians in the eighth century or later. The Buddhist seeks *nirvana*, or the absolute repose of being; a state in which he is freed not only from all earthly cares and distracting thoughts, but also from all cares and thoughts of whatever description. In fact, while Christianity seeks deliverance from selfishness, Buddhism seeks deliverance from selfhood, and aims to lose all consciousness, as the Sankhya doctrine of India, which is apparently the root of Buddhist theology, plainly teaches. In this respect the "passive" education comes most strongly into contrast with the "active" education. The former seeks to free itself from evil by passively renouncing not only all action, but life itself. The latter strives to conquer evil by action, and educates to a life which helps itself by helping others.]

CHAPTER III.

SECOND GROUP.—THE SYSTEM OF ACTIVE EDUCATION.

§ 195. Active education elevates man from his complete subjection to the family, caste, and asceticism, into a concrete activity guided by a definite aim which subordinates those institutions into means of its own development, and grants to each independence on condition of its perfect accord with the spirit of the whole. These aims are the military state, the future condition after death, and industry. There is always an element of nature present, which gives occasion to the activity; but this no longer appears, like the family, the caste, the egoistic personal seclusion of the cloister, as immediately dwelling within the individual, but as something outside of himself which limits him; and yet, as his destined career has an internal relation to him, is essential to him and assigns to him the object of his activity. The Persian has for his object of conquest, other nations; the Egyptian, death; the Phœnician, the sea.

[Active education in contrast to passive education directs its efforts outward with a view to accomplish some new conquest. Passive education was conservative, and aimed to crush out individuality by imposing on it burdensome codes of etiquette, ceremonies, and moral order. Active education has the opposite tendency. The Persian strives to prepare his youth for military conquest. The Phœnician educates for foreign commerce, the perils of the sea and hostile lands. The Egyptian makes this life a preparation for immortality, building gigantic tombs, and embalming the corporeal hull of the soul, so that it may serve its purpose again at the resurrection.]

I. *Military Education.*

§ 196. That education which would emancipate a nation from the passivity of isolation and one-sided development must throw it into a process of intercourse with other forms of civilization. A nation does not find its real limits in its territorial boundaries; it can leave its habitat and seek a new and distant one. Its true limit is made by another nation. The nation which feels its own genuine substantiality turns itself therefore against other nations in order to subject them and to reduce them to the condition of mere accidents of itself as substance. It begins a system of conquest which has in itself no limitations, but goes from one nation to another, and extends its course indefinitely. The final result of this attack on other nations is that it combines them against it, and is in its turn invaded and conquered.

The early history of the Persian is twofold: the patriarchal in the high valleys of Iran, and the religio-hierarchical among the Medes. We find under these circumstances a repetition of the principal characteristics of the Chinese, Indian, and Buddhist education; even the Indian is included, because in ancient Zend there were also castes. Among the Persians themselves, as they descended from their mountains to the conquest of other nations, there was properly only a military nobility. The priesthood was subjected to the royal power which represented the concrete might of the nation. Of the Persian kings, Cyrus attacked Western Asia; Cambyses, Africa; Darius and Xerxes, Europe; until at last the reaction of the spiritually higher nationality of Greece did not content itself with mere self-protection, but under the Macedonian Alexander returned the attack upon Persia itself.

[Intercourse with foreign nations is the prime source of national activity. The Persian desires to establish an unconditioned empire. To do this he must reduce to submission the tribes and states that border on his frontier. Out of the Euphrates Valley in earlier times the Chaldeans and Assyrians had made inroads upon the separate branches of the Aryan race, which are now united and form the Persian Empire. On the north and east the Mongolian tribes menaced the peace of his border-land. Under Cyrus the valley of the Euphrates, and later, all Syria and Asia Minor are subdued; under Cambyses, Egypt. But the Persian can not annihilate border-lands, although he removes them thousands of miles from his capital. Beyond Asia lies Europe. Greece contains another Aryan people in whom are beginning the impulses toward a new civilization far more favorable to individual development than anything that has yet appeared. Darius and Xerxes attempt to conquer this new limit, but fail at last. Greece, aroused by the contest, and learning to know its own power, returns the attack in the following century, and all the territory that Persia had conquered yields to Alexander and his generals.]

§ 197. Education enjoined upon the Persians (1) to speak the truth; (2) to learn to ride horseback, and to use the bow and arrow. There is implied in the first command a recognition and acknowledgment of the reality of things and events, the negation of all dreamy absorption, of all fantastical vagueness; and in this light the Persian, in contrast with the Hindoo, appears to be sober and reasonable. In the second command is implied warlike practice, but as yet that of the nomadic tribes. The Persian fights on horseback, and thus appears in contrast to the Indian hermit-seclusion and the quietism of the Lamas as restless and in constant motion.

The family increases in value as it rears a large number of warriors. To have many children was a blessing. The King of Persia gave a premium for all children over a certain number. Nations were assembled as nations for war; hence the immense multitude of a Persian army. Everything—family, business, possessions—must be regardlessly sacrificed to the one aim of war. Education, therefore, cultivated an unconditional obedience to the king; the slightest inclination to assert an individual independence was high treason and was punished with death. In China, on the contrary, duty to the family is paramount to duty to the state, or rather is itself duty to the state. The civil officer who mourns the loss of one of his family is released during the period of mourning from the duties of his function.

[The education of the Persians is said to have laid great stress on (1) speaking truth, and (2) learning to ride horseback, and use the bow and arrow. To speak the truth implies a respect for the facts and events of the world as they are. Under the passive peoples there prevailed a greater respect for human ordinances, etiquette, caste, etc. The Hindoo looked upon all nature as pure illusion—a sort of dream which is imposed upon man because of his fallen condition. East Indian poetry gives rein to the imagination, and allows truth to interpose no limits to its exaggerations. Hence truth-speaking seems to have great significance. It could not be encouraged among people who despised real facts and events and held in contempt all existence. We must not, however, count the civilizations of Brahminism and Buddhism as of no value. They are immense steps in advance of mere tribal civilization. In his first step away from mere savage life man exaggerates the importance of ethical usages and despises in a corresponding degree the facts and events of Nature. In mere tribal life the savage fears Nature, and has no peace from its inconstancy and dreadful might. After long progress he comes to revere human social order as superior. The members of the family are supplemented and rendered equal by mutual help, so that infancy, old age, sickness, calamity, and sex are robbed of their special terrors. The state performs a similar service in insuring the individual against vicissitude, and especially against violence from mankind. Civil society protects the individual from famine, in case of failure of crops in one particular locality. But notwithstanding the importance of social order, the nations of Eastern Asia go to extremes in their reverence for it. The Western Asiatic nations, whom Rosenkranz calls "active nations," correct this one-sidedness in various ways. The Persian trained his youth carefully in observing accurately the exact state of facts and events by insisting on scrupulous statements. He taught him to ride horseback and use the bow and arrow. Here the state as such became the most important institution, whereas in China the family, in India the divisions of civil society, in Thibet the church, were most important.]

§ 198. The theoretical education, which was limited to reading, writing, and to instruction in religious ceremonial, was in the hands of the magi, the number of whom was estimated at eighty thousand, and who themselves had enjoyed the advantages of a careful education, as is shown by their gradation into *Herbeds*, *Mobeds*, and *Destur-mobeds*, i. e., into apprentices, journeymen, and masters. The very fundamental idea of their religion was military; it demanded of man to fight on the side of the king of light, and guard against the princes of darkness and evil. It gave to him the honor of a free position between the world-moving powers and thus the possibility of a self-chosen career, by which means vigor and chivalrous feeling were developed. Religion directed the activity of man toward the realities on this planet, making it its object to increase the dominion of the good, by purifying the water, by planting trees, by extirpating troublesome wild beasts. Thus it increased bodily comfort, and no longer, like the monk, treated this as a mere negative affair.

[The Magi, a separate tribe, said to number eighty thousand, furnished the teachers of reading, writing, and religion. They had three degrees of advancement in culture among them—apprentice, journeyman, and master (*Herbed*, *Mobed*, and *Destur-mobed*). The religion of China has a family character—the worship of ancestors; the religion of Old Persia has a character tending to promote the interests of the state—a military tendency. Ahura-Mazda (Ormuzd), the good spirit, fights against Angra-Mainya (Ahriman), the evil spirit. The Persian religion teaches that life is a warfare, and that all good men must fight on the side of Ormuzd, the king of light. It was enjoined by religion to conquer the desert by planting trees and digging wells and increasing bodily comfort. This is in contrast to the spirit of Buddhism.]

II. *Priestly Education.*

§ 199. War achieves its purpose through its capacity to inflict death. It deals out death, and by its means decides who shall serve and who obey. But the nation that finds its activity in war, though it makes death the servant of its purpose, yet finds its own limit in death. Other nations are only its boundaries, which it can pass over by fighting with and conquering them. But death itself it can never escape, whether it come in the sands of the desert—that buried for Cambyses an army which he sent to the oracle of the Libyan Ammon—or in the sea, that scorns the rod * of the angry despot, or by the sword of the free man † who guards his household gods. On this account, a people stands higher that in the midst of life reflects on death, or rather lives for it. The education of such a nation must be priestly, because death is the means of the transition to the future life, and consequently it, like birth, becomes a sacrament. The family-state, the caste-state, the monkish-state, and the military-state are not hierarchies in the sense that the national life is directed by a priesthood. But in Egypt this was actually the case, because the chief educational tribunal was the death-court which judged only the dead, awarding to them or denying them the honor of burial as the result of their whole life. Its award, however, affected also the honor of the surviving family.

[War is directed against the limits of national sovereignty. Death is a natural limit to life. War succeeds because it deals out death to the enemy. While the Persian directs his energies

* Xerxes ordered the Hellespont to be scourged with rods because his bridge was broken by the waves.

† Say, at Marathon, Salamis, and Thermopylæ.

against the limit of the state, the Egyptian occupies himself with the consideration of the supreme limit of life itself. The leading idea of Egyptian civilization seems to be the preparation for death. The death-court that decided upon the merits of the life of each individual at his decease furnished the most important educative influence in the land. It established an ideal standard of living and gave daily illustrations of its application to particular examples. Those who approximated this ideal were awarded the honor of being embalmed—they were considered fit to dwell with Osiris in the "still kingdom of Amenti." The priestly caste in Egypt were the teachers.]

§ 200. General education here limited itself to reading, writing, and arithmetic. Special education consisted properly only in training the youth for a definite vocation within the circle of the family. In this fruitful and warm land the expense of supporting children was very small. The division into classes was without the cruel features of the Indian civilization, and life itself in the narrow valley of the Nile was very social, abounding in festivities, and in eating and drinking, and was brave and cheerful, because the familiarity with death heightened the force of enjoyment. In a stricter sense only, the warriors, the priests, and the kings had an education. The aim of life, which was to determine at death its eternal future, to secure for itself a passage into the still kingdom of Amenti, manifested itself externally in the care which they expended on the preservation of the dead hull of the immortal soul, and on this account devoted its temporal life to building tombs to last an eternity. The Chinese builds a wall to secure his family-state from attack; the Hindoo builds pagodas for his gods; the Buddhist erects for himself monastic cells; the Persian constructs in Persepolis the tomb of his kings, where they may retire in the evening of their lives after they have rioted in Ecbatana, Babylon, and Susa; but the Egyptian builds his own tomb, and carries on war only to protect it.

[The Egyptian finds it possible to conquer Nature and make it serve him. He builds canals and dikes to regulate the overflow of the Nile, and thereby get the utmost service from the fertilizing power of the fine soil that the river brings down to him from the mountains at the south. Observation of Nature, necessary for the purpose of utilizing the Nile freshets, leads him to a knowledge of astronomy, the construction of calendars, and to hydraulic engineering. He understands irrigation, the construction of canals, dams, and reservoirs. He invents the science of geometry, so far as it is required in surveying, because he has to recover his farm every year after the inundation, and fix anew its boundaries. Farms on the banks of the river are liable to be washed away by new channels cut through by freshets, or the old landmarks may be covered up or destroyed; hence he is led to a more careful system of laws on the subject of landed property, the rights and privileges appertaining to its use and its ownership. Egypt invents writing by hieroglyphics, and develops out of it two other systems, the syllabic and alphabetic. The priestly caste taught arithmetic, geometry, surveying and mensuration, civil engineering, reading and writing and music to youth of their own caste as well as to the caste of warriors. Plato, however, tells us that the children of the Egyptians were taught to read in classes. Diodorus says that even the artisans were taught to read. Perhaps this was necessary to the numerous artisans who engraved inscriptions on the temples and tombs. We learn that arithmetic was taught by means of games and plays, such as trading pieces of money, guessing at the number of grains of wheat held in the hand, or by arranging pupils in military lines. The cost of living was so cheap that four dollars in our money would have supported a single individual until twenty years of age.]

III. *Industrial Education.*

§ 201. The system of active education was to find its solution in a nation which wandered from the coast of the Red Sea to the foot of the Lebanon Mountains on the Mediterranean, and ventured forth upon the sea which before that time all nations had avoided as a dangerous and destructive element. The Phœnician was industrial, and needed markets where he could dispose of the products of his skill. But while he sought for them he disdained neither force nor deceit: he planted colonies; he stipulated that he should have in the cities of other nations quarters for himself; he induced the nations to adopt articles of luxury, and insensibly introduced among them his culture and even his religion. The education of such a nation must have seemed profane, because it fostered indifference toward family and one's native land, and made restless and even passionate activity subservient to gain. The practical understanding and utilitarianism rose to a high dignity.

[The Phœnician resembles the other active peoples in having for his supreme aim the conquest of a limit to his being. Industry aims to conquer Nature in so far as it limits our lives in the form of three wants—food, clothing, and shelter. In order to overcome these completely, man must lay under contribution all lands and all climates. One locality compensates for the deficiencies of another. Commerce, then, is the form of industry that aids most effectively the conquest over Nature. The Phœnician leaves his home and braves the ocean. Education must be of such a character that it will wean the youth from love of home. Tyre, Sidon, Byblus, Berytus, Tripolis, Aradis, were places of great security on the land side, while they afforded security for shipping on the seaward side. Manufactures of metallic goods, glass, linen textures dyed with the wonderful Tyrian purple, furnished the home productions with which to obtain the coveted articles of foreign peoples. Tin from Cornwall, amber from the Baltic, gold-dust from Western Africa, were brought home and used in manufactures. Trains of loaded camels pierced the deserts and arrived at the great cities on the Euphrates. Phœnician colonies settled Cyprus, Crete, Carthage,

Gades (Cadiz). The Phœnician carried the alphabetic writing of Egypt to all parts of Europe, for in commerce writing is indispensable.]

§ 202. Of the education of the Phœnicians we know only so much as to enable us to conclude that it was certainly various and extensive: among the Carthaginians, at least, that their children were practiced in reading, writing, and arithmetic, in religious duties; secondly, in a trade; and, finally, in the use of arms. Commerce became with the Phœnicians their chief occupation, and self-interest made them brave to plow the inhospitable sea and, led by curiosity, penetrate the horror of its vast distances, but yet conceal from other nations their discoveries and wrap them in a veil of fable.

It is a beautiful testimony to the quality of the Greek mind that Plato and others assign as a cause of the low state of arithmetic and mathematics among the Phœnicians and Egyptians the want of free and disinterested investigation.

[Education assumes a utilitarian character for a commercial people—especially arithmetic and penmanship form the commercial arts. Inasmuch as affection for home and parents would injure the quality of the sailor, education rooted out this affection. The fearful worship of Moloch, the fire-god, to whom they sacrificed children, laying them in his red-hot arms in the presence of mothers who were not permitted to express their pain by cries was a powerful means of educating parental and filial indifference necessary to produce a population of commercial adventurers. Their religious rites thus assisted to form the national character. Not only arithmetic and writing, but cunning and deceit were taught, as necessary for skillful bargains.]

CHAPTER IV.

THIRD GROUP.—THE SYSTEM OF INDIVIDUAL EDUCATION

§ 203. One-sided passivity as well as one-sided activity is subsumed under individuality, which makes itself into its own end and aim. The Phœnician made gain his aim; his activity was of a utilitarian character. Individuality as an educational principle is indeed selfish in so far as it endeavors to cultivate its own peculiarity, but it is at the same time noble. It desires not to *have*, but to *be*. Individuality also begins in what is natural, but it elevates nature by means of art to ideality. The principle of beauty gives place to the principle of culture, which renounces the charm of appearance for the knowledge of the true. The æsthetic individuality is followed by the practical, which has no longer any basis in natural relations, but proceeds from an artificial basis —a state formed for a place of refuge. In order to create an internal unity in this, a definite code of laws is framed; in order to assure its external safety, the invincible warrior is demanded. Education is therefore, more exactly speaking, training in juristic and military affairs. The morality of the state is undermined as it brings into its mechanism one nation after another, until it encounters an individuality, become dæmonic, which makes its war-hardened legions tremble with weakness. We characterize this individuality as dæmonic because it desires recognition simply for its own sake. Not for its beauty and culture, not for its knowledge of business and its bravery, only for its peculiarity as such does it claim value, and in the effort to secure this it is ready to hazard life itself. In its naturally growing existence this individuality is deep, but at the same time without self-limit. The nations educate themselves to this individuality when they destroy the Roman world—that of self-limit and balance—which they find.

[Individuality contains both passivity and activity. Rosenkranz understands by "individual education" that education which has for its sole aim the development of the individual, instead of seeking an external object for which it subordinates the individual. It desires not to *have*, but to *be*. The phases of "individual" education are three: (*a*) æsthetic education, which seeks to make a work of art out of man; it develops into a love of truth, and finally sets aside *seeming* for *being;* (*b*) practical education, that of Rome, deals not with the beautiful nor with the true, but with the realization of the will in its essence. The will of man is not revealed in caprice and arbitrariness, nor in mere customary usages. The essential forms are embodied in laws of justice and in rights. For these express what is and may be universal—the common ground of all particular volitions. Violate the law, and each man's deed is against the deeds of all other men. Without law the aggregate action of man tends toward self-nullification. The Roman principle in the world-history concerns the discovery and enunciation of the just self-limitation of will, and it has bequeathed to the world the code of laws and forms of municipal government which make possible modern civilization. The Greek has left us the ideal standard of the beautiful and the statement of the true, as well as the form of its investigation. Each of these activities involves the culture of the individual: (a) the graceful body; (b) the developed intellect; (c) the formation of character. The Greek individuality is undermined by the discovery of the principle of truth as higher than beauty. The Roman principle is undermined by the conquest of all nations; its success destroys it by removing the tension which had existed against other nations, and which had helped it to form the Roman character. It now encounters the third phase of individuality—that of the Gothic or Teutonic nations. These northern peoples do not make special individuality their object either in the form of the beautiful, of the true, or of the firm and just character. They make general individuality their object, without any special aims, or with any and all aims. Individuality of this sort is called "dæmonic" by Rosenkranz, because it does not consider any other motives than recognition of the peculiar self of the individual, counting as naught all possessions, wisdom, justice, sacred ordinances, and demanding recognition solely. This trait of the Gothic race reappears always when its individuals settle on a border-land or resort to partisan warfare. The chieftains of the Scottish border-land, the Norse sea-kings, the Crusaders, the knights of Charlemagne, the Cid—even the "cow-boy" desperadoes of our own border-land—exhibit this supreme love of individuality for its own sake. Rome conquered the northern peoples, and then taught them civil law and military tactics. They then assumed the mastership of the world, and modern history begins.]

I. *Æsthetic Education.*

§ 204. The system of individual education begins with the transfiguration of the immediate individuality into beauty. On the side of nature this system is passive, for individuality is given through nature; but on the side of spirit it is active, for spirit must determine to restrain itself within limits as the essence of beauty.

[Æsthetic individuality involves a passive side, in so far as it presupposes the body as an organic product of nature. It proceeds to cultivate its natural gifts by training through gymnastics, and this is its active side. Self-control, manifested physically, produces what we call gracefulness, and gracefulness is the Greek ideal of beauty. It may be defined as the bodily manifestation of freedom. Every limb of a Greek statue seems to be posed as it is because the soul within thus wills it. "Self-limitation" is a characteristic of Greek character—moderation, the golden mean, being its manifestation.]

§ 205. Here the individual is of value only in so far as he is beautiful. At first beauty is apprehended as natural, but secondly it is carried over into the realm of spirit (i. e., into the institutions of civilization), and the good is posited as identical with the beautiful. The ideal of æsthetic education demands always that there shall be also an *external* unity of the good with the beautiful, of spirit with Nature.

We can not here give in detail the history of Greek education. It is the best known among us, and the literature in which it is worked out is very extensive. . . . We must content ourselves with mentioning the chief epochs which follow from the nature of its principle.

[The beautiful was first realized in the living bodies of athletes (the "natural" phase of the beautiful). In the next place it was realized in social forms, civil and political. The "natural" phase of the beautiful was developed in the games. There were the great national games: the Olympian, celebrated once in four years; the Isthmian, once in two years; the Nemean, once in two years; the Pythian, once in four years; so that nearly every year there was a great national celebration in which it was determined who of all Greece should carry off the prize at wrestling, boxing, and throwing the discus, the spear, or the javelin; who could excel at running, leaping, the chariot-race, or the horseback-race. The preparation for these great national festivals took place in every village in the land every week and every day. The daily labor for the necessities of life was all well enough, but the Greek considered games of far greater importance. Games were in fact his highest religious ceremonies. For he believed that his gods were supremely beautiful human forms, in whose likeness human beings were intended to be. The games were instituted to celebrate this likeness of man to the gods as well as to develop and increase this likeness. The people attended these games and in time each and all became good judges of what is beautiful and graceful in human form just as a community that attends horse-races comes to know at a glance the good points of a horse. Neighboring villages unite for more general games on special occasions. Then the entire state has its festival. The victors in each state go up to those great national games founded by heroes and demi-gods in order to decide their relative claims for the leadership. Among a people thus educated as to the living work of art, it became possible for such artists to arise as Phidias, Polycletus, and Praxiteles. Their works could be appreciated as never since. The perfection in form and gracefulness of carriage reached by the victors in the games are fixed for eternity in shapes of stone, and no one is considered fully educated in any civilized land until he knows something about the Greek ideal of the beautiful. Greek education has thus resulted in preparing for us one phase of the world-education. The statues of gods and demigods that have come down to us cause our unbounded astonishment at their perfection of form. It is not their resemblance to living bodies, not their anatomical exactness that interests us, nor their so-called "truth to nature," but their gracefulness and serenity, their "classic repose." Whether these statues represent gods and heroes in action or in sitting and reclining postures, there is ever present this "repose," which means *indwelling vital* activity, and not mere rest as opposed to movement. They are full of movement, though at rest, and full of repose when in violent action. In their activity they manifest considerate purpose and perfect self-control. The repose is of the soul and not a physical repose. Even sitting and reclining figures—for example, the so-called Theseus from the Parthenon, or the torso of the Belvedere—are replete with will-power in every limb, so that the repose is seen to be voluntary self-restraint, and not the repose which accompanies the absence of vital energy.]

§ 206. Education was in Greece thoroughly national. Education gave to the individual the consciousness that he was a Greek and no barbarian, a free man, and so subject only to the laws of the state, and not to the caprice of any one person. Thus the nationality was freed at once from the despotic unity of the family and from the exclusiveness of caste, through the fact that it combined within itself the manifold talents of individuals of different races. Thus the Dorian race held as essential, gymnastics; the Æolians, music; the Ionians, poetry. The Æolian individuality was absorbed in the development of the two others, and the latter unfolded an internal antagonism. The education of the Dorian race was national education in the fullest sense of the word; in it a uniform public education was given to all in common, even including the young women; among the Ionic race it was also in its subjects taught truly national, but in its form it was select and private for those belonging to various great families and clans. The former, reproducing the Oriental phase of abstract unity, educated all in one mold; the latter was the nursery of particular individualities.

[Greek education gave the individual the consciousness of freedom from the despotism of arbitrary will. The laws were the will for all. Neither family nor caste prevailed over the individual. Since the Amphictyonic League united the different Greek states without consolidating them, the distinctions of individuality were preserved. While the Dorian races (of Sparta, Argos, and Messenia) held to gymnastics almost exclusively, the Æolians (of Bœotia and Thessaly) cultivated music as of equal importance, and the Ionians (of Athens and the islands of the Archipelago) included poetry as especially essential. The Dorians tended toward the Persian form of Orientalism, educating all in one mold and repressing individualism. But, as the main object of its education was individualism, it contradicted itself by forcing all into one type. Especially in Athens we find the nursery of individuality in all its peculiarity.]

§ 207. (1) Education in the heroic age was without any systematic arrangement, and left each one perfectly free. They told the histories of the adventures of other heroes, and by their own deeds gave material for similar histories to others.

The Greeks began where the last stage of the active system of education ended—with piracy and the seizure of women. Swimming was a universal practice among the sea-dwelling Greeks, just as in

England—the mistress of the ocean—rowing is the most prominent exercise among the students, and for its encouragement public regattas are held.

[In the heroic age education fitted the individual for adventures, chiefly in the interest of the welfare of Hellas, however. Surrounding peoples were called "barbarians," and were thought to possess no rights that the Greek was bound to respect. The heroes belong to the maritime states, and are associated with adventures on the sea. Hercules, who seems to have been suggested by the Phœnician Melkarth, is of a more humane type than the Phœnician educational ideal. There is a trace of a sun-myth in his twelve labors, showing Oriental origin, and doubtless the hero is a reminiscence, through several modifications, of the hero Izdubar and the famous god Mar-duk of the Euphrates Valley (the great "Tower of Babel" was dedicated to Mar-duk).]

§ 208. (2) In the period of state-education proper, education developed itself systematically; and gymnastics, music, and grammatics, or literary culture, constituted the general pedagogical elements.

[Besides gymnastics and music, grammatics, or study of letters and literature, is named as an element of the later education.]

§ 209. Gymnastics aimed not alone to render the body strong and agile, but, far more, to produce in it a noble carriage, a dignified and graceful manner of appearance. Each one fashioned his body into a living, divine statue, and in the public games the nation crowned the victor.

(Note on the Greek relation of ἀἴτης and εἰσπνήλας here omitted.)

[Objects aimed at in gymnastics. See commentary on §§ 204 and 205.]

§ 210. It was the task of music, by its rhythm and measure, to fill the soul with well-proportioned harmony. So highly did the Greeks prize music, and so variously did they practice it, that to be a musical man meant the same with them as to be a cultivated man with us.

Education in this branch was very painstaking, inasmuch as music exercises a very powerful influence in developing discreet behavior and self-possession into a graceful naturalness.

Among the Greeks we find a spontaneous delight in Nature—a listening to her voices, the tone of which reveals the internal qualities of things. In comparison with this tender sympathy of the Greeks with Nature—who heard in the murmur of the fountains, in the dashing of the waves, in the rustling of the trees, and in the cry of animals, the voice of divine personality—the sight and hearing of the Oriental people for Nature is dull.

[Music expressed to the ear what gracefulness did to the eye—a sense of rhythm. Rhythm is appearance of an internal measure, a principle that regulates and harmonizes external appearance. The Greek temple was a petrified hymn to the gods (Goethe said that architecture is "frozen music"). Music did not have the narrow meaning that it possesses in our language. It referred to the nine Muses and to all rhythmical culture. In Hegel's "Philosophy of History" is found the most wonderful characterization of the Greeks. The ear with which they listened to the tones of Nature—murmur of fountains, rustling of trees, cries of animals, etc.—revealed to them the spiritual beings which they conceived to be behind natural appearances. The faculty of thus interpreting Nature was called *μαντεία*, as Hegel (p. 245, English translation) calls to our attention.]

§ 211. The stringed instrument, the cithern, was preferred by the Greeks to all wind instruments because it was not exciting, and allowed the accompaniment of recitation or song, i. e., a simultaneous spiritual activity on the part of the performer, in poetry. Flute-playing was first brought from Asia Minor after the victorious progress of the Persian war, and was especially cultivated in Thebes. They sought in vain afterward to oppose the wild excitement raised by its influence.

[The cithern (*κιθάρα*, pronounced nearly like *guitar*, which is its modern equivalent) was first preferred. The flute, used after-

22

ward in Thebes, is spoken of by the ancients as dangerous to the virtues of the people. Aristotle ("Politics," book viii, chap. vi) says, "The flute is not a moral instrument, but rather one that will inflame the passions." This surprises us.]

§ 212. Grammar comprehended letters (γράμματα), i. e., the elements of literary culture, reading and writing. Much attention was given to correct expression. The fables of Æsop, the Iliad, and the Odyssey, and later the tragic poets were read, and partly learned by heart. The orators borrowed from them often the ornament of their commonplace remarks.

[The favorite reading-books were "Æsop," the "Iliad," and "Odyssey," and later the tragic poets, certainly a rich collection.]

§ 213. (3) The internal growth of what was peculiar to the Grecian state came to an end with the war for the Hegemony. Its dissolution began, and the philosophical period followed the political. The beautiful ethical life dissolved before the thoughts of the true, beautiful, and good. Individuality developed the habit of reflection, and undertook to subject freedom, the existing regulations, laws and customs, to the criticism of reason, and to inquire whether these were in and for themselves universal and necessary. The Sophists, as teachers of grammar, rhetoric, and philosophy, undertook to extend the cultivation of reflection; and this introduced instability where the moral customs had hitherto obtained unquestioning obedience. Among the women, the *Hetæræ* undertook the same revolution; in the place of the πότνια μήτηρ appeared the beauty, who stood apart from her sex in the consciousness of her charms and in the perfection of her varied culture, and exhibited herself to the public admiration. The tendency to idiosyncrasy often approached willfulness, caprice, and whimsicality, and opposition to the national moral sense. A Diogenes in a tub became possible; the genial but graceful frivolity of an Alcibiades charmed, even though it was openly condemned; a Socrates completed the rupture in the popular consciousness, and urged upon the system of the old morality the pregnant question, whether virtue could be taught? Socrates worked as a philosopher who was at the same time an educator. Pythagoras had imposed upon his pupils of both sexes the strict and narrow discipline of a common, exactly defined manner of living. Socrates, on the contrary, freed his disciples—in general, those who conversed with him—leading them to the consciousness of their own individuality. He introduced a revolution into the education of youth in that he taught them, instead of a thoughtless obedience to moral customs, to seek to comprehend things and events by their purpose in the world, and to rule their actions by deliberate consideration of ends and aims. Outwardly he conformed to the popular standard in politics, and in war (as at Marathon); but in the direction of his teaching he was subjective and modern.

[The Peloponnesian war broke up the internal unity of Greece and put an end to the worship of the beautiful. Teachers of grammar, rhetoric, and philosophy taught the youth to criticise existing customs and regulations. All simplicity disappeared. Individuality approached whimsicality. Socrates completed the revolution. He is the first to elevate blind adherence to custom to free moral action. He recognizes conscience or individual standard of right, and urges each one to rule his actions by reflection upon what is just and expedient. Before his time divination was resorted to, or an appeal was made to the oracle or to the auspices on the occasion of any new undertaking. The will looked to some external event—some sign, portent, or omen

—to guide its action. With Socrates begins the mode to which we are accustomed, the decision through reflection on several courses of action possible.]

§ 214. This idea, that virtue could be taught, was realized especially by Plato and Aristotle; the former inclining to Dorianism, the latter holding to the principle of individuality in nearly the modern sense. As regards the pedagogical means—gymnastics, music, and grammar—both philosophers substantially agreed. But, in the seizing of the pedagogical development in general, Plato held that the education of the individual belonged to the state alone, because the individual was to devote himself wholly to the state. On the other hand, while Aristotle also holds that the state should, as a general thing, conduct the education of its citizens, and that the individual should be trained for the interest of the state, yet he recognizes also the family, and the peculiarity of the individual, as positive powers, to which the state must accord relative freedom. Plato sacrifices the family to the state, and must therefore have sacred marriages, nurseries, and common and public educational institutions. Each one shall do only that which he is fitted to do, and shall work at this one employment so as to perfect his skill in it; but to what he shall direct his energies, and in what he shall be instructed, shall be determined by the government, and the individuality consequently is not left free. Aristotle also will have for all the citizens a uniform, common, and public education; but he allows, at the same time, independence to the family and self-determination to the individual, so that a sphere of private life presents itself within the state: a difference by means of which a much broader scope of individuality is possible.

These two philosophers have come to represent two very different directions in the science of education, which at intervals, in certain stages of culture, reappear—the one, the tyrannical guardianship of the state which assumes the work of education, tyrannical to the individual; and the other, the free development of the liberal system of state-education, which directs itself against idiosyncrasy and fate.

[Plato inclines to the Spartan form of civilization, and would have strict control exercised by wise men in power. Aristotle inclined to the direction of greater individualism, and his views are approximately those of the present day.]

§ 215. The complete dissolution of the principle of æsthetic individuality takes place when the individual, in the decay of public life, in the disappearance of all beautiful morality, isolates himself, and seeks to gain in his isolation such strength that he can bear the changes of fortune with composure—"ataraxy." The Stoics sought to attain this end by turning their attention inward into pure internality, and thus, by preserving the self-determination of abstract thinking and willing, maintaining their equanimity: the Epicureans endeavored to do the same, with this difference, however, that they strove after a positive satisfaction of the senses by filling them with concrete pleasurable sensations. As a consequence of this, the Stoics withdrew from practical life in order to maintain their independence of external conditions, and to preserve their mental quiet unbroken. The Epicureans lived in companies, because they heightened the results of their pleasure-seeking principle through harmony of feeling and through the sweetness of friendship. In so far the Epicureans were Greeks and the Stoics Romans. With both, however, the beauty of manifestation was secondary to the immobility of the inner feeling. The plastic union of the good and the beautiful was destroyed by the extremes of thinking and feeling. This was the advent of the Roman principle among the Greeks.

[With the principle of Stoicism the Greek has finally deserted the æsthetic standpoint and arrived at the Roman principle. To be imperturbable ("ataraxy") in the midst of calamity is the object of both Stoics and Epicureans. The former strives, by cultivating his will through self-denial and his intellect through reflection, to build for himself a world in the depths of his soul secure from external events. The Epicurean seeks to make the most of the world as it actually is, and to make sure of happiness, but he takes care to hold his feelings under restraint, and, like the Stoic, to create his happiness by thinking and willing.]

§ 216. The educational significance of Stoicism and Epicureanism consists in this, that, after the public moral life was sundered from the private, the individual began to educate himself, through philosophical culture, into stability of character, for which reason the Roman emperors particularly disliked the Stoics. At many times, a devotion to the Stoic philosophy was sufficient to make one suspected. But, at last, a noble emperor, in order to win himself a hold in the chaos of things, was forced himself to become a Stoic, and took refuge in the inaccessible calm of the depths of thought occupied in reflecting on its own nature, and of the will engaged in restraining itself by ethical maxims. Stoics and Epicureans both had what we call an ideal. The Stoics used for this ideal the expression, "kingdom"; as Horace says, sarcastically, "*Sapiens est rex nisi—pituita molesta est.*"

[With Stoicism and Epicureanism, education assumes a new significance, because both depend on careful training of intellect and will. The early stages of Greek life were spontaneous; education simply enjoined the following of blind custom. Hereditary instincts rendered it all easy and natural. Greece came under Roman power, and this contradiction between native Greek customs and the course of educated thought and feeling became very marked. Marcus Aurelius, the Stoic emperor, whose "Meditations" we prize so much, rendered Stoicism acceptable with the government of Rome.]

CHAPTER V.

SYSTEM OF INDIVIDUAL EDUCATION (*continued*).

II. *Practical Education.*

§ 217. The outcome of the dissolution of the beautiful individuality is the earnest individuality that directs all its labor to the achievement of purposes useful to the state, which, on the one hand, considers carefully end and means, and, on the other hand, seeks to realize the end through the corresponding means, and in this effort subordinates mere beauty of form to usefulness. The practical individuality is therefore directed to the achievement of an external object, since it is not its own purpose like the beautiful, as it was even in the case of the Stoics and Epicureans, but has an external object, and finds its satisfaction not so much in this after it is attained as in the striving for its attainment.

[The Roman makes usefulness rather than beauty the supreme end. He looks upon things and events as means to ends. But the end or object for which all things, even the lives of individuals, are means, is Rome. While the individuality of the Greek is educated for beauty, and hence for its own culture and not for an external end and aim, the Roman individuality is educated for the preservation and prosperity of the state. But in this we must not forget that the Roman differs from the Persian who is educated for the conquest of boundaries and the extension of the sway of the nation. The Persian does not distinguish between the state in the abstract and the king in the concrete. But Romans always make this distinction, and never confound the abstract sovereignty to which all owe their lives and property with individuals in authority. Even the most absolute dictator is simply a means and not an end; he must "see that the republic does not suffer detriment." Therefore it is that the Roman education is an "individual system," and not a one-sided "active" or "passive" system. The historical myths and legends relate that Rome was settled by fugitives and outlaws on the border-land of the Sabines, the Latins, and the Etruscans. This *colluvies*, as Livy calls it, the dregs of the surrounding peoples, must unite for its own safety, and form a government on a purely artificial basis. All other nations had united on a religious basis. But these peoples had different religions and different manners and customs. The political bond, pure and simple, is set up as the highest. It becomes the object of religion in fact. Another interesting feature is the fact that compact or contract is the essence of the Roman spiritual life. Founded not on religion, but on mutual agreement for common safety, the Roman state exists as a sort of higher will of each individual. Two or more wills unite and consolidate in a sort of higher, resultant will. Such is a contract. To sum up Roman education in a word, one may say that his idea of the all-importance of a contract and the implicit obedience which the individual should render it, is the great educative influence always present with the Roman in the republic. On the basis of this idea arises the noble patriotism which the citizen displays when he offers up his life and property for the safety and honor of Rome. On the same basis arises the opposite feeling of private right, the intense enjoyment of private property, and the network of civil laws which protect it. The Roman unites in his consciousness these two antithetic notions: (a) utter devotion of life and property for the state; (b) absolute freedom and independence within the limits of his private property. In his mind he reconciles and adjusts these two relations—the one *for Rome*, the other *for himself*. This makes the Roman character peculiar in the history of the world. There is this dualism in it.]

§ 218. The education of this system begins with strict simplicity. But, after it has attained its object, it gives itself up to the pursuit of æsthetic culture as a recreation, not for the sake of producing works of art, but in order to enjoy them and without any further object. What was to the Greeks a real delight in the beautiful became therefore with the Romans simply an æsthetic amusement, and as such must finally become wearisome. The Roman earnestness of individuality made for itself a new object in mysticism, which was distinguished from the original one in that it concealed in itself a mystery and exacted an activity that was partly theoretical and partly ascetic.

[Æsthetic culture, which was religion with the Greeks, therefore becomes mere idle amusement with the Romans. There are three epochs in Roman education: (1) the strictly simple education of the republic; (2) the education for amusement and the enjoyment of fine arts; (3) the education into secret rites and mysteries which took place in the latter days, when the special religions of all nations had been mingled, and a tendency to eclecticism prevailed.]

§ 219. (1) The first epoch of Roman education, as properly Roman, was the juristic-military education of the republic. The end and aim of the Roman was Rome; and Rome, as from the beginning an eclectic state, could endure only through the adaptation of its laws and external politics to hold together the composite elements of the nation, and subordinate each interest to the interest of the whole. It bore the same contradiction within itself as in its external attitude. The latter forced it into an attitude of violence against neighboring nations; the plebeians were likewise opposed to the patricians in the same attitude of violence, for they robbed them gradually of all their privileges. On this account education directed itself partly to giving a knowledge of the law, partly to training for war. The boys were obliged to commit to memory and recite the laws of the Twelve Tables, and all the young men were subject to military service. The Roman possessed no individuality of native growth, but one formed through the intermingling of various national stocks; fugitives collecting on the Roman hills furnishing the population. This developed a very great energy. Hence from the first he was attentive to his own conduct; he watched jealously over the limits that bounded his rights from the rights of others, measured his strength, moderated himself, and constantly guarded himself. In contrast with the careless cheerfulness of the Greeks, he therefore appears gloomy.

The Latin tongue is crowded with expressions which paint presence of mind, effort at reflection, a critical attitude of mind, the importance of personal control: as *gravitas morum*, *sui compos esse*, *sibi constare*, *austeritas*, *vir strenuus*, *vir probus*, *vitam honestam gerere*, *sibimet ipse imperare*, etc. The Etruscan element imparted to this earnestness a peculiarly stiff, ceremonial, solemn character. The Roman was no longer, like the Greek, unembarrassed in the presence of naturalness. He was ashamed of nudity; *verecundia*, *pudor*, were genuinely Roman. *Vitam præferre pudori* was disgraceful. On the contrary, the Greek gave to Greeks a festival in exhibiting the splendor of his naked body, and the inhabitants of Crotona erected a statue to Philip solely because he was perfectly beautiful. Simply to be beautiful, only beautiful, was enough for the Greek. But a Roman, in order to be recognized, must have done something for Rome: *se bene de republica mereri*.

[Rome, being an eclectic state, could exist only by subordinating all interests to the supreme one of the safety of the state. The individual may cherish all other interests as private interests, but must not allow them to interfere with the public cause. Here, for the first time, is freedom of the individual in such matters as manners and customs and modes of religious worship that were peculiar to the separate tribes which united to form Rome. Each family had its own "household gods." Strange, too, we find ancestor-worship in Rome in almost as pure a form as it exists in China. It seems to have been arrested in its development by the establishment of an artificial abstraction, the republic as absolute. Education had to make the youth acquainted with the written law of the "Twelve Tables," which recited the fundamental limitations of private freedom and possession that are rendered necessary to secure the public weal. These laws concerned chiefly the forms of transference of property and the forms of recovery. The individuality of the Roman is realized in private property through the fact that the supreme power, political and religious, re-enforces his private will and protects it in its rights within the limits prescribed in the code of laws. Private ownership in this sense is a participation on the part of the particular will of the individual in the universal or collective will of the state. The other side of education was the preparation for military service.

Most remarkable is the vocabulary of Latin words expressing the *gravity*, *soberness*, *austerity*, *probity*, *honesty*, *self-restraint*, *composed* manners, etc., of this people. His (the Roman's) mind is divided between the private and the public interests, and always under a sort of constraint—never spontaneous and free like the Greek in early ages before Greek philosophy had superinduced reflection. All modern peoples that have entered civilization inherit from Rome this double consciousness of the self and the public interest, but not in the contradictory form which it once assumed. Christianity solved its contradiction by giving to it an infinite ground in the doctrine of the divine-human and of the atonement.]

§ 220. In the first education of children the Roman mother was especially influential, so that woman with the Romans took generally a more moral, a higher, and a freer position. It is worthy of remark that, while the beautiful woman set the Greeks at variance, among the Romans, through her ethical authority, she acted as reconciler.

[Woman in Greece as the ideal of the beautiful in the person of Helen set states at variance. In Rome the daughters of the Sabines, stolen by the Romans, reconciled the conflicting armies. In Rome woman took a higher and freer position.]

§ 221. The mother of the Roman helped to form his character; the father undertook the work of instruction. When, in his fifteenth year, the boy exchanged the *toga prætextata* for the *toga virilis*, he was usually sent to some relative, or to some respectable jurist, as his guardian, to learn thoroughly, under his guidance, the laws and political usages of the state; with the seventeenth year began military service. All education was for a long time entirely a private affair. On account of the necessity of the mechanical unity which war demands in its evolutions, the greatest stress was laid upon obedience. In its restricted sense instruction was given in reading, writing, and arithmetic; the last being, on account of its usefulness, more esteemed by the Romans than by the Greeks, who gave more time to geometry. The schools, very characteristically, were called *Ludi*, because their work was, in distinction from other occupations, regarded simply as a recreation, as play.

The Roman recognized with pride this distinction between the Greek and himself; Cicero's introduction to his "Essay on Oratory" expresses it. To be practical was the one result aimed at by the reflective character of the Romans, which was always proposing to itself new objects and seeking the means for their attainment; which loved moderation, not to secure beauty thereby, but respected it as a means for a happy success (*medium tenuere beati*); which did not possess serene self-limitation, or σωφροσύνη, but rather carefully estimated *quid valeant humeri, quid ferre recusent;* but which, as a matter of course, went far beyond the Greeks in persistency of will, in *constantia animi.* The schools were at first held publicly in booths at the intersection of streets; hence the name *trivium.* Very significant for the Roman is the predicate which he conferred upon theoretical subjects when he called them *artes bonæ*, *optimæ*, *liberales*, *ingenuæ*, etc., and brought forth the practical element in them (their relation to the will).

[The influence of the Roman mother over her son is well portrayed in Shakespeare's "Coriolanus." At fifteen the Roman youth studied the laws; at seventeen entered the army. Obedience emphasized. Branches of study. Schools called by the Romans places for *sport and recreation* (*ludi*); by Greeks, places of *leisure* (σχολή). The difference between the Roman and the Greek in the matter of self-possession of individuality; the Roman has constancy of purpose; the Greek, serene self-limitation, i. e., moderation and self-control in his reaction against impulses and external incitements.]

§ 222. (2) But the practical education could no longer keep its ground after it had become acquainted with the æsthetic. The conquest of Greece, Asia Minor, and Egypt made necessary, in a practical point of view, the acquisition of the Grecian tongue, so that these lands, so permeated with Grecian culture, might be governed effectively. The Roman of family and property, therefore, took into his service Greek nurses and teachers who should give to his children, from their earliest years, instruction in the Greek tongue. It is the first instance in the history of education in which a nation has undertaken to teach a foreign tongue to its youth.

Moreover, the usefulness of it in political and other affairs caused the study of Greek rhetoric, so that not only in the deliberations of the senate and in the assemblies of the people, but in pleadings before the courts, the Roman citizen might gain his cause by its aid. Whatever effort the Roman government made to prevent the invasion of the Greek rhetorician was all in vain. The Roman youth sought this very useful knowledge even abroad, e. g., in the flourishing school of rhetoric on the island of Rhodes.

At last, even the study of philosophy commended itself to the practical Roman, in order that he might obtain consolation amid the disappointments of life. When his practical activities did not bring him any result, he devoted himself in his poverty to abstract contemplation. The Greeks desired philosophy for its own sake; the ataraxy of the Stoics, Epicureans, and skeptics even wished to be considered the result of a necessary principle; but the Roman, on the contrary, wished to lift himself by philosophemes above trouble and misfortune.

This direction which philosophy took is noteworthy, not alone in Cicero and Seneca, but at the fall of the Roman Empire, when Boëthius wrote in prison his immortal work on the "Consolation of Philosophy."

[After the conquest of Greece and the necessary introduction of the study of the Greek language in order to rule Egypt, Asia, and places where that language had been carried by the Alexandrian conquests, the Roman education changes rapidly, and introduces literary studies. The useful art of rhetoric, so necessary to the politician and the barrister, initiated this change. Greek teachers of rhetoric taught the most eminent Roman politicians. Apollonius of Rhodes taught both Cicero and Cæsar. Afterward the poets and historians, and finally the philosophy of Greece, came to be studied.]

§ 223. The earnestness which pursued a definite object degenerated into its opposite. The idleness of the wealthy Roman, who felt himself to be the lord of a world without limits, led to desire for enjoyment and dissipation, which, in its entire want of moderation, abused Nature. The most elegant form of the education that became prevalent at this period was that in *belles-lettres*, which also for the first time came to belong to the sphere of education. There had been a degeneration of art in India and Greece, but never an artistic trifling. But in Rome there arose a pursuit of art in order to win a certain consideratio in social position, and to create a species of recreation adapted to the *ennui* of a soul satiated with sensual debauchery. Such a treatment of art is unworthy, for it no longer recognizes its independent significance, but subordinates it as a means to personal gratification. Literary *salons* then appear.

In the introduction to his "Catiline," Sallust has painted excellently this complete revolution in the Roman education. The younger Pliny in his letters furnishes ample material to illustrate for us this pursuit of *belles-lettres.* In Nero it became insanity. We should transgress our prescribed limits did we enter here into particulars. Its analysis shows the perversion of the æsthetic into the practical, the æsthetic losing thereby its proper nature. But the Roman could not avoid this perversion, because, according to his original tendency, he could not move except toward the *utile et honestum.*

[Mere literature, as means of amusement, and trifling with matters of art, now entered the education of the idle Roman possessed of wealth. He did not attain the genuine æsthetic, but rather destroyed it by perverting its aim to mere amusement. The Greek had produced it in a religious mood. The Roman enjoyed it as an idle pastime.]

§ 224. (3) But this pursuit of fine art, this mere showy display, must at last weary the Roman. He sought for himself an object to which he could devote himself again with some degree of exertion. His dominion over the world was assured, and conquest as an object could no more charm him. National religion had fallen with the destruction of the national individualities. The soul looked out over its political life into an empty void. It sought to establish a relation between itself and another world filled with imaginary spiritual powers. In place of the depreciated nationality and its religion there enters the eclecticism of mystic orders. There had been, it is true, here and there, in national religions certain secret signs, rites, words, and meanings; but now, for the first time in the history of the world, there appeared secret organizations as educational societies, which concerned themselves only with the private individual and were indifferent to nationality. Everything had been profaned by the roughness of violence. They believed no longer in the old gods, and the superstitious faith in ghosts and evil spirits became only a thing fit to frighten children with. Thus they took refuge in secrecy, which for *blasé* men had a piquant charm.

[When the Roman Empire had conquered the world, she had at the same time destroyed the peculiar idiosyncrasy of the city of Rome which made it politically sacred. The rights of citizenship were conferred by the emperors on the inhabitants of cities in all parts of the world. The peculiar religions of the conquered nations were adopted and recognized and their gods transported to Rome and set up in the Pantheon. Such toleration of all religions enforced on the peoples composing the Empire necessarily sapped the foundations of religious education and caused a wide-spread indifference as to sacred matters. One set of heathen gods is just as good as another, and neither of them receives the worship of the educated Roman. Accordingly, the religious sentiment takes refuge in a sort of mystic pantheism, using especially Persian and Egyptian forms. The worship of Mithras and Isis became common.]

§ 225. The education of the mysteries was twofold, theoretical and practical. In the theoretical we find a regular gradation of symbols and symbolical acts through which one seemed gradually to approach the revelation of the secret; the practical contained a regular gradation of ascetic actions [disciplinary training] alternating with an abandonment to wild orgies. These two forms of education elevated one from the rank of the novice to that of the initiated. The degrees of the orders formed an instrumentality for the development of ethical growth, and this form has been retained in the education of all such secret worship, *mutatis mutandis*, down to the Illuminati.

In the Roman Empire, its Persian element was the worship of Mithras; its Egyptian, that of Isis; its Grecian, the Pythagorean doctrines. All these three, however, were much mingled with each other. The Roman legions, who really no longer had any native country, spread these artificial religions throughout the whole world. The breaking away from established forms led often to clairvoyance, which was not yet understood, and to belief in miracles. Apollonius of Tyana, the messiah of heathenism, is the principal figure in this group; and, in comparison with him, Jamblichus appears only as an enthusiast, and Alexander of Abonoteichus as an ordinary impostor.

[Secret societies with graded symbolism and secret initiations celebrated the esoteric or *inner meaning* which was supposed to underlie all religions, especially the Persian and Egyptian. Those who seized the deep meaning called themselves *the illuminated.* In 1776 Adam Weishaupt founded the Illuminati referred to in the text. Apollonius of Tyana (A. D. 30–70) collected a mass of doctrines from the East, resembling what passes for "esoteric Buddhism" or "theosophy" in our literature of 1886. Jamblichus was an extravagant Neo-Platonist, holding the doctrines of the pre-existence of the soul and the descent of creation by a lapse ("fall" or degradation) from the Absolute. Alexander of Abonoteichus (in Paphlagonia), a notorious sorcerer, about the middle of the second century A. D., who gave himself out for a prophet. His life was written by Lucian.]

III. *Abstract Individual Education.*

§ 226. What the declining nations in their despair sought for in these mysteries was individuality, which in its special singularity is conscious of the universality of the rational world of institutions as its own essence. This individuality existed more immediately in the Germanic race, but, nevertheless, on account of its peculiar nature, it attained its true actualization first in Christianity. It can be here only pointed out that the Germanic people most thoroughly, in opposition to Nature, to men, and to the gods, felt themselves to be independent, as Tacitus says, "*Securi adversus homines, securi adversus Deos.*" This individuality, which had for its object only itself, must necessarily be destroyed, and was saved only by Christianity, which overcame and enlightened its dæmonic and defiant spirit. We can not speak here of a system of education. Respect for personality, the free acknowledgment of the claims of woman, the loyalty to the leader chosen by themselves, loyalty to their chosen companions (the idea of comradeship)—these features all deserve to be well noted, because from them arose the feudalism of the middle ages. What Cæsar and Tacitus tell us of the education of the Germans expresses only the free play allowed itself by individuality, which in its rudimentary savage state had no other form in which to manifest itself than wars of conquest.

To the Roman there was something dæmonic in the German. He perceived dimly in him his future, his master. When the Romans first met the Cimbri and Teutons in the field, their commander had to accustom them gradually to the fearful sight of the wild, giant-like forms.

[The individualism of the Germanic race is called "abstract" by Rosenkranz because that race loved individuality pure and simple. They cared neither for men nor gods, having that intoxication of bravery which utter desperation gives. The Germanic individuality is here called dæmonic (not *demonic*), in the Greek sense of "possessed by a spirit." It is a sort of madness or frenzy—the Berserker rage, described in Kingsley's "Hypatia," as possessing the Norsemen in battle. (See § 203.) They had loyalty to their friends and leaders, and acknowledged the claims of woman. The tragedy of Brunhild in the old Norse Edda shows how deeply prophetic was their sentiment regarding woman.]

CHAPTER VI.

THE SYSTEM OF THEOCRATIC EDUCATION.

§ 227. The system of national education was founded on the substantial basis of the family institution; its second phase is the division of the nation by means of division of labor which it makes permanent in castes; its third stage presents the free antithesis of the laity and clergy; next it makes war, immortality, and trade, by turns, its end; after this, it sets up beauty, patriotic duty, and the immediateness of individuality, as the essence of human nature; and at last dissolves the unity of nationality in the consciousness that all nations are really one since they are all human beings. In the intermixture of races in the Roman world arises the conception of the human race, the *genus humanum*. Education had become eclectic: the Roman legions leveled the national distinctions. In the wavering of all objective morality, the necessity of self-education in order to the formation of character appeared ever more and more clearly; but the conception, which lay at the foundation, was always, nevertheless, that of Roman, Greek, or German education. But in the midst of these nations another system had striven for development, and this did not base itself on the natural bond of nationality, but made this, for the first time, only a secondary thing, and made the direct relation of man to God its chief idea. In this system God himself is the teacher. He manifests to man his will as law, to which he must unconditionally conform, for no other reason than that he is the Lord and man is his servant who can have no other will than His. The obedience of man is, therefore, in this system mere mechanical submission to authority, until through experience he gradually attains to the knowledge that the will of God has in it the very essence of his own will. Descent, talent, events, work, beauty, courage—all these are indifferent things compared with the subjection of the human to the divine will. To believe in God is the way to be well-pleasing to him. Without this unity with God, what is natural in national descent is of no value. According to its form of manifestation, Judaism is not so advanced as the Greek spirit. It is not beautiful, but rather grotesque. But in its essence, as the religion of the contradiction between the absolute, divine ideal and the finite and the imperfect existence of the world, it takes a step beyond Nature, which it perceives to be created by an absolute, conscious, and reasonable will; while the Greek concealed in a myth concerning the birth of Gæa, his mother-earth, the fact of the dependence of all Nature on a higher source. The Jews have been preserved in the midst of all other civilizations by the elastic power of the thought of God as one who was free from the control of Nature. The Jews have a patriotism equal to that of the Romans. The Maccabees, for example, were not inferior to the Romans in greatness.

Abraham is the genuine Jew because he is the genuinely faithful man. He does not hesitate to obey the horrible and inhuman command of his God. Circumcision was made the token of the national unity, but the nation may assimilate members to itself from other nations through this rite. The essential condition of membership in the chosen people always lies in belief in a spiritual relation to which the natural relation is secondary. The Jewish nation makes proselytes, and these are widely different from the *Socii* of the Romans or the *Metoeci* (Μέτοικοι) of the Athenians.

[Quite in contrast to the "individual" education is the system of "theocratic" education. The "unity of nationality is dissolved in the consciousness that all nations are really one since they are all human beings." This refers to the last stage of Roman history. The Romans had conquered all nations and imposed upon them the Roman law and the double consciousness (above described) of public and private rights. Upon the conquest of a new country, its youth, able to bear arms, were conscripted into the army and sent to some remote part of the empire where they were opposed to a foe so unlike themselves in language and customs as to cause them to cleave loyally to the Roman standard as the only means of self-preservation. Besides, it was only through Rome that they could ever hope to hear from their native land or return to it. By this plan the conquered peoples became thoroughly intermingled throughout the army. Those who fought side by side learned to respect each other. Slowly there arose the idea of the *genus humanum*, the idea of all men as of one blood.

While this leveling of national distinctions had gone on within the Roman Empire, there arose another movement parallel to it, but in the deepest recesses of the human spirit. It was the theocratic education that developed the idea of the personal God, who is not a special limited God, but the God of all people. While Greek poetry is beautiful, Hebrew poetry is sublime. It presents the strong contrast between a Creator of infinite power and his finite works. God is above and apart from all Nature. The Persian makes Ahura-Mazda identical with the natural element, light. But the Bible says that light was created by a mere word of the Divine Person.]

§ 228. To the man who knows Nature to be the work of a single, transcendent, rational Creator, she loses independence. He is negatively freed from her control, and sees in her only a means. As opposed to the heathen conceptions richly endowed with the poetic imagination, this seems to be a backward step, but for the emancipation of man it is a progress. He no longer fears Nature, but her Lord, and admires Him so much in his works that prose rises to the dignity of poetry even in this teleological contemplation (which celebrates the purpose of Nature rather than Nature herself). Since man stands above Nature, education is directed to morality as such, and expresses itself in manifold qualifications, by means of which the distinction of man from Nature is definitely stated. The ceremonial law appears often arbitrary, but in its prescribed ceremonies it offers man the satisfaction of placing himself as will in relation to will (human will in relation to Absolute Will). For example, if he is forbidden to eat any specified part of an animal, the ground of this command is not merely natural (i. e., based on hygienic reasons)—it is the will of the Deity. Man learns, therefore, in his obedience to such directions, to free himself from his self-will, from his natural appetites. This thorough renunciation of mere subjectivity (selfishness) is the beginning of wisdom, the purification of the will from all individual egotism.

The Decalogue contains the rational substance of the law expressed for all time. Many of our modern much-admired authors exhibit a superficiality bordering on shallowness when they confine their comments to the absurdity of the miracles, and omit all notice of the profound depth of the moral struggle of the Jewish people, and fail to see the practical rationality of the ten commandments.

[When a religion teaches man that Nature is only a created object, and that the Creator is a conscious person, he does not any longer worship forces and material forms, but sees in them only a means for the realization of spiritual ends. With such a belief education is directed toward what is ethical. In obeying the "law" man obeys the will of deity and not a mere blind necessity of unconscious Nature.]

§ 229. Education in this theocratical system is in one respect patriarchal. The family is very prominent, because it is considered to be a great happiness for the individual to belong from his earliest life to the company of those who believe in the true God. In another respect it is hierarchical, inasmuch as its ceremonial law develops a special function, to be filled by those whose duty it is to see that obedience is paid to its multifarious regulations. And, because these are often perfectly arbitrary, education must, above all, see that they are committed to memory so thoroughly that they may always be remembered. The Jewish monotheism shares this necessity with the superstition of heathenism.

[In the theocratic system education is at first patriarchal because the family is the link that connects the individual with the faithful chosen people. Secondly, the education is provided by the priests who have to preserve the ceremonial law in its purity, and see to its observance. What is prescribed by divine command must be committed to memory; hence the tendency in this species of education to exclusive cultivation of the memory.]

§ 230. But the technique proper of the ceremonial mechanism is not the most important educational element of the theocracy. We find this in its historical significance, since its history throughout has an educational character. For the people of God show us always, in their intercourse with Him, a progress from the external to the internal, from the lower to the higher, from the past to the future. Their history, therefore, abounds in situations very interesting in an educational point of view, and in characters which are eternal models.

[To the command to obey is added a promise of material prosperity and a threat of punishment. The history of the chosen people shows a gradual progress away from the state of mind which looks to material reward for obeying spiritual laws.]

§ 231. (1) The will of God as the absolute authority is at first to this people, as law, external. But soon God adds to the command to obedience, on the one hand, the inducement of a promise of material prosperity, and on the other hand the threat of material punishment. The fulfillment of the law is also encouraged by reflection on the profit which it brings. But, since these motives are all external, we rise finally into the insight that the law is to be fulfilled, not on account of those motives, but because it is the will of the Lord; not alone because it is conducive to our happiness, but also because it is in itself holy, and written in our hearts: in other words, man proceeds from the standpoint of abstract legality, through the reflection of eudæmonism (i. e., the expectation of selfish gain for our obedience), to the internality of moral sentiment—the course of all education.

This last standpoint is especially represented in the excellent collection of aphorisms of Jesus Sirach—a book rich in pedagogical insight, which paints with master-strokes the relations of husband and wife, parents and children, master and servants, friend and friend, enemy and enemy, and the dignity of labor as well as the necessity of its division. This priceless book forms a companion-piece from the theocratic standpoint to the "Republic" and "Laws" of Plato, in which he treats the province of ethics.

[The history of the Jews shows the discipline that they undergo. They come to see that the law must be obeyed, not because it brings prosperity, but because it is the law of holiness and its fulfillment makes men resemble God. In the progress of this nation we see three stages which are repeated in all individuals who become thoroughly educated: (1) abstract legality, mechanical obedience without insight or purpose; (2) "the reflection of eudæmonism"—"reflection," because the doer sees in his deed his own profit or gain, i. e., a reflection of self as in a mirror; (3) to the internality of moral sentiment, obedience to the law, because it leads to holiness or union with God. See the book "Ecclesiasticus" in the "Apocrypha," "containing the Wisdom of Jesus, the Son of Sirach," for this insight into the law of holiness.]

§ 232. (2) The progress from the lower to the higher appeared in the conquering of the natural individuality. Man, as the servant of Jehovah, must have no will of his own; but selfish naturalness arrayed itself so much the more vigorously against the absolute "Thou shalt," allowed itself to descend into alienation from the law, and often reached the most unbridled extravagance. But since the law with its inexorable strictness always remained the same, contrasting its persistence with the inequalities of human acts, it forced man to come back to it, and to conform himself to its demands. Thus he learned self-criticism, thus he rose from the natural into the spiritual. This progress is at the same time a progress from necessity to freedom, because self-criticism gradually opens a way into the insight that the will of God is the true outcome of man's own self-determination. Because God is one and absolute, there arises the expectation that his will will become the basis for the will of all nations and men. The criticism of the understanding must recognize a contradiction in the fact that the will of the true God is the law of only one nation. Other nations, moreover, were repelled from the Jews by reason of their worship of God as a gloomy mystery, and they detested that race as *odium generis humani*. And thus is developed the thought that the isolation of the believers will come to an end as soon as the other nations recognize their faith as the true one, and are received into it. Thus here, in the deepest penetration of the soul into itself, as among the Romans in the fusion of nations, we see appear the idea of the human race.

[Progress appeared in another respect in the degree to which the people could subdue their natural appetites and lusts and submit to the law of Jehovah. The ideal standard of conduct being furnished by the law, each Jew could criticise his own life by it. This criticism, moreover, gave him insight into the fact that the law of holiness was at the same time the true outcome of his own self-determination—that is to say, the true means of his own perfection, and not an arbitrary regulation of Jehovah forced on man against his true interests. Again, as a consequence of this insight, it became evident that the law is the means of perfection for all men, and that Jehovah is the God of all nations, and not the God of the Jews alone, and that He ought to be recognized by all people. When this is done the chosen people will be no longer exclusive. At this point the Jewish theocracy has reached the idea of the human race as belonging to one religion, and from a different standpoint has come to the same result that the Roman civilization has done.]

§ 233. (3) The progress from the past to the future developed an ideal of a servant of God who fulfills all the law, and therefore blots out the empirical contradiction involved in the fact that the "Thou shalt" of the law did not attain adequate reality. This Prince of Peace, who shall gather all nations under his banner, can therefore have no other thing predicated of him than holiness. He is not beautiful as the Greeks represented their ideal, not brave and practical as was the venerated *Virtus* of the Romans; he does not place an infinite value on his individuality as the German does; but he is represented as insignificant in appearance, as patient, as humble, as he who, in order to reconcile the world, takes upon himself the infirmities and disgrace of all others. The heathen nations have only a lost paradise behind them; the Jews have one also before them. From this belief in the Messiah who is to come, from the certainty which they have of conquering with him, from the power of esteeming all present things of small importance in view of such a future, springs the indestructible nature of the Jews. They ignore the fact that Christianity is the necessary result of their own history. As the nation of the future, they are the world-historical nation *par excellence*, the nation among nations, whose education — whenever the Jew has not changed and corrupted his nature through modern culture—is still always patriarchal, hierarchal, and mnemonic (dwelling on the memory of its past history).

[The "Prince of Peace" is to gather all peoples under his banner of holiness. The Messiah is to come and restore the lost paradise. In view of this ideal, which has the Absolute God for the guaranty of its realization, the Jew regards his nation as the nation of the future, and endures the trials of the present with infinite fortitude. The same ideal in Christianity creates the martyrs whose stubborn individuality endures not only persecution but death cheerfully. This education, therefore, furnishes the deepest ground for individuality—sought by the Greeks, Romans, and Teutonic peoples with only partial success. It is the basis for all future education. All men are of one blood, and all have the same destiny, namely, holiness, or participation in the divine nature.]

CHAPTER VII.

THE SYSTEM OF HUMANITARIAN EDUCATION.

§ 234. The systems of national and theocratic education came to the same result, though by opposite ways, and this result is the conception of a human race in the unity of which the distinctions of different nations combine and complement each other so as to form a perfect whole. But with them this result is a mere ideal, and they remain in their actual state without realizing it. They picture to themselves the ideal of the advent of the Messiah. But these ideals exist only in the mind, and the actual condition of the people sometimes does not correspond to them at all, and sometimes only in a slight degree. The idea of spiritual perfection had in these presuppositions the possibility of its concrete actualization; one individual man must become conscious of the universality and necessity of the will as being the very essence of his own freedom, so that all external authority should be canceled in the self-rule of spirit, which is a law unto itself. Natural individuality appearing as national traits was still acknowledged, but was deprived of its abstract one-sidedness. The divine authority of the truth of the individual will is to be recognized, but at the same time freed from its estrangement toward itself. While Christ was a Jew and obedient to the divine law, he knew himself as the universal man who determines for himself his own destiny; and, although distinguishing God, as subject, from himself, yet holds fast to the unity of man and God. The system of humanitarian education began to unfold from this principle, which no longer accords the highest place to the natural unity of national individuality, nor to abstract obedience to the command of God, but to that freedom of the soul which knows itself to be unconditioned by aught in time or space. Christ is not a mere ideal of thought, but is known as a living member of actual history, whose life, sufferings, and death for freedom form the guaranty of its absolute justification and truth. The æsthetic, philosophical, and political ideal are all found in the universal nature of the Christian ideal, on which account no one of them appears one-sided in Christian life. The principle of human freedom excludes neither art, nor science, nor politics.

[The national systems begin with China, and end with Rome. Their outcome is the same as that of the theocratic system of education—the conception of a human race in which the differences and distinctions of nations are swallowed up and harmonized. A new system of education arose in the Roman Empire, and in the new nations that sprang from its ruins—a system founded on the Christian idea. What there was positive in all former educational ideals is contained in the Christian ideal. The brotherhood of all men and the common heritage of an infinite destiny make the attainment of all kinds of perfection possible. Art, science, politics, morality, and industry, are included, but harmonized by the new ideal. This new ideal may be stated in the formula: *The goal of progress* in Christian civilization is the greatest perfection of the whole, and the simultaneous realization of the good of the whole race in each individual. The earlier stages of human civilization accepted, as goal, the perfection of institutions as a whole at the expense of individuality. Complete subordination, which was necessary for the perfect working of the patriarchal state, could not be attained without a suppression of independence on the part of the single individual. Progress is marked by the rise of institutions which secure their greatest perfection through the greatest development of the individual. For example, the education of all people up to the point of independent self-activity is necessary for an ideal representative democracy.]

§ 235. In its conception of man the humanitarian education provides for separate nationalities (local, independent self-governments), thus securing the good feature in "national" education, and likewise for the subjection of all men to the divine law, which was taught in the theocratic system, but it will no longer permit the former to grow into an isolating exclusiveness, and the latter into a despotism which includes the former as an unessential element. But this principle of humanity and human nature took root so slowly that the two elements, out of which it developed, were revived within it in their peculiar one-sidedness, and had to be again overcome and united anew. These stages of culture were the Greek, the Roman, and the Protestant Churches, and education was metamorphosed to suit the formation of each of these.

For the sake of brevity we shall confine ourselves in what follows to pointing out general characteristics; the unfolding of details is intimately bound up with the history of politics and of civilization. We shall be contented if we correctly indicate the general course of their history.

[Humanitarian education (*Humanitäts-Erziehung* = humanity-education) took root so slowly that the two phases which were united within it often fell out of harmony and developed one-sidedly, now one predominating and now the other. It became often necessary to overcome these extreme tendencies and restore equilibrium. First, there would be a sort of relapse out of the Christian ideal into a heathen ideal, and the national system of education would be approached. Then a reaction would set in, and an extreme reached closely resembling the theocratic system. The three phases of the Church—Greek, Roman, and Protestant—suggest the three forms of individualism: (a) the æsthetic, (b) the practical or political, (c) the chivalric.]

§ 236. Within education we can distinguish these three stages of development as three epochs: the monkish, the chivalric, and that education which is to fit one for civil life. Each of these endeavored to express all that belonged to humanity as such; but it was only after the recognition of the moral nature of the family, of labor, of culture, and of the conscious equal title of all men to their rights, that this became really possible.

[Rosenkranz distinguishes three epochs in humanitarian education: (a) the monkish; (b) chivalric; (c) citizen.]

I. *The Epoch of Monkish Education.*

§ 237. The Greek Church seized the Christian principle still abstractly as deliverance from the world, and therefore, in the education proceeding from it, it arrived only at the negative form, defining the universality of the individual man (i. e., his essence, his true destiny) as the renunciation of self. In the dogmatism of its teaching, as well as in the ascetic severity of its practical conduct, it was a reproduction of the theocratic principle. But when this had assumed the form of national centralization, the Greek Church dispensed with the ascetic severity, and, as far as regards its form, it returned again to the quietism of the Orient.

[The Greek Church laid emphasis on the principle of renunciation which is only one of the elements of the Christian ideal. Its education, accordingly, took a negative tendency toward the passive systems of the extreme East. Its asceticism also reproduced the theocratic principle. Passivity and quietism, the complete subjugation of self, the renunciation of all secular aims, the world, the flesh, and the devil, the withdrawal from civilization as something repugnant to holiness, characterize this first epoch. Holy men retired to the deserts and lived as hermits.

Then they lived in Christian societies in artificial hermitages, cells constructed within high monastic walls. Then in the Roman epoch the monks came out of their cells and entered society to elevate it—under the leadership of St. Dominic and St. Francis. It was discovered that quietism and withdrawal from the world left the mass of mankind to spiritual degradation. Christ had not withdrawn to the desert, but had come nigh humanity in its busy haunts and sought to convert it. So the Dominicans turned toward science and learning and became the teachers of the wealthy and powerful classes. The Franciscans became popular preachers, going among the poor and lowly, and carrying the gospel. Then came Protestantism, taking the further step of recognizing the secular in itself, considered as a necessary element of the Christian ideal of humanity.]

§ 238. The monkish education is in general identical in all religions, in that, through its concentration of its entire attention upon itself in its practical activity, and the stoicism of its way of thinking, through the cloister-seclusion of its external existence and the mechanism of a thoughtless subjection to a general rule as well as to the special command of superiors, it fosters a spiritual and bodily dullness. The Christian monachism, therefore, as the perfect realization of the ideal of monachism, is at the same time the complete exposure of the defect of the principle, because, in merely renouncing the world instead of conquering it and gaining possession of it, it contradicts the very principle of Christianity.

[The defect of monachism, as measured by the entire scope of Christianity, has been seen: it renounces the world instead of conquering it.]

§ 239. We must notice, as the fundamental error of this whole system, that it does not in free individuality seek to produce the ideal of divine-humanity, but to copy its historical manifestation in an external reproduction. Each human being must complete the Atonement by offering up as sacrifice his own individuality. Each biography has its Bethlehem, its Tabor, and its Golgotha.

[Monachism aims rather to copy an historic past than to reincarnate its divine principle in a new present life. Bethlehem, Tabor, and Golgotha, doubtless come, or should come, into every complete life, but under new forms peculiar to the occasion.]

§ 240. Monachism looks upon the freedom from one's self and from the world, that Christianity demands, only as an entire renunciation of self, which it seeks to compass, like Buddhism, by the vows of poverty, chastity, and obedience, which must be taken by each individual.

This rejection of property, of marriage, and of individual volition, is at the same time the negation of work, of the family, and of responsibility for one's actions. In order to avoid the danger of avarice and covetousness, of sensuality and of nepotism, of error and of guilt, monachism seizes the convenient device of complete severance from all the objective world without being able fully to carry out this negation. Monkish education must, in consequence, be very particular about an external separation of its disciples from the world, so as to make the task of alienation from the world easier and more decided. It therefore builds cloisters in the solitudes of the desert, in the depths of the forest, on the summits of mountains, and surrounds them with high windowless walls; and then, so as to carry the isolation of the individual to its farthest possible extreme, it constructs, within these cloisters, cells, in imitation of the caves of the first hermits—a seclusion the immediate consequence of which is boundless and most paltry curiosity.

[Christian monachism resembles in many of its forms that of Buddhism. In fact, the Abbé Huc, who visited Thibet in 1845, found so many ceremonies of Lamaism nearly identical with corresponding ones of the Catholic Church that he was obliged to infer that they had been borrowed from the latter. This is not improbable, when we consider the extent to which Christian monachism spread over Western Asia in the first four centuries. The peculiar form of Buddhism known as Lamaism is of later origin than the Christian Hermit epoch, and indeed at least one century later than St. Benedict's reform in monachism. In 622 Buddhism was introduced into Thibet, and Lhasa (Lassa) founded—the date of the birth of Mohammed. Its transformation into Lamaism may have been as late as the eleventh century.

Three vows—poverty, chastity, and obedience—indicate the attitude toward the secular world. The three chief secular institutions: (a) the family is attacked by the second vow, which aims at celibacy; (b) civil society, or the institution for the production and distribution of property by means of industry, is attacked by the first vow, which renounces property; (c) the state is attacked by the third vow, which renounces allegiance to any but its religious superiors. That this extreme of quietism was a necessary resort in the epoch when it was established may be granted without question. The Church has, however, found it from time to time desirable to restrict this form of life. It aims to restrict monastic life to those who have made a hopeless failure in a secular life, and by it save them from despair and sin. In early ages it was thought to be the only life of holiness; now it is thought to be auxiliary to holiness in some cases.]

§ 241. Theoretically, monkish education seeks, by means of complete silence, to place the soul in a state of spiritual immobility, which, through the want of all interchange of thought, at last sinks into entire apathy and antipathy toward all intellectual culture. The chief feature of this practical culture is caused by the mistaken idea that one should ignore Nature, instead of morally freeing himself from her control. As Nature again and again asserts herself, the monkish discipline proceeds to ill-treat her, and strives through fasting, through sleeplessness, through voluntary self-inflicted pain and torture, not only to subdue the wantonness of the flesh, but to destroy the love of life till it shall become a positive loathing of existence. In and for themselves the objects renounced by the monkish vow—property, the family, and individual choice—are not immoral. The vow is, on this account, very easy to violate. In order to prevent all temptation to this, monkish education invents a system of supervision, partly open, partly secret, which deprives one of all freedom of action, all freshness of thinking and of willing, and all poetry of feeling, by means of the perpetual shadow of spies and informers. The monks are well versed in all police-arts, and the well-graded series of supervisors and general inspectors in the hierarchy spurs them on always to distinguish themselves in these arts of espionage.

[Monkish discipline of fasts, vigils, and penances. Necessity of espionage—the support of individual resolution by the supervision of one's companions and superiors.]

§ 242. The gloomy breath of this education penetrated all the relations of the Byzantine state. Even the education of the emperor was infected by it; and in the strife for freedom waged by the modern Greeks against the Turks, the priors of the cloisters were the real leaders of the insurrection. Independence of individuality, as opposed to monkish self-abnegation, was compelled more or less to degenerate into the crude form of soldier and pirate life. But this principle of free individuality was not left to manifest itself in this unlawful manner; on the contrary, it was built up positively into humanity; and this the German world, under the guidance of the Roman Church, undertook to accomplish.

[Deserted by the religious element, secularity in the Eastern Empire took on irregular and barbarous forms. In the West, under the "Holy Roman Empire," whose seat was in Germany, secularity came to be more penetrated by the influence of the Church, and thus arose the epoch of chivalric education.]

II. *The Epoch of Chivalric Education.*

§ 243. The Romish Church annulled the principle of abstract substantiality of the Greeks (i. e., that suppressed individuality in behalf of divinely ordained religious ceremonies) through the practical aim which she set up in the principle of sanctity in works, and by means of which she raised up German individuality to the idealism of chivalry, i. e., a free military service in behalf of Christendom.

[By the principle of sanctity in works (Pelagianism), the Church raised German individuality to the idealism of chivalry. This seems strange to ordinary Protestant views. The Roman Catholic principle, however, corrected in this way the faulty abstraction of the Greek Church.]

§ 244. As a matter of course the system of monkish education which was taken up into this epoch as one of its elements was modified to conform to it; e. g., the Benedictines were accustomed to labor in agriculture and in the transcribing of books, and this contradicted the idea of monachism, since that in and for itself tends to an absolute forgetfulness of the world and a perfect absence of all activity in the individual. The begging orders were public preachers, and made popular the idea of love and unselfish sacrifice for others. They gave an impulse to self-education, especially by holding up the ideal of the life of Christ; e. g., in Tauler's classical book on the "Imitation of the Life of Jesus," and in the work of Thomas-à-Kempis, which resembles it. Through a constant contemplation of the mental picture of Christ, who suffered and died for love, they sought to find content in divine rest and self-forgetfulness.

[Monachism in the West was modified by the mentioned principle of sanctity in works, so that *ora et labora* became the motto. Industry was admitted side by side with religious ceremonial. Agriculture, copying of manuscripts, some of the trades, etc., were followed by the monks. It retained, however, elements of quietism.]

§ 245. German chivalry sprang from feudalism. The education of those pledged to military duty had become confined to practice in the use of arms. The education of the chivalric vassals pursued the same course, refining it gradually through the influence of court society and through poetry, which devoted itself either to the art of relating graceful tales, or to the glorification of woman. Girls were brought up without especial care. The boy until he was seven years old remained in the hands of women; then he became a lad (a young gentleman), and learned the art of offensive and defensive warfare, on foot and on horseback; between his sixteenth and eighteenth year, through a formal ceremony (the laying on of the sword), he was duly authorized to bear arms. But whatever besides this he might wish to learn was left to his own caprice.

[The education of chivalry was confined to practice in the use of arms, to knightly etiquette, and poetry.]

§ 246. In contradistinction to the monkish education, chivalry placed an infinite value on individuality, and this it expressed in its extreme sensibility to the feeling of honor. Education, on this account, endeavored to foster this consciousness of self-importance by means of the social isolation in which it placed the knightly order. The knight did not delight himself with domestic affairs, but he sought for him who had been wronged, since in helping him to his rights he could find enjoyment as a conqueror. He did not live in simple marriage, but strove for the piquant pleasure of making the wife of another the lady of his heart, and this often led to moral and carnal infidelity. And, finally, the knight did not obey alone the general laws of knightly honor, but he strove, besides, to discover for himself unusual tasks, which he should undertake with his sword, in defiance of all criticism, simply because it pleased his caprice so to do. He *sought adventures*.

[While the monkish education repressed individuality, chivalry placed unbounded value on it. Monachism did not, it is true, repress essential individuality, after the manner of Oriental systems. It gave the soul assurance of infinite individuality as its eternal reward. In distinguishing between holiness and finite aims, however, it went to an extreme in repressing the latter. The knight took no pleasure in the prose of common life. He sought adventure. He must find some person who had been robbed or kidnapped whose wrongs he would undertake to right. He looked about for some odd and peculiar enterprise, so that he might realize his individuality in its pursuit. Eccentricity was supposed to be essential to individuality.]

§ 247. The reaction against the numberless fantastic extravagancies arising from chivalry developed the idea of the spiritual chivalry which was to unite the cloister and the town, absolute self-denial and military life, separation from the world and the sovereignty over the world. Although this was an undeniable advance, it was an untenable synthesis which could not long delay the dissolution of chivalry, which, as the rule of the stronger, led to the destruction of all regular culture founded on principles, and brought on a protracted period of absence of all education. In this perversion of chivalry to a grand vagabondism, and even to robbery, noble souls often rushed into ridiculous excesses. The downfall of chivalry prepared the way for citizenship, whose education, however, did not, like the πόλις and the *civitas* of the ancients, limit itself to the narrow bounds of special local interests, but, through the presence of the principle of Christianity, accepted the whole circle of humanity as the aim of its culture.

[Knight-errantry developed into a more rational form of chivalry, namely, the orders devoted to special religious purposes. But these did not retard the decay of the entire institution of chivalry. The Crusades furnished the highest opportunity for the spirit of knightly individuality, and, when they had succeeded in giving a new consciousness to Christendom by uniting the East and West, there was nothing left for chivalry to do. It degenerated into a grand vagabondism. The Crusades impoverished royal treasuries, and weakened the power of the aristocracies. But the cities gained immensely, because they furnished troops and money to carry on the wars. Their charters were made strong and liberal. They were the nurseries of freemen. The growth of cities put an end to chivalry, and inaugurated the present epoch of education, that whose object is citizenship.]

CHAPTER VIII.

THE SYSTEM OF HUMANITARIAN EDUCATION (*continued*).

III. *The Epoch of Education fitting one for Civil Life.*

§ 248. THE condition of cities had gradually improved through trade and industry, and this state of affairs now found in Protestantism its spiritual confirmation. Protestantism, as the self-assurance of the individual that he was directly related to God without dependence on the mediation of any man, adopted the principle of the autonomy of the soul, and began to develop Christianity, as the principle of humanitarian education, into concrete actuality, and to free it from the creations of the imagination, with which monasticism and chivalry had clothed it. The cities were not merely, in comparison with the clergy and the nobility, the "third estate"; but the citizen who himself managed his political affairs, and defended his interests with arms, developed into the order of state-citizen, which absorbed the clergy and nobility, and the state-citizen found his ultimate ideal in pure humanity conscious of its rationality.

[The growth of citizenship found a special confirmation in the Protestant movement, whose most important feature was the recognition of secularism as one essential phase of Christian civilization.]

§ 249. The phases of this development are (1) civil education as such, within which we find also the chivalric education metamorphosed into the so-called nobility education, these two forms, however, being controlled, as to education, within Catholicism by Jesuitism, within Protestantism by pietism. (2) Against this exclusive tendency toward the Church, we find reacting on the one hand the devotion to a study of antiquity, and on the other the friendly alliance with immediate actuality, i. e., with Nature. We can name these periods of the history of education those of its ideals of culture. (3) But the true aim of all culture must forever remain moral freedom. After education had arrived at a knowledge of the meaning of idealism and realism, it must seize as its absolute aim the moral emancipation of man into humanity; and it must subordinate its culture to this aim, inasmuch as technical dexterity, social accomplishment, proficiency in the arts, and scientific insight, can attain to their proper rank only through moral purity.

[The three phases of development of this epoch are: (1) The education of the citizen as opposed to the education of the nobility, both controlled by religious education—Jesuitism within Catholicism and Pietism within Protestantism. (2) A counter-movement arose as a reaction against the too exclusive control of the Church, on the one hand devoted to the study of ancient languages and history, on the other hand devoted to natural science. (3) The further progress of education unites and reconciles these two tendencies.]

1. *Civil Education as such*

§ 250. The one-sidedness of monkish and chivalric education was overcome by civil education in so far as it set aside the celibacy of the monk and the estrangement of the knight from his family, doing this by increasing the hold of family life upon the individual; for it set up, as its standard of perfect living, the positive morality of marriage and the family in the place of the negative duty of holiness of the celibate; while, instead of the poverty and idleness of monkish piety and instead of chivalric wealth, it taught that property and labor were worthy objects of man—i. e., it advocated the self-determined morality of civil society and of its transactions; and, finally, instead of the slavery of the conscience, in the form of implicit obedience to the command of others, and instead of the freakish self-sufficiency of the caprice of the knights, it demanded obedience to the laws of the commonwealth as representing his own self-conscious, actualized, practical reason, in which laws the individual can recognize and acknowledge himself.

As this civil education left free the enjoyment of the body, sensuality was without bounds for a time, until, after men became accustomed to labor and to know their privileges and capacities for physical satisfaction, they gradually learned a moderation which sumptuary laws and prohibitions of gluttony and drunkenness could never create from the external side. What the monk inconsistently enjoyed with a bad conscience, the citizen, like the preacher in Ecclesiastes, could take possession of as a gift of God. After the first millennium of Christianity, when the earth had not, according to the current prophecies of the millennialists, been destroyed, and after the great plague in the fourteenth century, there was felt an immense pleasure in living, which manifested itself externally in the fifteenth century in delicate wines, dainty food, great eating of meat, drinking of beer, and, in the domain of dress, in trunk-hose, peaked shoes, plumes, golden chains, bells, etc. There was much venison, but as yet no potatoes, no tea and coffee. The temper of men was quarrelsome. [Reference here to Sebastian Brant, etc., omitted.]

[Civil education (*a*) overcomes the estrangement of the knight from his family and of the monk from secularity. It sets up marriage and the family as the ethical ideal; (*b*) it opposes the poverty of the monk and the wealth of the knight by claiming for labor and its productions a higher place; (*c*) instead of obedience to the spiritual superior and the caprice of the knight, it required obedience to the laws of the commonwealth as laws demanded by the reason and self-interest of all. Great sensuality prevailed for a time after the advent of this epoch.]

§ 251. In contrast with the heaven-seeking of the monks and the sentimental love-making of the knight, civil education established, as its principle, usefulness, which investigated in things their adaptation to various purposes in order to gain such mastery over them as was found possible. The understanding was trained with all exactness, that it might clearly perceive the objects in the world. But since family-life did not allow the self-concentration of the individual ever to become as great as was the case with the monk and the knight, and since the cheer of a sensuous enjoyment in cellar and kitchen, in clothing and furniture, in social games and in gorgeous pageants, penetrated the whole being with soft pleasure, there was developed a sense of propriety and sobriety, a sort of house-morality, and, united with the prose of labor, a warm and kindly disposition, which left room for innocent merriment and roguery, and found its serious transfiguration in the staid and solemn demeanor at church. Beautiful burgher-state, thou wast weakened by the Thirty Years' War, and hast been only accidentally preserved sporadically in Old England and in some places in Germany, only to be at last swept away by the flood of modern world-pain, political sophistry, and anxiety for the future!

[Usefulness, or adaptation of finite things to rational purposes, was set up as the principle. The extremes of individualism were tempered by the family influence at home and by the influence of the clergy and the ceremonies of the Church.]

§ 252. The citizen paid special attention to public education, heretofore wholly dependent upon the Church and the cloister; he organized city schools, whose teachers, it is true, for a long time possessed only superficial culture, and were often employed only for uncertain or short terms. The society of the brotherhood of the Hieronymites introduced a better system of instruction before the close of the fourteenth century, but education had often to be obtained from the so-called traveling scholars (*vagantes*, *bacchantes*, *scholastici*, *goliardi*, etc.). The teachers of the so-called *scholæ exteriores*, in distinction from the schools of the cathedral and cloister, were called here *locati*, there *stampuales*—in German,

Kinder-Meister. The institution of German schools soon followed the Latin city schools. In order to remove the anarchy in school matters, the citizens aided the rise of universities by donations and foundations, and sustained the street-singing of the city scholars (*currende*), an institution which was well-meant, but which often failed of its end because on the one hand it was often misused as a mere means of subsistence, and on the other hand the sense of honor of those for whom it was established not unfrequently became, through their manner of living, lowered and degraded. The defect of the monkish method of instruction became ever more apparent, e. g., the silly tricks of their mnemotechnique, the utter lack of anything which deserved the name of any practical knowledge. The necessity of instruction in the use of arms led to democratic forms. Printing favored the same. Men began to concern themselves about good text-books. Melanchthon was the hero of the Protestant world, and as a pattern was beyond his time. His "Dialectics," "Rhetoric," "Physics," and "Ethics," were reprinted innumerable times, commented upon, and imitated. After him Amos Comenius, in the seventeenth century, had the greatest influence through his "Didactica Magna" and his "Janua Reserata." In a narrower sphere, treating of the foundation of philology in the gymnasiums (classical schools), the most noticeable is Sturm, of Strasburg. The universities in Catholic countries limited themselves to the scholastic philosophy and theology, together with which we find slowly struggling up to notice the study of Roman law and medicine in Bologna and Salerno. But Protestantism first raised the university to any real universality. Tübingen, Königsberg, Wittenberg, Jena, Leipsic, Halle, and Göttingen were the first schools for the study of all sciences, and for their free and productive pursuit.

[Here begins the organization of the school as an independent institution. Traveling scholars. "Outside schools," as distinguished from those of the cathedral and cloister. Endowments of universities by wealthy citizens. Melanchthon's text-books for Protestant schools. Comenius (1592–1671) shows in all directions the influence of his study of Lord Bacon's works. In the "Advancement of Learning" one finds the basis of the *Janua Linguæ Latinæ Reserata* of Comenius, as well as his system of classification and grading of pupils, and of his course of study. "Know all things (learning); master all things and one's self (virtue); find the relation of all to God (piety)": these Comenius held to be the objects of the school.

John Sturm, of Strasburg (1507–1589), long before Comenius, had laid the foundation of what has become the traditional course of instruction and methods of study in the classical schools for preparation for college. Scholastic philosophy and theology still held the chief place in Catholic universities. The German universities became the first schools for the study of all science.]

§ 253. The cities, which at first appeared with the clergy and the nobility as the third estate, formed an alliance with monarchy, and both together produced a transformation of the chivalric education. Absolute monarchy reduced the knights to mere nobles, to whom it conceded the prerogative of appointment as spiritual prelates as well as officers and counselors of state, but only on the condition of the most complete submission; and then, to satisfy them, it invented the artificial social revels of splendid court-life, and a charming and imposing array of beauty. In this condition, the education of the nobles was essentially changed in so far as to cease to be merely military. To the practice of arms, which, moreover, was made of very much less consequence by the democratic device of fire-arms, must be now added a special training of the mind which could no longer dispense with some knowledge of history, heraldry, genealogy, literature, and mythology. Since the French nation gave tone to the style of conversation, and after the time of Louis XIV controlled the politics of the Continent, the French language, as conventional and diplomatic, became a constant element in the education of the nobility in all the other countries of Europe.

Practically, the education of the noble endeavored to equip the individual with accomplishments, so that he should, by means of the important quality of an advantageous personal appearance and the prudence of his agreeable behavior, make himself into a ruler of all other men, and even of his equals in rank—i. e., he should copy in miniature the manners of an absolute sovereign. The practical knowledge of men was on this account made of the highest importance, and, under the form of ethical maxims, taught how to discover the weak side of every man, and so be able to outwit him. *Mundus vult decipi, ergo decipiatur.* According to this, every man had his price. They did not believe in the Nemesis of a divine ordination; on the contrary, disbelief in the higher justice was taught. One must be so elastic as to suit himself to all situations, and, as a caricature of the ancient ataraxy, he must acquire as a second nature a manner perfectly indifferent to all changes, the impassibility of an aristocratic repose, the amphibious cold-bloodedness of the "gentleman." The man of the world, like a worldling, sought his ideal in endless dissimulation, and this, as the flowering of his culture, he made his chief end. Intrigue, in love as well as in politics, was the soul of the nobleman's existence.

They endeavored to procure refinement of manners by sending the young man away with a traveling tutor. This was very good, but degenerated at last into the mechanism of the mere sight-seeing tourist. The noble was made a foreigner, a stranger to his own country, by means of his abode at Paris or Venice, while the citizen gradually outstripped him in genuine culture.

[The citizen-class appeared as a "third estate" between the nobles and the clergy (as explained in the commentary on § 247). The power of the king increased, and, assisted by the cities, was able to reduce the haughty nobles to obedience to law and order. The education of the nobility now ceased to be exclusively military. History, heraldry, literature, etc., began to be studied. Especially important is the fact that the French language became the court language for diplomacy as well as for polite intercourse.

The nobleman was educated to make himself a ruler over men. Great attention was given to his personal carriage. Certain worldly-wise maxims, entirely unscrupulous as to moral contents, became current. "The world wishes to be deceived, therefore let it be deceived." "Every man has his price." This worldliness assumed the form of a versatile diplomacy which was able to pursue its ends through dissimulation, preserving, under all its different faces, the impassivity of aristocratic repose, which was the ideal of the "gentleman."

The self-estrangement (see §§ 23, 24, commentary) necessary for culture was sought in foreign travel and residence abroad, besides, in the use of the French language when at home, in London, or Vienna.]

§ 254. The education of the citizen as well as that of the noble was taken possession of, in Catholic countries by the Jesuits, in Protestant countries by the Pietists: by the first, with a military strictness; by the second, in a sociable and gentle form. Both, however, agreed in destroying individuality, inasmuch as the one degraded man into a will-less machine for executing the commands of others, and the other deadened him in cultivating the feeling of his sinful worthlessness.

[Two religious systems of education: (*a*) the Jesuits; (*b*) the Pietists.]

(*a*) *Jesuitic Education.*

§ 255. Jesuitism combined the maximum of worldly freedom with an appearance of the greatest piety. Proceeding from this standpoint, it devoted itself in education to elegance and showy knowledge, to diplomacy and what was suitable and convenient in morals. To secure future power, it adapted itself not only to youth in general, but especially to the youth of the nobler classes. To please the latter, the Jesuits laid great stress upon a fine deportment. In their colleges dancing and fencing were well taught. They knew how well they should by this course content the noble, who had already usurped the name of education for these technical accomplishments useful in giving formal expression to personality.

In instruction they developed so exact a mechanism that they gained the reputation of having model school regulations, and even Protestants sent their children to them. From the close of the sixteenth century to the present time they have based their teaching upon the *Ratio et institutio studiorum Societatis Jesu* of Claudius of Aquaviva. Following that, they distinguished two courses of teaching, a higher and a lower. The lower included nothing but an external knowledge of the Latin language, and some fortuitous knowledge of history, of antiquities, and of mythology. The memory was cultivated as a means of keeping down free activity of thought and clearness of judgment. The higher course comprehended dialectics, rhetoric, physics, and morals. Dialectics was expounded as the art of sophistry. In rhetoric, they favored the polemical and emphatic style of the African fathers of the Church and their gorgeous phraseology; in physics, they followed Aristotle closely, and especially encouraged reading of the books "De Generatione et Corruptione" and "De Cœlo," on which they commented after their fashion; finally, in morals casuistic skepticism was their central point. They made much of rhetoric on account of their sermons, giving to it careful attention. They laid stress on declamation, and introduced it into their showy public examinations through the performance of Latin school comedies, and thus amused the public, disposed them to approval, and at the same time quite innocently practiced the pupil in the art of assuming a feigned character.

Diplomatic conduct was made necessary to the pupils of the Jesuits as well by their strict military discipline as by their system of mutual mistrust, espionage, and informing. Implicit obedience relieved the pupils from all responsibility as to the moral justification of their deeds. This exact following out of all commands, and refraining from any criticism as to principles, created a moral indifference, and, from the necessity of having consideration for the peculiarities and caprices of the superior on whom all others were dependent, arose eye-service. The coolness of mutual distrust sprang from the necessity which each felt of being on his guard against every other as a tale-bearer. The most deliberate hypocrisy and pleasure in intrigue merely for the sake of intrigue—this subtilest poison of moral corruption—were the result. Jesuitism had not only an interest in the material profit, which, when it had corrupted souls, fell to its share, but it also had an interest in the educative process of corruption. With absolute indifference as to the idea of morality, and absolute indifference as to the moral quality of the means used to attain its end, it rejoiced in the efficacy of secrecy, and the accomplished and calculating understanding, and in deceiving the credulous by means of its graceful, seemingly scrupulous, moral language.

It is not necessary to speak here of the morality of the order. It is sufficiently recognized as its fundamental contradiction, that while it taught that the idea of morality insists upon the eternal necessity of conformity to duty in every deed, on the other hand it taught that in actual practice this conformity to moral precept should be made to depend on circumstances. As to discipline, they were always guided by their fundamental principle, that body and soul, as in and for themselves one, could vicariously suffer for each other. Thus penitence and contrition were transformed into a perfect materialism of outward actions, and hence arose the punishments of the order, in which fasting, scourging, imprisonment, mortification, and death were formed into a mechanical artificial system.

[The Jesuit system of education, organized in 1584 by Claudius of Aquaviva, was intended to meet the active influence of Protestantism in education. It was remarkably successful, and for a century nearly all the foremost men of Christendom came from Jesuit schools. In 1710 they had six hundred and twelve colleges, one hundred and fifty-seven normal schools, twenty-four universities, and an immense number of lower schools. These schools laid very great stress on emulation. Their experiments in this principle are so extensive and long-continued that they furnish a most valuable phase in the history of pedagogy in this respect alone. In the matter of supervision they are also worthy of study. They had a fivefold system, each subordinate being implicitly obedient to his superior. Besides this, there was a complete system of espionage on the part of teachers and pupil monitors.]

(*b*) *Pietistic Education.*

§ 256. Jesuitism would make machines of man, Pietism would dissolve him in the feeling of his sinfulness: either would destroy his individuality. Pietism proceeded from the principle of Protestantism, as, in the place of the Catholic Pelagianism with its sanctification by works, it offered justification by faith alone. In its tendency to internality, i. e., to laying stress on the inward state of the heart and the attitude of the will, was its just claim. It would have even the letters of the Bible learned with religious emotion. But in its execution it fell into the error of one-sidedness in that it placed, instead of the actual freedom accorded to the individual by the spirit of Christianity, the imprisonment of a limited personality, supplanted free individuality by the personality of Christ in an external manner, and thus brought back into the very midst of Protestantism the principle of monachism—an abstract renunciation of the world. Since Protestantism had destroyed the idea of the cloister, it could produce estrangement from the world only by exciting public opinion against such social amusements and culture as it stigmatized as *worldly* for its members, e. g., card-playing, dancing, the theatre, etc. Thus it became negatively dependent upon works; for since its followers remained in constant relation with the world, so that the temptation to backsliding was a permanent one, it must watch over them, exercise an indispensable moral-police control over them, and thus, by the distrust of each other which was involved, take up into itself the Jesuitical practice, although in a very mild and affectionate way. Instead of the forbidden seclusion of the cloister, it organized a separate company, which, in its regularly constituted assembly, we call a conventicle. Instead of the cowl, it put on its youth a dress like that of the world in its cut, but scant and drab-colored; it substituted for the tonsure a fashion of cutting and parting the hair, and it often went beyond the obedience of the monks in its expression of pining humility and punctilious submission. Education within such a circle could not well recognize Nature and history as revelations of God, but it must consider them to be obstacles to their union with God, from which death alone could completely release them. The soul, which knew that its home could be found only in the future world, must feel itself to be a stranger upon the earth, and from such an opinion there must arise an indifference and even a contempt for science and art, as well as an aversion for a life of active labor, though an unwilling and forced tribute might be paid to it. Philosophy especially was to be shunned as dangerous. Bible-reading, the catechism, and the hymn-book, although quite mechanically used, were the one thing needful to the "poor in spirit." Religious poetry and sacred music were, of all the arts, the only ones deserving of any cultivation. The education of Pietism endeavored, by means of a carefully arranged series of symbolic expressions, to create in its disciples the feeling of their absolute nothingness, vileness, godlessness, and abandonment by God, in order to lift them out of the abyss of despair in regard to themselves and the world, and bring them into a warm, dramatic, and living relation to Christ—a relation in which all the erotic passion of the mystical fervor of the mendicant-friars was renewed in a somewhat milder form and with a strong tendency to a sickening sentimentality.

[The Protestant counterpart of Jesuitism was Pietism, in which there was a tendency toward relapse into the principle of monachism. It laid so much stress on the letter that there was not strength enough left to duly emphasize the spirit. J. Spener (1635–1705) and A. H. Francke (1663–1727) were the founders of this movement. It came so far as to be hostile toward the cultivation of the intellect and practical will. There should be no æsthetics except in the matter of sacred songs ("psalm-tunes"); no science, and no history except sacred history. The Quakers and the Puritans who settled in America brought with them some of the features of the Pietists. The truth of Pietism was its struggle to realize the living presence of God in the affairs of men. The truth of Jesuitism was the importance to the Church of preventing a separation between secular education and religious education. The Church, during its first twelve centuries, had held aloof from the secular. From the thirteenth to the sixteenth centuries it had striven to bring the Church into the secular, and thereby to guide and mold it. The Jesuit movement was a renewal of the Dominican and Franciscan movements (see commentary to § 234) of the thirteenth century. Then the danger came from Arabian schools of science and philosophy in Spain; now it was Protestantism, with its doctrine of the right of individual judgment.]

CHAPTER IX.

THE SYSTEM OF HUMANITARIAN EDUCATION. III. *The Epoch of Education fitting one for Civil Life* (concluded).

2. *The Ideal of Culture.*

§ 257. CIVIL education arose from the recognition of marriage and the family, of labor and enjoyment, of the equality of all before the law, and of the duty of self-determination. Jesuitism in the Catholic world and Pietism in the Protestant were the reaction against this recognition—a return into the asceticism of the middle ages; not, however, in its purity, but mitigated by some regard for worldly affairs. In opposition to this reaction the interests of citizen-life produced another, in which it undertook to save individuality by means of a different kind of alienation. On the one hand, it became absorbed in the study of the Greek and Roman world; on the other hand, it occupied itself with the practical interests of the present. In the former case, it placed man outside of his present world in a distant past which held to the present no immediate relation, in the latter case took him out of himself and occupied his attention with the affairs which were to serve him as means of his comfort and enjoyment. In the former it created an abstract idealism—a reproduction of the ancient view—in the latter it set up an abstract realism in a high appreciation of things which ought to be considered of value only as a means. In the one direction, individuality was lost in the contemplation of extinct nations; in the other, it was lost in a world of business. In one case, the ideal was that of the æsthetic republicanism of the Greeks; in the other, the utilitarian cosmopolitanism of the Romans. But, in reaction against these two extremes, there arose a form that united them and reconciled them in a humanity that treated even the beggar and the criminal with pity and mercy.

[Civil education rested on these four things recognized by the new spirit of civilization: (a) marriage and the family; (b) labor and enjoyment of its products; (c) equality of all before the law, no personal tyranny; (d) the duty of thinking for one's self and acting according to the dictates of one's own conscience. Jesuitism and Pietism were the Catholic and Protestant reactions against this new spirit. A counter-reaction against these now set in: the study of the Greek and Latin classics on the one hand and a study of natural science on the other. These were (a) the humanist ideal, and (b) the philanthropic ideal.]

(a) *The Humanist Ideal.*

§ 258. The Oriental-theocratic education is preserved in Christian education through the Bible. Through the mediation of the Greek and Roman Churches the views of the ancient world were taken up, but not entirely assimilated. To accomplish this latter function was the problem of humanist education. It aimed to teach the Latin and Greek languages, expecting thus to secure as effect a purely human character in a broad, cosmopolitan sense. The Greeks and Romans being sharply marked nationalities, how could one cherish such expectations? It was possible only relatively in contrast, partly to an urban population from whom all genuine political sense had departed, partly in contrast to a church limited by a confessional, to which the idea of humanity as such had become almost lost in dogmatic differences of opinion on trifling details. The spirit was renewed in the first by the contemplation of the pure patriotism of the ancients, and in the second by the discovery of rational insight among the heathen. In contrast to the provincial Philistinism and against the want of refined ideals and the lack of refined taste, was arrayed the power of culture derived from the contemplation of antique art. The so-called uselessness of learning dead languages imparted to the mind, it knew not how, an ideal drift. The very fact that it could not find immediate profit in its knowledge gave it the consciousness that there is something of a higher value than material profit. The ideal of the humanities was the truth to nature which was found in the monuments of the ancient world. The study of language as form, must lead one involuntarily to the actual seizing of its meaning. The Latin schools grew into *Gymnasia*, and the universities contained not merely professors of eloquence, but also teachers of philology.

[The study of the Latin and Greek classics was supposed to secure the development of a pure humanity, or in other words to develop human nature in its entirety. The Greeks and Romans had been true to nature, and the study of their languages and literatures would do most to set the youth into harmony with himself. These reasons are not quite so satisfactory as those which ground the importance of classic study on the fact that modern civilization is derivative; resting on the Greek for its æsthetics and science; resting on the Roman for its legal and political forms. A study of Latin and Greek gives the modern youth a "self-estrangement" which ends by his becoming familiar with the view of the world held at Rome and Athens. When he can see the world from the standpoints of those peoples who were competent by their original genius to invent art and science and jurisprudence, our modern youth finds himself returned from out his "self-estrangement" with the capacity to see and comprehend those important strands of his civilization that were before invisible to him or seen only dimly. The study of Latin and Greek is the study of the embryology of our civilization.

In this view we are interested especially in the history of the modern study of the classics. Trotzendorf (1490–1556), who went to Wittenberg in 1518 and taught with Melanchthon, and was rector of the *Gymnasium* at Görlitz for twenty-five years, is one of the most important names. Sturm is another (see § 252, commentary). The powerful effect of classic study in giving the youth possession of himself has been noted for centuries. The explanation of it has varied. In the expression "humanities" (*humaniora*, or *literæ humaniores*) is suggested the theory that the classics are especially adapted to *humanize* the youth. If this means that they give him an insight into human nature as nothing else does, the expression is very apt. Human nature has shown itself especially in the Greek and Roman peoples, rising to wonderful heights of intellect and will-power. But this does not state so directly the present value of those languages as the view above presented, namely, that they give the pupil the point of view of the original inventors of art, science, and jurisprudence, and hence their study is to all modern civilized peoples (whose culture is derivative) a study of their own spiritual embryology, and therefore indispensable for direct self-knowledge. The vague expression "discipline of mind" has been much used to express the valuable result of classic study, but it does not hint at the genuine source of the culture as the word *humanities* does.]

(*b*) *The Philanthropic Ideal.*

§ 259. The humanitarian tendency reached its extreme in the complete forgetting of the present, and the neglect of its just claim. Man discovered at last that he was not at home with himself, although he had made himself at home in Rome and Athens. He spoke and wrote Latin, if not like Cicero, at least like Muretius, but he often found himself awkward in expressing his meaning in his mother-tongue. He was often very learned, but he lacked judgment. He was filled with enthusiasm for the republicanism of Greece and Rome, and yet at the same time was himself exceedingly servile to his excellent and august lords. Against this gradual deadening of active individuality, the result of an abnormal study of the classics, we find now reacting the education of the age of revolution, which we generally call the philanthropic education. It sought to make men friendly to the immediate course of the world. It placed over against the learning of the ancient languages for their own sake the acquisition of the branches useful in earning one's living—mathematics, physics, geography, history, and the modern languages, calling these the reality-studies ("*Realien*"). Nevertheless, it retained chief place in the instruction in the Latin language because the Romance languages have sprung from it, and because, through its long domination, the entire terminology of science, art, and law, is derived from it. Philanthropic education desired to develop the social side of its pupils through a compendium of practical knowledge and personal accomplishments, and to lead him out of the hermit-like sedentary life of the book-pedant into the fields and the woods. It desired to imitate life even in its method, and to instruct entertainingly in the way of play or by conversation. It would add to the printed words and names the objects themselves, or at least their representation by pictures; and in this direction, in the literature which it prepared for the entertainment of children, it sometimes strayed into childishness. It performed a great service when it gave to the body its due, and introduced simple, natural dress, bathing, gymnastics, pedestrian excursions, and thereby hardened it against the influences of wind and weather. As this system of education, so friendly to children, believed that it could not soon enough begin to honor them as citizens of the world, it committed the error of presupposing as already finished in its children much that it itself should have gradually developed; and as it wished to educate the pupil into the general ideal of humanity rather than into that of a particular province or sect, it became indifferent concerning the concrete distinctions of nationality and religion. It agreed with certain philologists in placing, in an indirect manner, Socrates above Christ, because he had worked no miracles, and taught only morality. In such a dead cosmopolitanism, individuality disappeared in the indeterminateness of a general "humanity," and saw itself forced to agree with the humanistic education in proclaiming the truth of nature as the educational ideal, with the distinction that, while humanism believed this ideal realized in the Greeks and Romans, Philanthropinism found itself compelled to presuppose an abstract natural man, and often manifested a not unjustifiable pleasure in recognizing in the Indian of North America, or the savage of Otaheite, the genuine man of Nature. Philosophy developed these abstract views into the idea of a rational political state-government, which should incorporate within its organism the scientific knowledge of whatever is rational, and should adopt as reforms all changes demanded by the growth of such science.

The course which the development of the philanthropic ideal has taken is as follows: (1) Rousseau, in his writings, "Émile" and the "Nouvelle Héloïse," first preached the evangel of natural education, the emancipation from historic precedents and tradition, the negation of existing culture, and the return to the simplicity and innocence of Nature. Although he often himself testified in his experience his own proneness to evil in a very discouraging manner, he fixed as an almost universally accepted axiom in French and German pedagogics his principal maxim, that man is by nature good. (2) The reformatory ideas of Rousseau met with only a very infrequent and sporadic introduction among the Romanic nations, because among them education was too dependent on the Church, and retained its cloister-like seclusion in seminaries, colleges, etc. In Germany, on the contrary, they were put into practice, and the *Philanthropina*, established by Basedow in Dessau, Brunswick, and Schnepfenthal, made experiments, which nevertheless very soon departed somewhat from the extreme views of Basedow himself, and had many excellent results. (3) Humanity exists *in concreto* only in the form of nations. The French nation, in their first Revolution, tried the experiment of emancipating themselves from historic tradition, of leveling all distinctions of culture, of enthroning a despotism of reason, and of organizing itself as humanity, pure and simple. The event showed the impossibility of such an undertaking. The national energy, the historical impulse, the love of art and science, came forth from the midst of the revolutionary movement which was directed to their destruction more vigorously than ever. The *grande nation*, their *grande armée*, and *gloire*—that is to say, glory for France—supplanted all the humanitarian phrases. In Germany the philanthropic circle of education was limited at first to the higher ranks. There was no exclusiveness in the *Philanthropina*, for there nobles and citizens, Catholics and Protestants, Russians and Swiss, were mingled; but these were always the children of wealthy families, and to these the plan of education was adapted.

Then appeared Pestalozzi and directed education also to the lower classes of society—those which are called, not without something approaching to a derogatory meaning, *the people*. From this time dates popular education, the effort for the intellectual and moral elevation of the hitherto neglected atomistic human being of the non-property-holding multitude. There shall in future be no dirty, hungry, ignorant, awkward, thankless, and will-less mass, devoted alone to an animal existence. We can never rid ourselves of the lower classes by having the wealthy give something, or even their all, to the poor; but we can rid ourselves of them in the sense that the possibility of culture and independent self-support shall be open to every one, because he is a human being and a citizen of the commonwealth. Ignorance and rudeness, and the vice which springs from them, and the malevolent frame of mind that hates civil laws and ordinances and generates crime—these shall disappear. Education shall train man to self-conscious obedience to law, as well as to kindly feeling toward the erring, and to an effort not merely for their punishment, but for their improvement. But the more Pestalozzi endeavored to realize his ideal of human dignity, the more he comprehended that the isolated power of a private man could not attain it, but that the nation itself must make the education of its people its first business. Fichte by his lectures first made the German nation fully accept these thoughts, and Prussia was the first state which, by her public schools and her military preparation for defense, led the way with clear consciousness in providing for national education; while among the Romanic nations, in spite of their more elaborate political formalism, it still depends partly upon the Church and partly upon the accident of private enterprise. Pestalozzi also laid a foundation for a national pedagogical literature by his story of "Leonard and Gertrude." This book appeared in 1784, the same year in which Schiller's "Robbers" and Kant's "Critique of Pure Reason" announced a new phase in the drama and in philosophy.

The incarnation of God, which was, up to the time of the Reformation, an esoteric mystery of the Church, has since then become continually more and more an exoteric problem of the state.

[In the schools of Trotzendorf and Sturm the youth were trained as though they were to live in Rome or Athens. A wise insight into the principle of self-estrangement takes note of the importance of so conducting the return from it that the pupil does not get set in foreign ways so firmly that he never returns to his present environment. The danger of humanism is that it makes the means into the end, and does not provide for a return out of the Latin and Greek world to the modern world. The moderns, represented by (a) the natural sciences, (b) the modern languages and literatures, and (c) modern history, constitute the return phase of this course of study. It is not a question of preferring one for the other: they are parts of one whole. Any school education, no matter how meager, should have discipline studies and information studies—or self-estrangement studies and familiar-reality studies. The latter studies—the "moderns" or the "information" studies are advocated by the "philanthropic" or "philanthropinist" educators under the name of "*real*" studies. The outcome of these two extremes, separately carried out, results, curiously enough, in setting up an ideal human nature. Humanism sets up the Greek and Roman humanity, while Philanthropinism, or realism, sets up an imaginary "natural man" unspoiled by artificial culture: (1) Rousseau preached the evangel of "return to Nature." It is amazing to see how universally his maxim has been adopted, and how thoughtlessly it is used. There is a confusion here between "nature" as it exists in real forms in time and space, and "nature" as it exists as an ideal, which is not yet realized. Human nature is not a *real* form in time and space, like a rock or tree, but is brought forth by self-activity, self-development. Moreover, human nature is a participation on the part of one individual in the results that his race have brought forth. Education seeks to render the individual able to participate in the experience of all men—giving him the result of their perception and reflection, of their deeds and the consequences for weal or woe that flowed from them. Civilization is not an artificial structure in the sense that Rousseau dreamed it to be, but it is the gigantic revelation, of what is in human nature as a possibility, worked out *in extenso* in time and space.

(2) Rousseau's educational ideas were suppressed among the Romanic nations, but were put into practice in Germany, especially by Basedow in his "Philanthropinum." In France they were not acted upon in education, but they produced a far more startling effect in exploding the French Revolution.

(3) The French tried to emancipate themselves from historic tradition and to live "according to Nature," but with most dismal results. It is likely to prove useful for many centuries as an educational spectacle. The nation discovered its "state of nature" to be a "self-estrangement," from which it slowly returned through the process of Bonapartism to Bourbonism; again to make new departures and new returns before finally reaching the true state of *human* nature.

Perhaps the happiest result of Rousseau is his effect on Pestalozzi. The education of the people *as* people—popular education that reaches all classes—owes to Pestalozzi the greatest debt, and through him to Rousseau still a large obligation. We shall in the future rid ourselves of the "dirty, hungry, ignorant, thriftless, thankless, and will-less masses devoted to a merely animal existence." They will all be developed in youth in the school and made self-active and intelligent, and by this means become self-helpful. Pestalozzi made the problem clear to all Europe. Fichte persuaded Prussia to adopt public education as a state policy. Since the Franco-Prussian War, public schools for the education of the people have spread very widely throughout Europe.

Since Pestalozzi, and with him as one of the greatest of educational reformers, has appeared Friedrich Froebel. His mission was directed to providing a proper form of school education for the younger children not qualified to enter the primary school. The school has begun hitherto with teaching the "conventionalities of intelligence," reading, writing, etc. Froebel would have the younger children receive a symbolic education, plays, games, and occupations which symbolize the primitive arts of man. Play should be the activity utilized for the first education of the child.]

3. *Free Education.*

§ 260. The ideal of culture of the humanist and the philanthropic education was taken up into the conception of an education which recognizes the family, social station, the nation, and religion as positive elements of the practical spirit, but which will require that each of these shall be defined from within through the idea of humanity, and brought into reciprocal relation with all the others. Physical development shall become the object of a national system of gymnastics, adopted universally by the people, and including the drill in the use of arms. Instruction, in respect to a general encyclopedic culture, ought to be the same for all, and parallel to this should run a system of special schools to prepare for the special vocations of life. The method of instruction ought to be the simple exposition of the special idea of each branch, and this should not be sacrificed any longer to the formal breadth of a literary treatment of many things which may find outside the school its opportunity, but within it has no meaning except as the history of a science or an art. Moral culture must be combined with family affection and the knowledge of the laws of the commonwealth, so that the collision between individual morality and objective legality may ever more and more disappear. Education ought, without violently estranging the individual from the internality of the family, to accustom him gradually to the life of the people as it actually exists, because a knowledge of human nature [as one obtains it by associating with all classes in public schools] furnishes the standpoint whence to obtain a just survey of the whole, and is the only thing which can prevent the cynicism of private life, the one-sidedness of knowledge and perverseness of will, and the spirit of caste, which has so extensively prevailed. The individual ought to be educated into a self-consciousness of the essential equality and freedom of all men, so that he shall recognize and acknowledge himself in each one and in all. But this essential and solid unity of all men must not degenerate into the insipidity of a humanity without distinctions, but instead it must realize the form of a concrete individuality and nationality, and transfigure the idiosyncrasy of its nation into a broad humanity. The unrestricted striving after beauty, truth, and freedom, presently and of its own accord, and not merely through ecclesiastical intermediation, will lead to religion.

The education of the state must furnish a preparation for the unfettered activity of self-conscious humanity.

[In the "free education" of the future, whose object shall be the emancipation of each individual, there must be schools that give a common general education, supplemented by special schools for the special vocations of life. The education by the newspaper is one of the most noteworthy phenomena of our time. Where all the people read and where the vast majority of the people live in cities or near railroad-stations in the country, the daily newspaper brings to each person at his breakfast a survey of the entire world. Compared with the village gossip in olden times, this general survey is a miraculous instrument of education in the humanizing direction. While it educates it governs, and few nations now exist that do not consider very carefully how their conduct will appear, when it, by the telegraph and the daily newspaper, is placed under the inspection of the entire world. Modern literature, which follows the daily newspaper into every family, contributes an increasingly powerful element in education. The prose novel makes every one familiar with the peculiarities of foreign people, and a genuine human interest in the details of life, as they exist among all nations has arisen. This is producing universal toleration for differences of custom and views of the world, and on the other hand rapidly drawing together all peoples who have become reading peoples.

These instrumentalities, the printing-press, railroads, telegraphs, and postal systems, which facilitate travel and personal acquaintance, and still more the intercommunication and acquaintance by the printed page, are hastening forward that stage of public opinion which demands in the name of Christian civilization that each individual shall share in the heritage of realized wisdom of the entire race.]

THE END.